IMAGES
of America

LATONIA

ON THE COVER: Harry Kleine and two children, his son Raymond (center) and a cousin Norma Meier (left), won second prize for their decorated automobile in the 1915 Covington Centennial celebration. Latonia had become part of Covington in 1909. Kleine gave flute lessons and owned candy stores, where he sold the sweets he manufactured in his candy factory on Park Avenue by the railroad tracks. He owned Kleine's Sweet Shoppe adjoining the Derby Theater at Fortieth Street and Decoursey Avenue, and the Latonia Sweet Shoppe at Inez and Decoursey Avenues. Kids could come to the sweet shops to get candy to take to the movies at the old Grand Theatre next to Ritte's Bowling Alley and at the Derby Theater, formerly the Delbee. He also put in a popcorn stand and an ice ball machine in a tiny space next door to the Latonia Bakery. The Latonia Sweet Shoppe was later purchased by Howard Litzler, but it fell victim to World War II rationing and shortages and had to close. (Courtesy of the author's collection.)

IMAGES
of America

LATONIA

Lisa C. Gillham

ARCADIA
PUBLISHING

ISBN 978-0-7385-5446-4

Published by Arcadia Publishing
Charleston, South Carolina

Printed in the United States of America

Library of Congress Catalog Card Number: 2008925854

For all general information contact Arcadia Publishing at:
Telephone 843-853-2070
Fax 843-853-0044
E-mail sales@arcadiapublishing.com
For customer service and orders:
Toll-Free 1-888-313-2665

Visit us on the Internet at www.arcadiapublishing.com

I dedicate this book to my grandmother, Fern Smith Gillham, who told me the stories of her family and of Latonia, which have shaped my life, and to my parents, Charles and Marcia Gillham, who brought me up to recognize good stories and magical places.

Contents

ACKNOWLEDGMENTS

Collecting the material for this book has been a wonderful experience. Not only was I doing one of my favorite things—looking at old pictures—I was doing it with a variety of kind and interesting people. People shared with me their family photographs and their memories and stories. This is most valuable stuff, perhaps the most valuable. I came to recognize the faces and learn the names of various grandmas and grandpas, and how they fit in the story of Latonia. This exchange is intimate, and I feel that with each loan of photographs I also gained a friend. I'd like to offer special thanks to Mary Cecil, Virginia Kupper Kaufman, Charles Gillham, Bill Beuttel, Judy Mark, Carol Dick, Jim Feldman, Tricia Dorman, Lorna Petty Harrell, Mary Martha Siefert Kaiser, Betty Lee, Karl Lietzenmayer, Tom Martin, Dr. Bruce Snider, Cliff Adams, Wanda Painter, Bob Regan, Jim Skyrm, Trinity United Methodist Church, St. Mark United Church of Christ, Latonia Baptist Church, Betty McCoy, Tom Mitchell, Philip Zumdick, Ben and Jim Baker, Geoff Grissom, and John Kennedy. Also I want to thank Bernie of the Northern Kentucky Views Web site (www.nkyviews.com) for graciously allowing me use of his images, and the Covington Fire Department for directing me to their historical photograph collection. My thanks go to the Kenton County Public Library for granting me access to their fine local collection, and to Tim Hyde and the Greater Cincinnati Railway Museum for their support. I'm grateful to Carrie Daniels and the L&N Railroad Company Collection, University of Louisville Archives and Records Center, Louisville, Kentucky, for generously allowing me use of their images. Finally, to my mother Marcia, for proofreading and major support, and to Luke Cunningham, my patient and supportive editor at Arcadia Publishing, I'd like to express special thanks.

INTRODUCTION

Latonia is a neighborhood within Covington, Kentucky, with 150 years of history. It had a racetrack and a busy Main Street. It still has trains running through it and all kinds of houses: big, little, and mostly old. Most of all, it has a mythos, an ineffable quality that gets into many of those who live here, making them need to remember and to tell stories.

Saloon keepers, ministers, doctors, businessmen, and jockeys have left their mark on Latonia. Yet women, mostly housewives, created Latonia day by day. They made it a place where their children, grandchildren, and great-grandchildren would want to stay or a place to which they would return. Most of them are known only by the family names that are still familiar here—no first names, only Mrs. or Grandma.

The Latonia Racetrack took its name from a nearby mineral springs resort called Lettonia Springs. The name references the Roman water goddess, Latona, and plays on the name of the hotel's owner, Mr. Letton. The springs were discovered in about 1829, and, soon after, the resort was thriving. It had a three-story, 50-room hotel with a ballroom. Wealthy Southern families came to escape summer's heat and epidemics, and it was the farthest north they could bring their slaves. The Civil War curtailed spa business, and by 1891, the resort was abandoned.

Rail lines first came to the area in 1854. The Louisville, Cincinnati, and Lexington Railroad and the Kentucky Central intersected in Latonia, creating a desirable location for industry. They were bought out by the L&N in 1881 and 1890, respectively. Coal transport was the major business for the L&N, bringing open coal cars through Latonia from the mining regions of southeastern Kentucky. The tracks, now owned by CSX, still cross the middle of town.

The area was known as the Milldale Magisterial District—an unincorporated section of Kenton County with a population of about 700. The name "Milldale" probably comes from Charles Mills, who owned much of what is now Latonia and operated an early distillery near the railroad. Latonia, which took its name from the racetrack, was incorporated in 1896, after some years of confusion over the town's status.

J. T. Earle was the first (and only) mayor of Latonia, but he ran afoul of many voters when he opposed the racetrack and liquor in Latonia, both of which were well loved by its citizens.

Latonia's biggest claim to fame was the racetrack, a national destination. The Latonia Racetrack opened in 1883 and was one of the finest tracks in the country. In its heyday, the track was more popular than Churchill Downs. It was graced with a beautiful Victorian clubhouse and grandstand, a lake, and handsomely planted grounds.

The track drew the cream of society. Alice Roosevelt, daughter of former president Theodore Roosevelt, visited the track with her fiance, Nicholas Longworth. Lesser lights of the social galaxy visited routinely. Each day, a horse-drawn omnibus left the elegant St. Nicholas Hotel in downtown Cincinnati, loaded with the town's upper crust heading for the Latonia Racetrack.

It also drew the requisite bookies, conmen, hookers, and petty thieves. Latonia's mayor J. T. Earle complained the bookmakers encouraged men to skip their jobs and deprived them of money that should have gone to their families. He wrote that "we are compelled to put on extra police and nearly every citizen sleeps on his revolver while the races are here, and especially the day or two before they leave."

The community profited from the racetrack, however. It was definitely good for business.

There has been uncertainty about why Madison Pike was also known as the "3L Highway." It does, indeed, stem from the Latonia Racetrack and companion racetracks in Lexington and Louisville that could be reached by that road. One could take racehorses on the 3L circuit or follow it to watch one's favorite thoroughbreds.

The old racetrack began to decline during the Depression, due to a combination of factors. The final blow came when the management, which also owned Churchill Downs, decided to put their resources behind that track. Latonia closed in 1939.

The activity surrounding the racetrack drew people interested in making Latonia home, and development took off in earnest. In 1893, the electric streetcar replaced the old mule-drawn streetcars, making it easier to commute to Covington every day. Latonia was becoming a streetcar suburb. Wealthy landowners created residential developments, like John Coppin's Lakeview Park and George Mason's Dinmore Park.

Latonia incurred debt for the street, sidewalk, and other municipal infrastructure improvements, and it caused city officials to consider annexation by Covington. By 1908, Latonia had a population of 8,000 and was $100,000 in debt, though a Covington audit showed it to be three times that figure. Some Covington officials were hesitant about annexation, but in 1909 Latonia became part of Covington. Although only a city for 15 years, many residents still say, a hundred years later, they live in Latonia.

The heart of Latonia is Ritte's Corner. It is a five-way intersection in the center of the historic business district and the intersection of two major roads, Taylor Mill Road and Decoursey Avenue. Five buildings originally anchored it, though one has been torn down. On the northeast corner was Henry Ritte's Saloon—hence the name.

In its heyday, Ritte's Corner was the center of life in Latonia. On evenings and weekends everyone would "go uptown," as was the common saying, to Ritte's Corner. There was something for everyone: movie houses, ice cream and sweet shops, and drinking establishments.

During World War I, a fountain was erected in the center of Ritte's Corner in honor of the first Latonia boy to go to war. One could watch racehorses, even Kentucky Derby winners, being walked up to drink. It even had a low bowl so that dogs could get a drink.

The railroad was as important as the racetrack in the development of Latonia. Many railroad workers settled in Latonia and reared families whose descendants live here still. The L&N was woven through life in Latonia, even for those who did not depend on it for a living. The trains were ever present. The sound was so familiar that people would not really hear it, and yet they would miss it if they moved away. Over the years, there were accidents when a vehicle or person would be hit by a train—the most tragic, of course, when it was a child.

The L&N brought special events and celebrities to Latonia. The circus would come with its own carnival-red cars, and once the great Sarah Bernhardt came to Latonia in her private train car. Racetrack fans, horsemen—and horses—came to town on the train, too.

Churches were established early in Latonia's history, such as Trinity United Methodist, Holy Cross, Latonia Christian, St. Mark's Church of Christ, and Latonia Baptist. Several offered services in German until World War I. Calvary Baptist and Runyon Memorial followed later. In recent decades, many new churches have made homes in Latonia.

Milldale's first schools were two rooms, heated by potbellied stoves. The one at Tibbatts Street and Southern Avenue was enlarged to become the Latonia Firehouse. The other was at Graff and what is now Thirty-fourth Street. Now used as a church, it is the only one of Latonia's public schools still in existence. Latonia later built three full-size schools, one on Golding Street (Locke), one on Graff Street, and one on Clifton. Latonia also had its own Colored School from 1883, when the racetrack opened, until 1913, when it was consolidated into Covington's system. Before 1900, many top jockeys and horsemen were African American, and their children needed a school.

Holy Cross Elementary opened in 1891, and later Holy Cross District High School opened. After Covington annexed Latonia, it constructed new wings onto the old public schools, and renamed them Eighth, Ninth, and Tenth Districts.

World War I was the first war that had a major impact on Latonia. Many young men served, and some died. The worst effect on Latonia was the terrible anti-German sentiment that swept Northern Kentucky and focused national attention on Latonia in what was known as the "Schoborg trial." World War II also saw many Latonia boys serve, and some did not return. During both wars, Blue Star flags were displayed in the windows of families who had soldiers in the war, and those on the home front did what they could to help the war efforts.

Prohibition had a big impact on Latonia. Saloons switched to serving soft drinks, and business dropped. Speakeasies, however, did excellent business. Almost everyone in town was making home brew, or homemade wine. Some enterprising neighbors had stills, which called for a high level of secrecy. Before the end of prohibition, Latonia had seen several exploding stills, Henry Ritte's Saloon had closed, and the Monte Casino monks left their hillside vineyards.

The Great Depression hit Latonia even harder. Workers were laid off, and families lost their homes. The Latonia Deposit Bank failed, then the Southern Exchange Bank went into the same building but did not survive the Depression either. It signaled the death knell for the racetrack. The L&N kept many of its workers, but they suffered demotions or less desirable shifts. Hobos were common sights in Latonia. They came to the back doors, and most families would make them a meal to eat outside. Home building stopped, sometimes in mid-construction.

After World War II, many Latonians moved out to the suburbs, as commonly happened in most of the older towns nationwide. An oil refinery replaced the racetrack. New schools were coming. The magnificent Coppin mansion fell to make way for a new Ninth District Elementary, and Latonia Elementary took houses from a whole quare block to combine the old Eighth and Tenth Districts.

From the late 1960s into the 1980s, Latonia experienced decline. In the 1980s, the Latonia Business Association (LBA) and the City of Covington began efforts to revitalize. By the 1990s, new life was growing as some residents refurbished historic houses. Ritte's East Neighborhood Group started in 1995 and gave revitalization efforts a big push.

By 2000, positive change had taken hold. Ritte's Corner had run down slowly, but, in recent years, life is returning rapidly. The Ritte's East Neighborhood Group partnered with VFW Post 6095 and together raised over $60,000 to erect a memorial fountain plaza for the Korean War with help from the City of Covington. Three of the four remaining buildings have since been handsomely restored.

The Latonia Business Association regrouped, and, in 2007, Latonia West, a second neighborhood association, got off to an active start. New restaurants have opened, and a pocket park is in the works. Ritte's East and the LBA have partnered to sponsor a mosaic gateway sign designed by Latonia artist Charles Gillham and made by Covington artists Rosemary Topie and Jackie Slone. Ritte's Corner now sports banners bearing a similar design by Gillham, in another collaboration between the groups. Latonia West and LBA have set up a handsomely landscaped gateway sign on Madison Pike. More people are restoring historic homes, and young people are moving here.

This book features images from the late 19th century through World War II plus a brief look at the 1950s. Its underlying theme is "home." Latonia has been and is thought of that way by so many. Generations of families have lived here, and many who live here now can point out the homes where their parents or grandparents lived. I am the fifth generation of my family to live here.

All my life, my grandmother told me the stories of her family and of Latonia, which were clearly the center of her universe. I lived in New York City and other places for a long time, and eventually I wanted to settle down. I looked all over the country and finally realized that I was looking everywhere else for my family home back in Latonia. This is where my stories are, and the stories are all about home.

One

HOME AND FAMILY

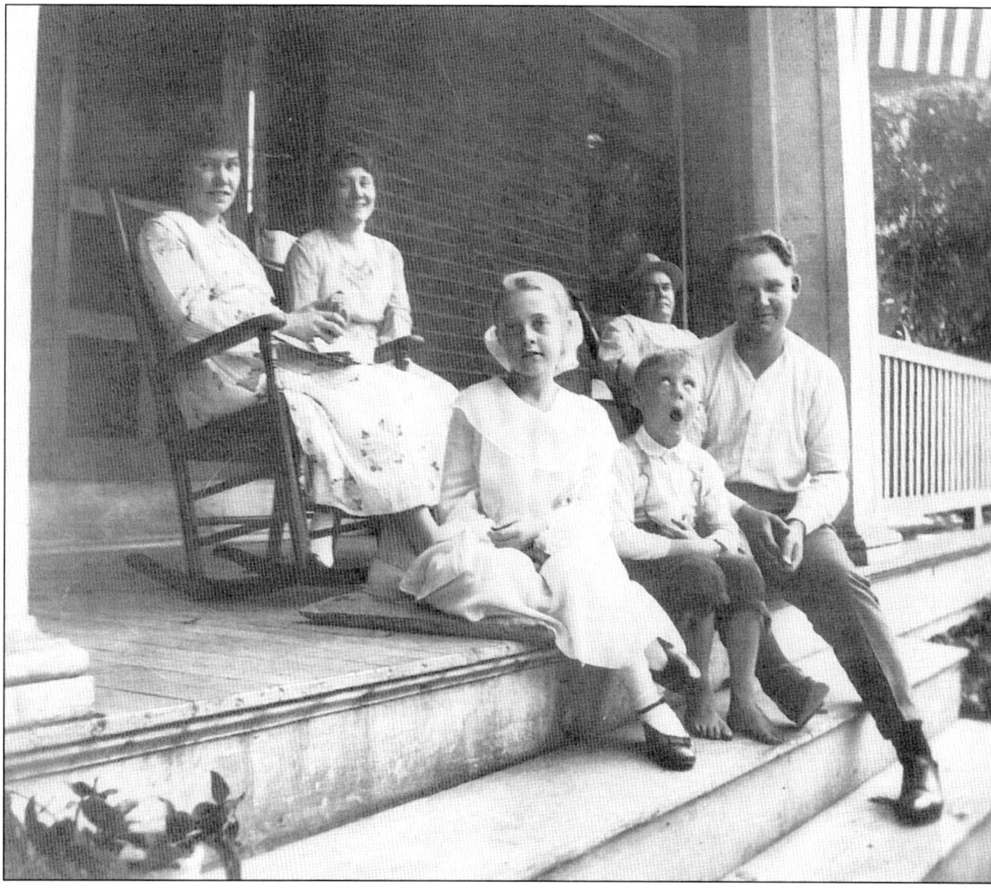

This was home in the stories told to the author by her grandmother, Fern. Here at 215 East Thirty-sixth Street (originally Franklin Street) still stands the house where Lizzie and George Smith reared six children. They built the house in about 1904, and it was the place to which their children returned in times of trouble. Life happened here, and the front porch was its focus. On this porch, Chicago baseball players gathered with top jockeys to drink beer with George and his sons and visit the family. From this porch, Fern watched as her husband crawled beneath a steaming derailed train to direct its righting. Here Harry Smith died in a rocking chair in the hot summer of 1934. It was where the family gathered, where George sat in his rocker strumming his guitar and whistling, and where they all sit unseen to this day. This c. 1912 photograph shows, from left to right, (seated on the step) Georgia Roe, Richter Roe, and Georgie Smith; (seated in rockers) Fern Smith, Myrtle Smith Roe, and George Smith, their "Papa." (Courtesy of the author's collection.)

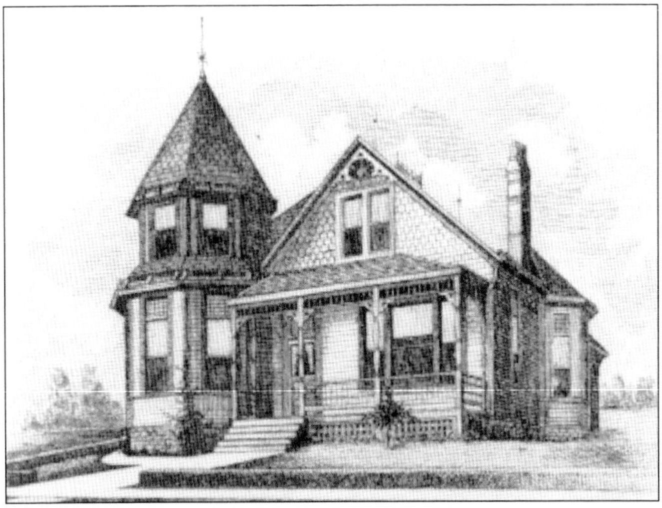

Johann Heinrich Kruse built his "country villa" on Park Avenue in 1892 when Latonia, then known as Milldale, was still sparsely populated. An executive at Covington's Bavarian Brewery, he was instrumental in the development of Milldale and later Latonia. In addition to his work at Bavarian Brewery, he served on the town councils of both Milldale and Latonia and owned extensive real estate holdings. (Courtesy of the author's collection.)

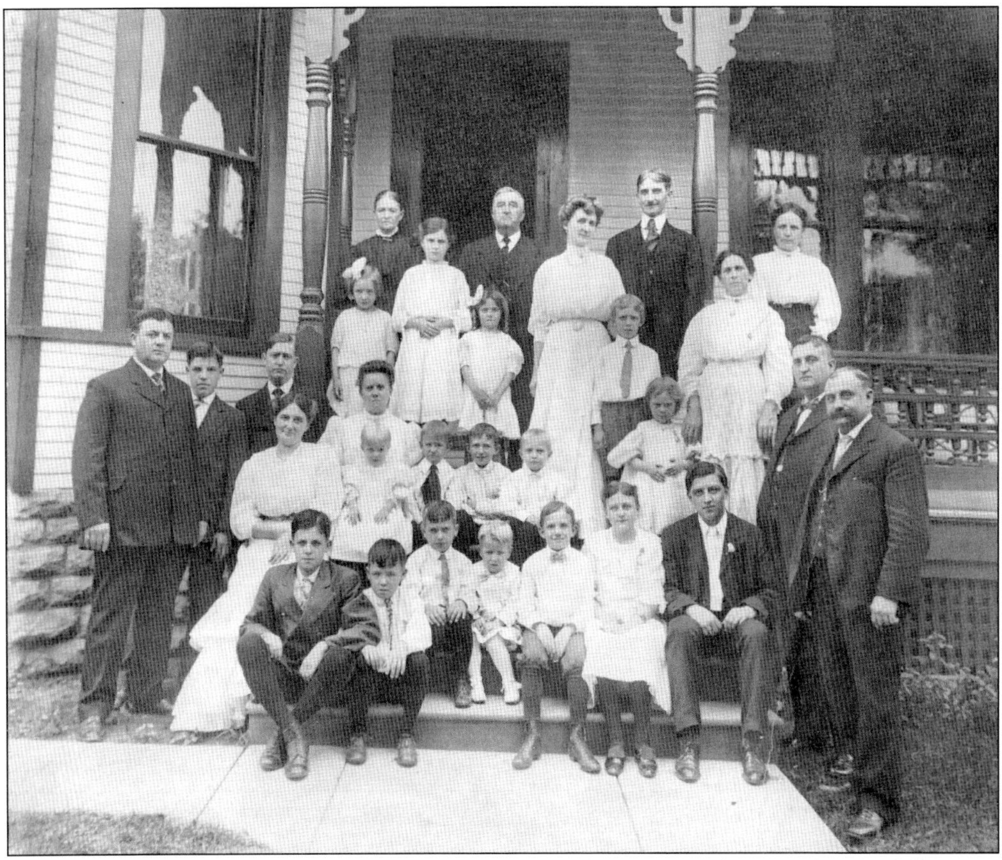

Kruse's extended family gathers on his front porch in this *c.* 1910 photograph. The following, from left to right, are: (fourth row, standing on the porch) Elizabeth and Johann Gerhard Kruse, Henry's parents; Henry (Heinrich); and an unidentified woman; (third row) Helen, Margaret, and Elizabeth, Henry's daughters; Catherine, his wife; Clifford, their son; and an unidentified woman. The rest are unidentified but are probably Henry's siblings and their families. The author now lives in this house. (Courtesy of the author's collection.)

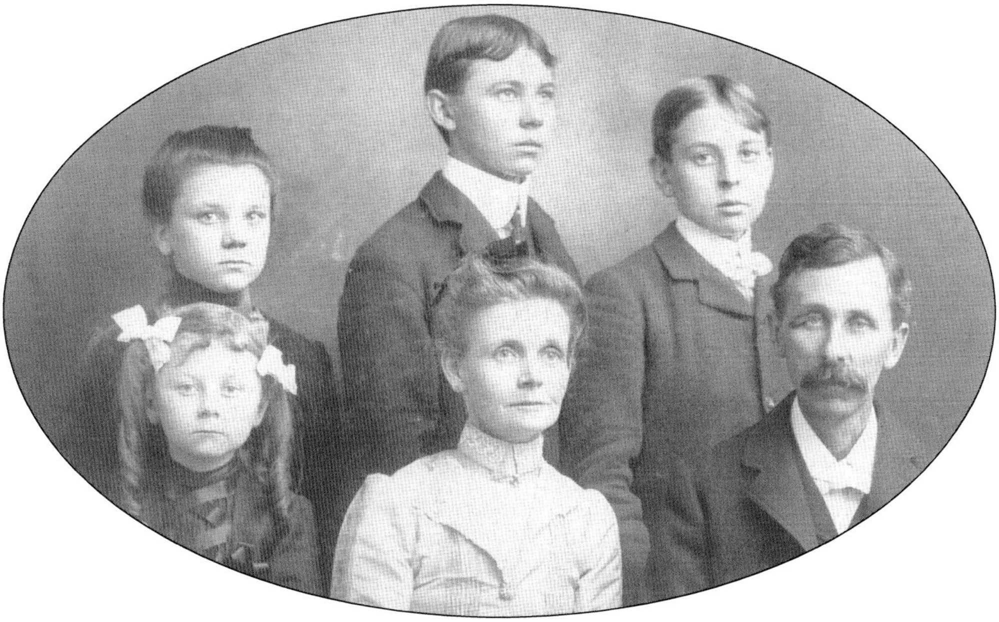

The family of William Fillmore Gillham lived on Glenn Avenue in a section of Latonia known as Dinmore Park. W. F., as he was known, owned the Gillham Coal Company, which was located in Covington first on the Licking River and later on Washington Street. From left to right are (first row) daughter Emma, Flavia Curtiss Gillham, and W. F.; (second row) children Cokie (Corcoran), Alfred, and Charles Gillham. (Courtesy of the author's collection.)

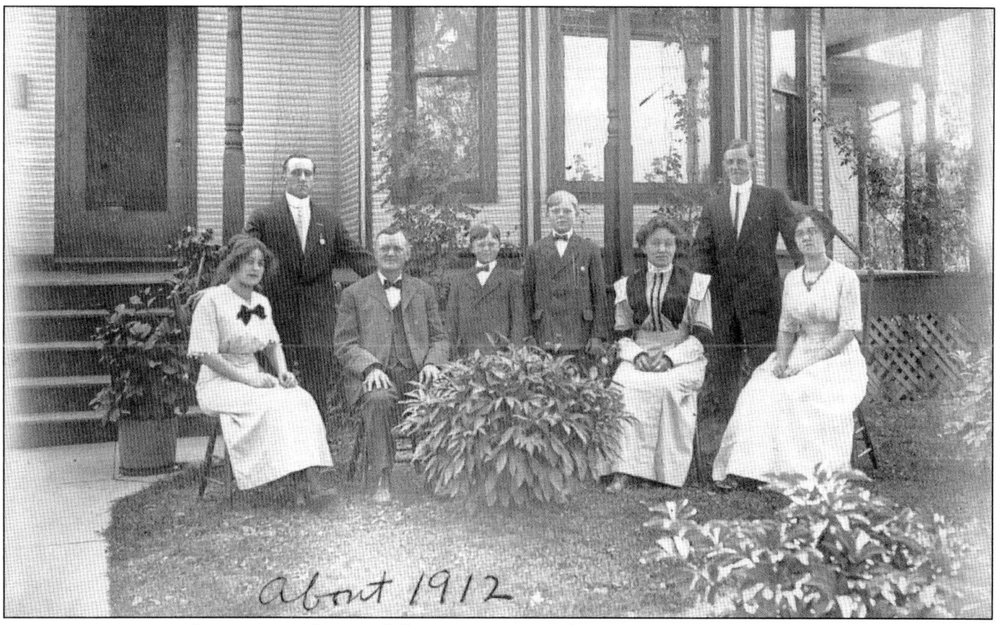

Here is the Beuttel family in front of their home on Glenn Avenue, around 1912. The Beuttels co-owned a bakery business with the Schmidt family. Mary Beuttel was an able businesswoman who handled the company's accounts and investments. Pictured from left to right are Elsie, Bill, William (father), George, Carl, Mary Bauer (mother), Walter, and Mayme. Bill Beuttel later served as mayor of Covington from 1940–1945. (Courtesy of Bill Beuttel.)

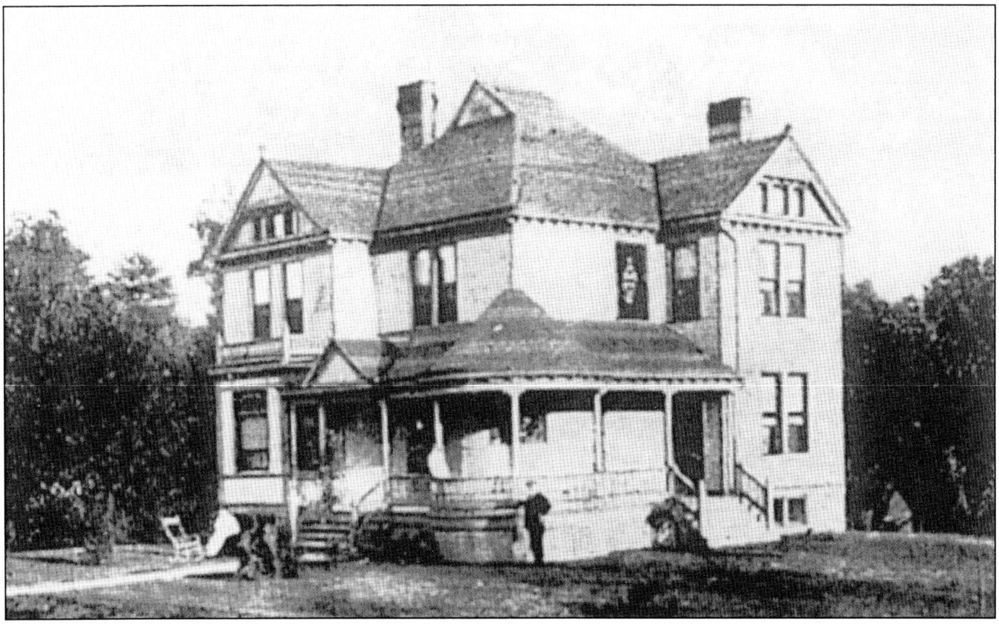

James Thomas Earle, the first—and only—mayor of Latonia, built this house on Southern Avenue near Myrtle Avenue in 1897. J. T., employed by the C&O Railroad, became president of Latonia's First National Bank, Latonia Board of Education, Latonia Grocery Company, and the Latonia Commercial Club. In 1905, he was elected mayor, but his brief tenure was controversial. (Courtesy of Karl Lietzenmayer.)

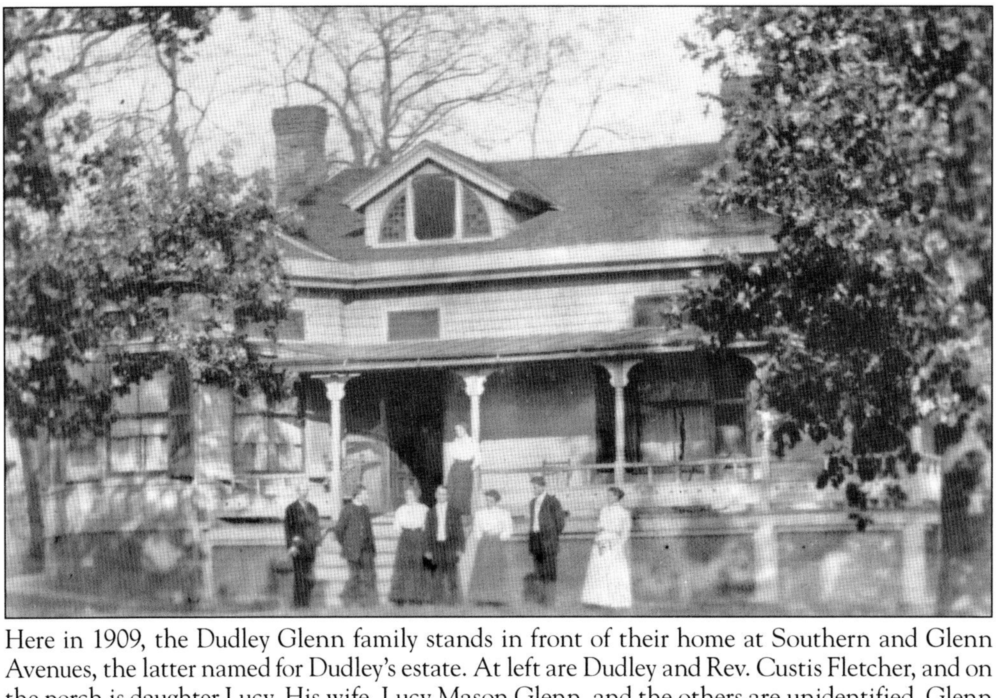

Here in 1909, the Dudley Glenn family stands in front of their home at Southern and Glenn Avenues, the latter named for Dudley's estate. At left are Dudley and Rev. Custis Fletcher, and on the porch is daughter Lucy. His wife, Lucy Mason Glenn, and the others are unidentified. Glenn was an early trustee, or councilman, of Latonia and rose to prominence in politics. (Courtesy of Karl Lietzenmayer.)

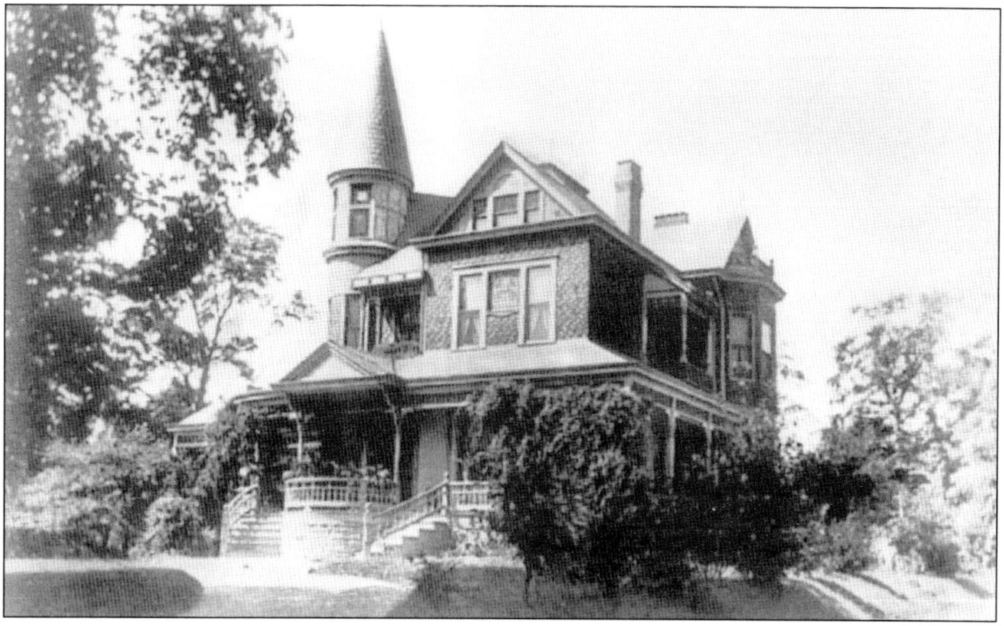

This mansion belonged to the family of John R. Coppin, who owned Coppin's, Covington's largest department store, as well as a subdivision near his home on Latonia's west side. This house faced a lake where neighbors were welcomed to ice skate. In 1957, the Covington Board of Education bought the mansion and demolished it to make way for Ninth District School. The drained lake is now a sports field. (Courtesy of the author's collection.)

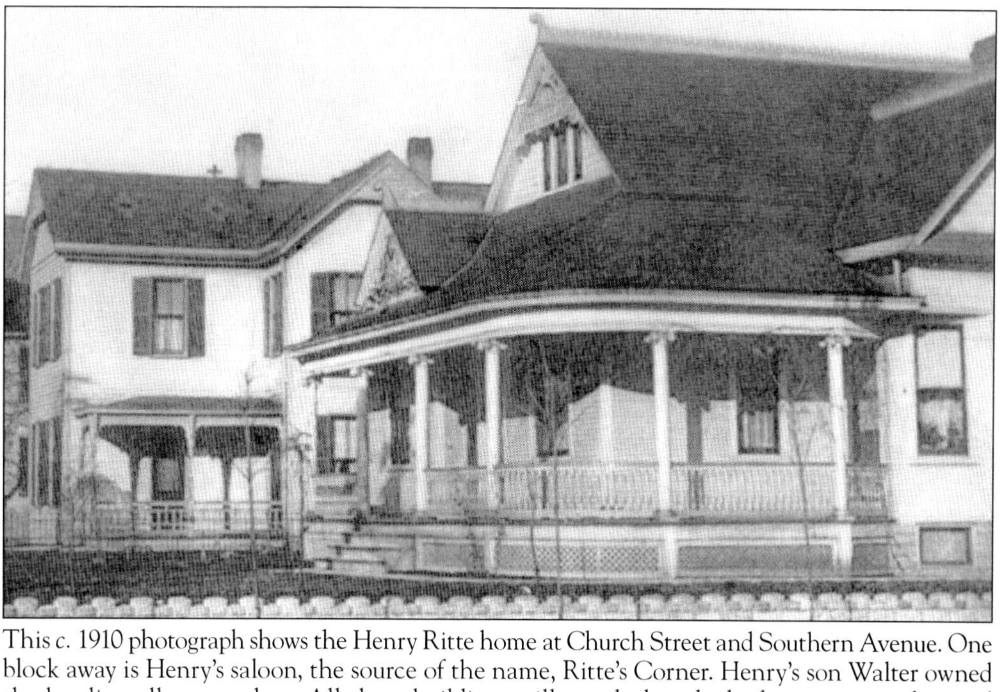

This c. 1910 photograph shows the Henry Ritte home at Church Street and Southern Avenue. One block away is Henry's saloon, the source of the name, Ritte's Corner. Henry's son Walter owned the bowling alley next door. All three buildings still stand, though the home was modernized recently. By 1928, Henry built a Tudor-style house behind the family home but facing Southern Avenue, and Walter took over the family home. (Courtesy of the author's collection.)

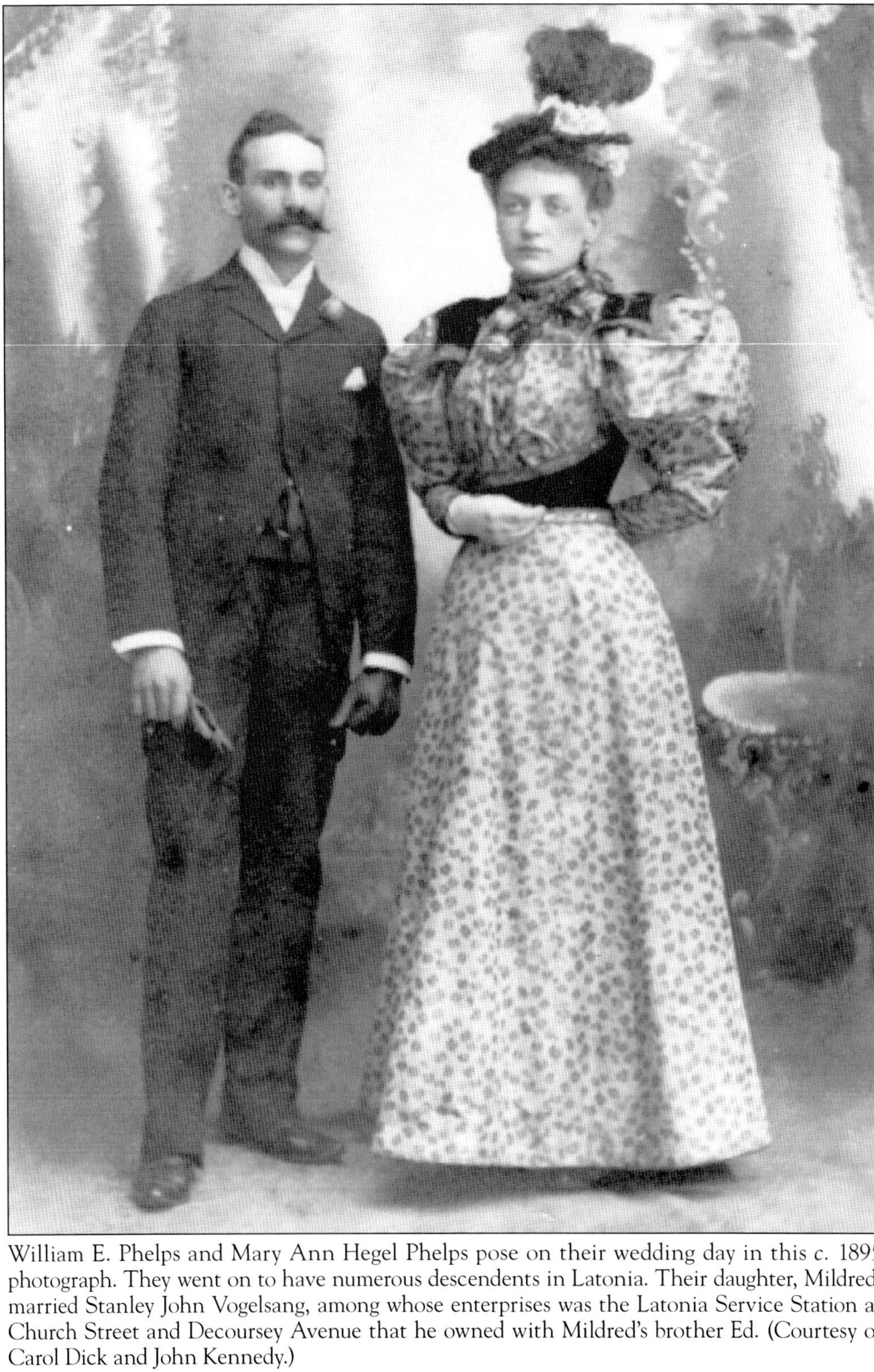

William E. Phelps and Mary Ann Hegel Phelps pose on their wedding day in this *c.* 1895 photograph. They went on to have numerous descendents in Latonia. Their daughter, Mildred, married Stanley John Vogelsang, among whose enterprises was the Latonia Service Station at Church Street and Decoursey Avenue that he owned with Mildred's brother Ed. (Courtesy of Carol Dick and John Kennedy.)

Carrie Beets Connley holds Harold, her second son with Dr. J. E. Connley, a dentist. The Beets family owned a lumberyard and lived two blocks from Carrie and Doc. Harold, with his brother Jack, grew up to open a funeral parlor in his family home. The funeral home is still known as Connley's, though the family no longer owns it. The large Beets home succumbed to St. Mark's Church's need for parking. (Courtesy of the author's collection.)

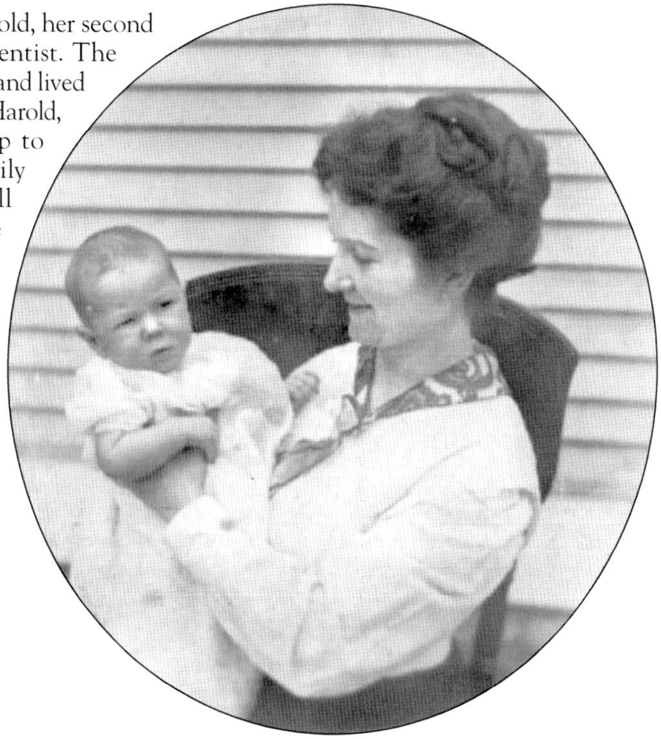

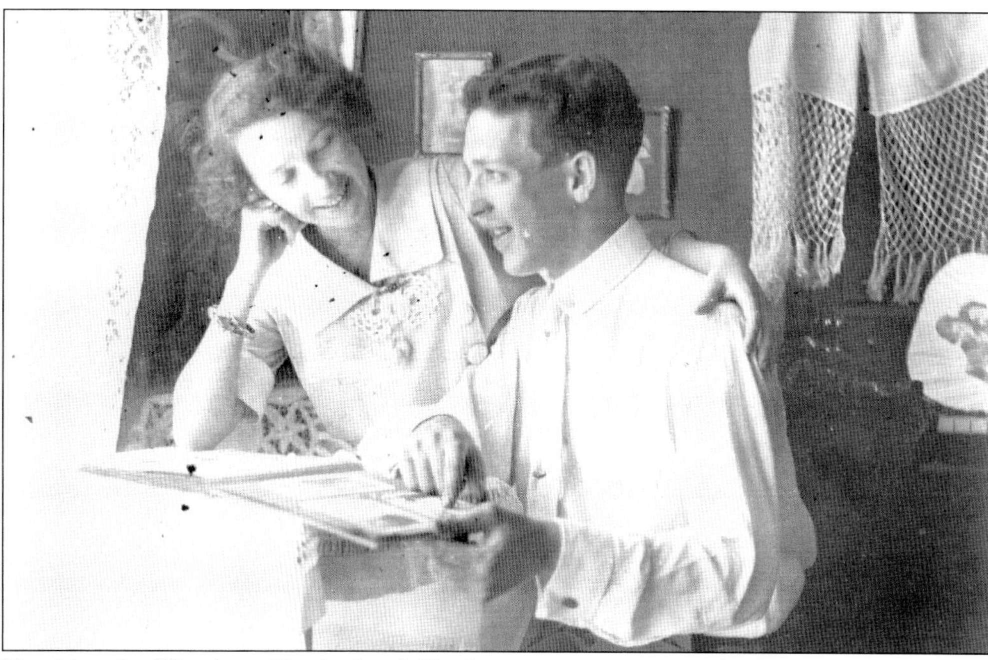

Flora Nienaber Warnke and her husband, Charles, enjoy a moment together looking at a photograph album. They lived at Forty-second and Church Streets. Judging from her photograph album, theirs was a happy union. Charles worked on the railroad and was a member of the Freemasons. Flora worked as a "floor lady" at Distillery Company No. 2, near the Latonia Depot. (Courtesy of Jim Feldman.)

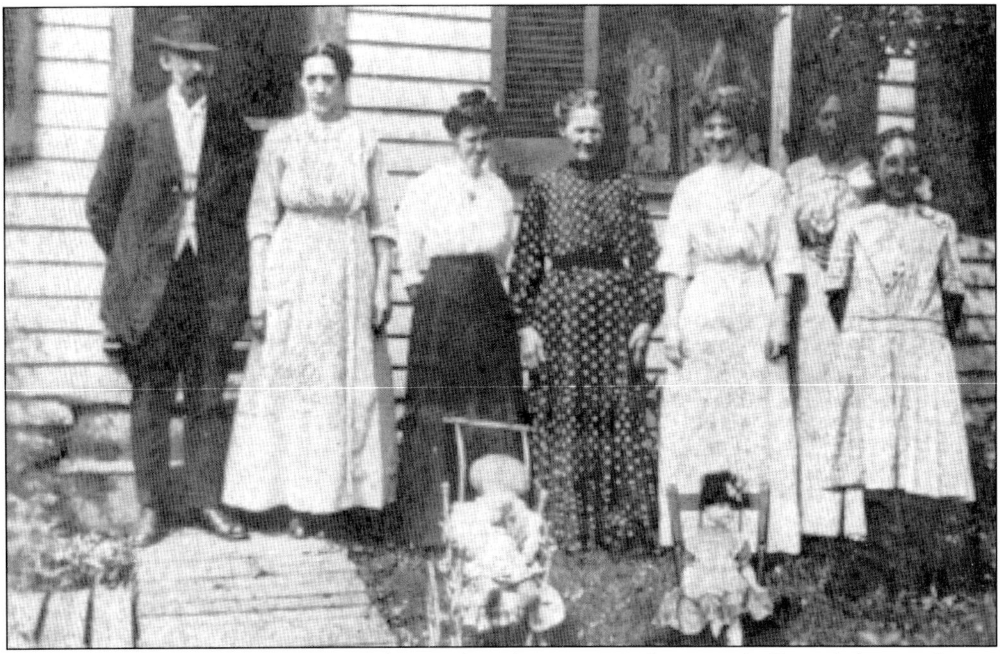

Members of the Osborn family are featured in this *c.* 1910 photograph. From left to right are ? Chrisman and his wife, Addie Osborn Chrisman; unidentified; Nancy Jane Skirvin Osborn, mother of Addie; unidentified; Cora, Addie's sister; and (at far right) her daughter Dolly Dimples Osborn. The "children" in front are family dolls. (Courtesy of Tricia Dorman.)

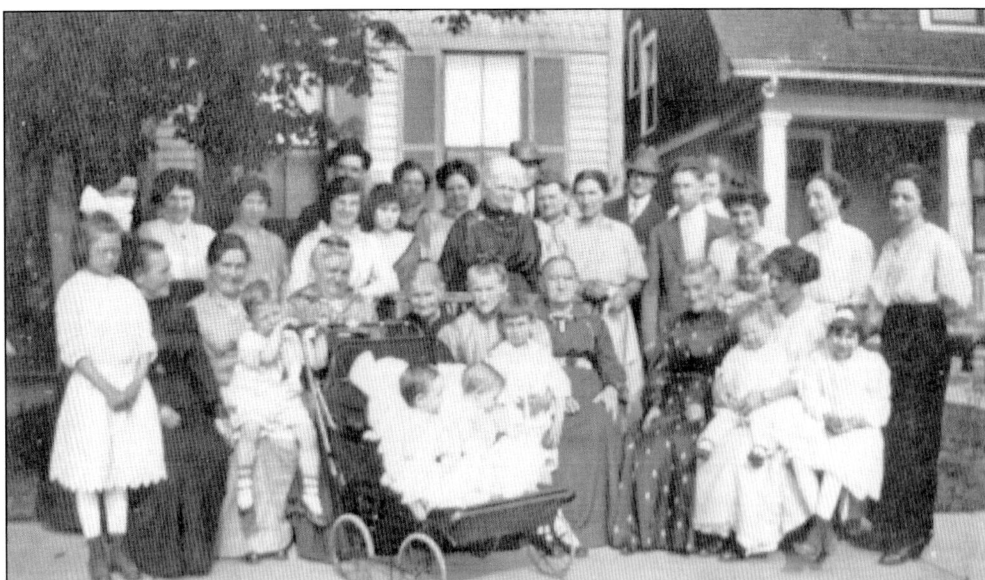

Family gathers at the Lincoln Avenue home of Elizabeth and Henry Hufnagel around 1905. Elizabeth, widowed then, lived there with sons Frank (an L&N fireman), and George and John (L&N engineers). Families represented are Hufnagels, Feltens, and Martins. In the baby carriage are Madeline (left) and John Martin (right). The house, built in 1891 and still standing, later became home to the family of Charley Mulvey, stationmaster of the nearby depot. (Courtesy of Tom Martin.)

Frederick and Catherine Siefert hold their baby Catherine outside their bakery at Thirty-eighth Street and Decoursey Avenue, which Fred opened in 1935. He married Catherine Legner in 1938, and, the following year, Catherine was born. In about 1940, they bought a building in Covington for a home and bakery, where they had three more children. Notice Vogelsang's Latonia Service Station in rear. (Courtesy of Mary Martha Siefert Kaiser.)

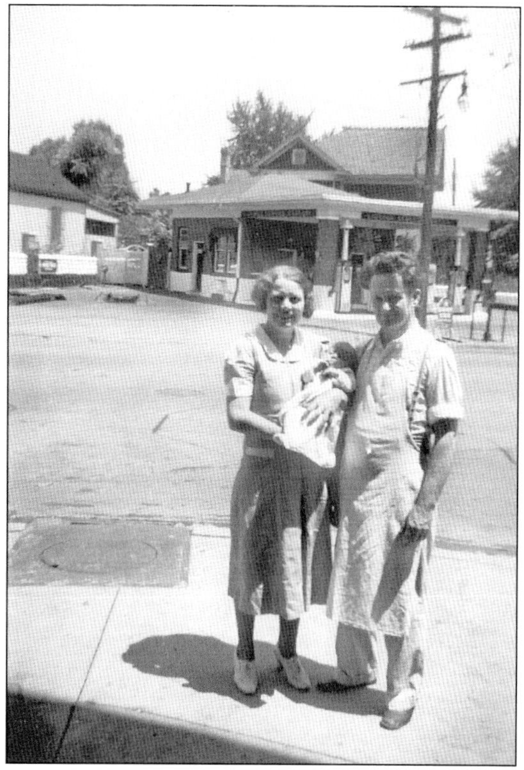

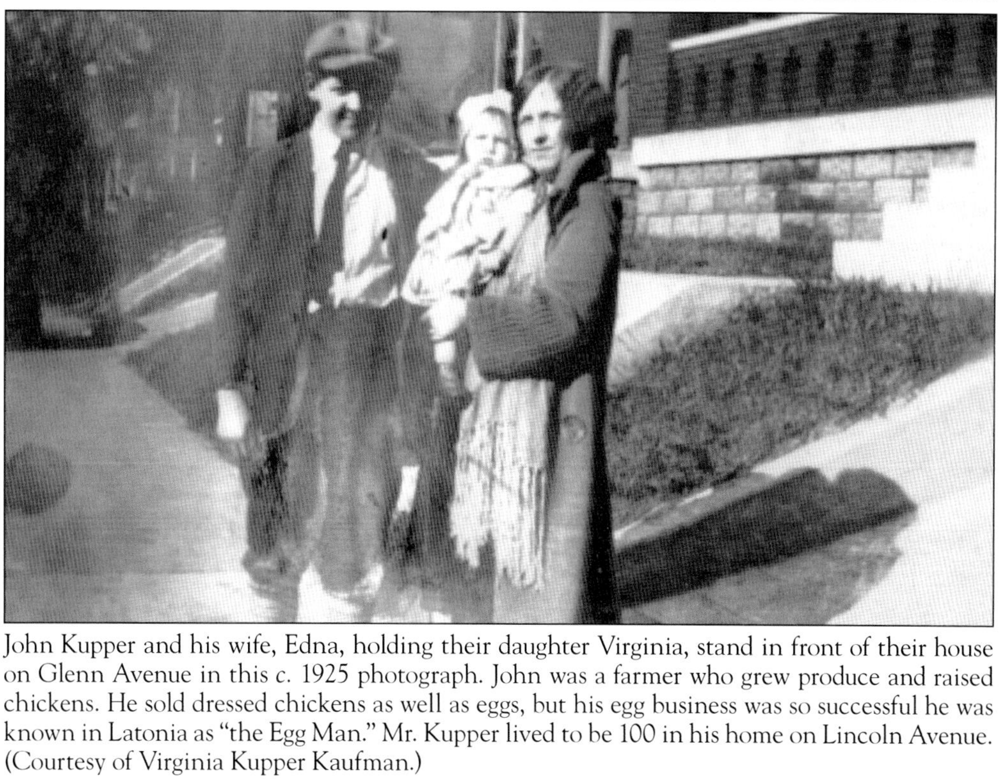

John Kupper and his wife, Edna, holding their daughter Virginia, stand in front of their house on Glenn Avenue in this c. 1925 photograph. John was a farmer who grew produce and raised chickens. He sold dressed chickens as well as eggs, but his egg business was so successful he was known in Latonia as "the Egg Man." Mr. Kupper lived to be 100 in his home on Lincoln Avenue. (Courtesy of Virginia Kupper Kaufman.)

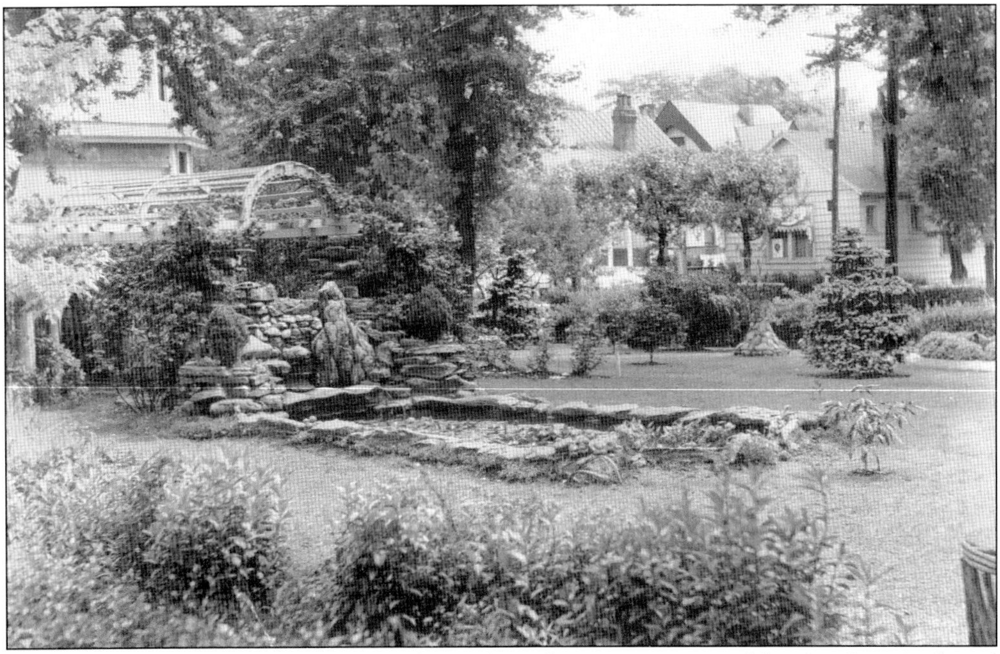

This view, taken around 1930, shows the garden of Dr. Lucas Lee and his family at Park and Southern Avenues. Dr. Lee was a prominent dentist and property owner in Latonia, and his garden was his passion. He had extensive stonework added to the Queen Anne–style home, including the rustic stone fishpond pictured. The pergola connected to a stone patio and greenhouse. The house was previously owned by Henry Kruse. (Courtesy of Betty Lee.)

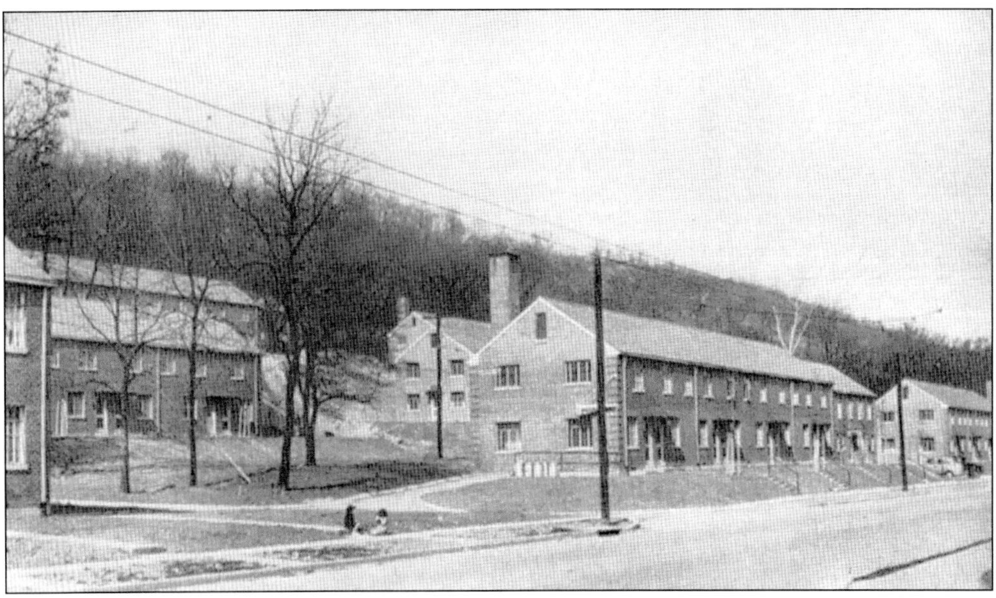

Latonia Terrace, a federally sponsored public housing project, was constructed around 1940 on Madison Pike. Part of Franklin Roosevelt's New Deal, it provided housing for low-income people in response to the Depression when so many lost their homes. It was built on the site of Parker's farm, and the old farmhouse was standing when construction began. (Courtesy of www.nkyviews.com.)

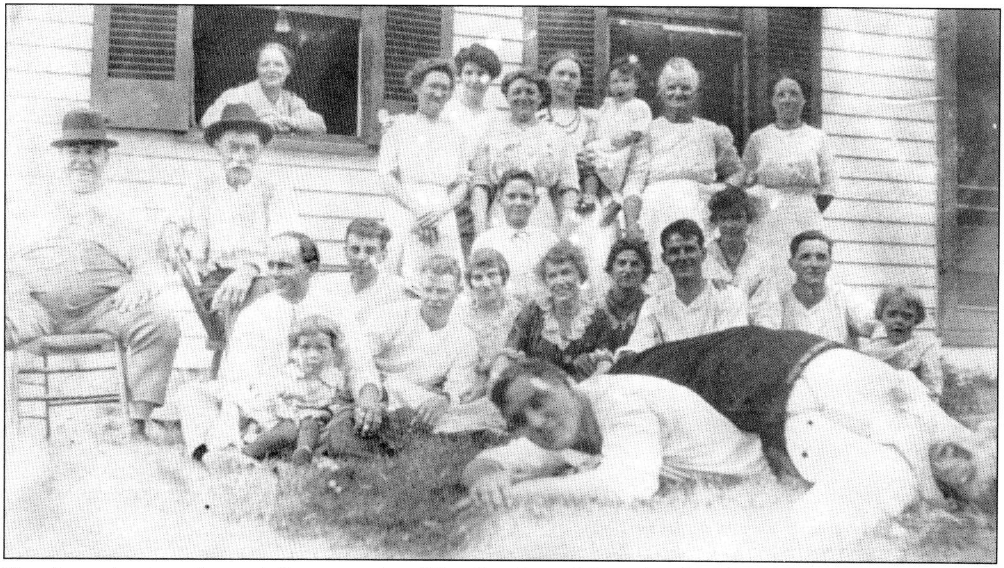

Family gatherings have different styles. The Smith and Luzader families (above) enjoy a picnic in this c. 1914 photograph. The following, from left to right, are: (in chairs) George Smith, known as "Big Smitty" for obvious reasons; Henry Luzader, George's father-in-law; (standing) Lizzie Luzader Smith, Frederica Dias Smith, and Annie Luzader May. Standing second from right is Lizzie's great-aunt Dora Leistner. Seated third from left is Charley Gillham, then Georgie Smith, Janet Smith, Fern Smith Gillham, Ethel Luzader Seale, and Hayden Seale. On the ground in front are actor Harry Smith and a pal hamming it up as usual. Below is the Hengehold family gathered for a formal family portrait in front of the original Holy Cross Church, which was then used as the school. The building was razed in 1914 to accommodate the new school. (Above, courtesy of the author's collection.; below, by photographer August Koenig, courtesy of Kenton County Public Library.)

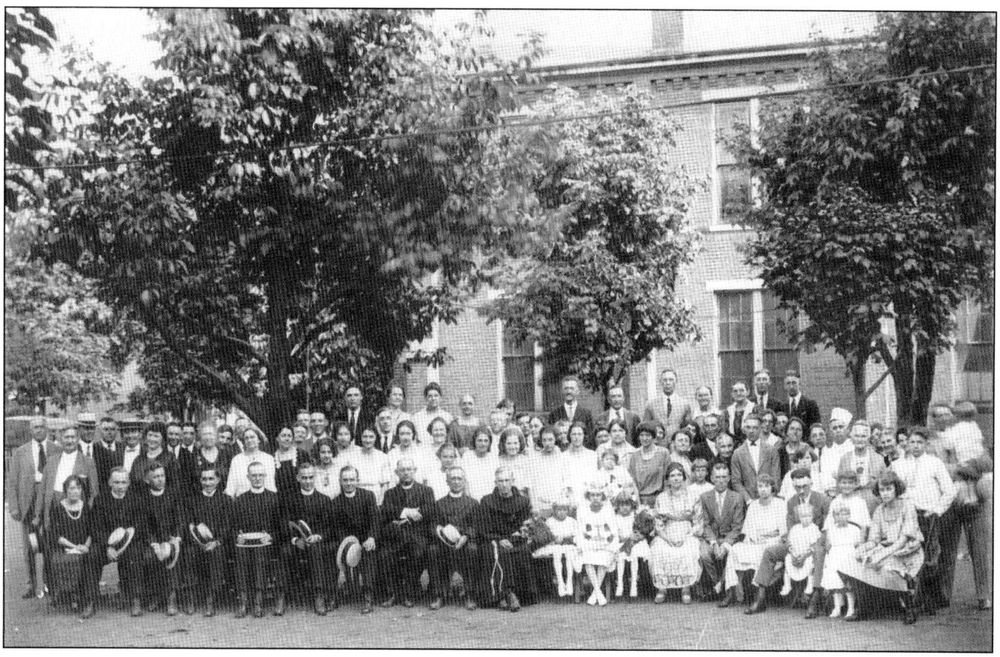

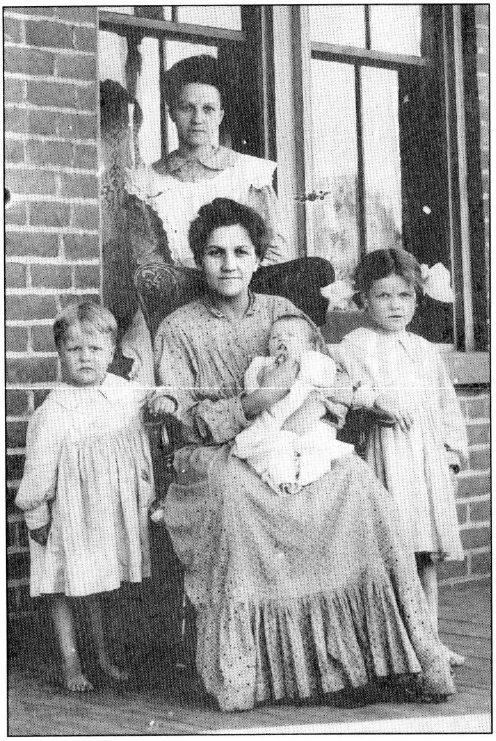

Lillian Hartman MacMannis holds her youngest son, known as "Junior," in this c. 1928 photograph. Behind her is her daughter Louise (Smith). At right is her daughter Helen, and, at left is her son Joseph. They lived on Huntington Avenue across from the infirmary. Lillian's husband, George MacMannis, worked for the L&N as a hostler, caring for engines at Decoursey yards. (Courtesy of the author's collection.)

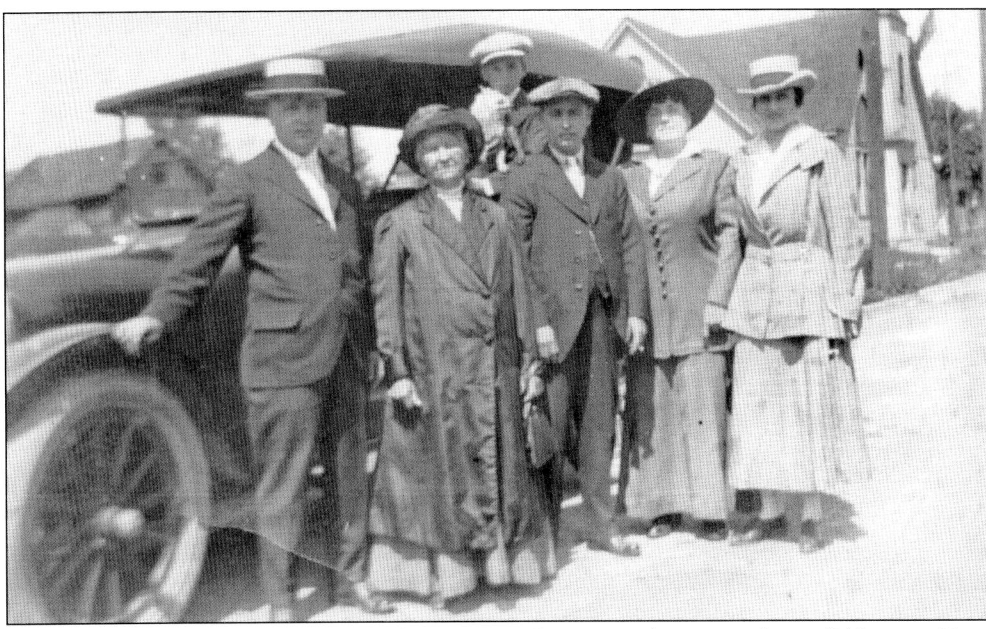

The Carroll family poses on Thirty-sixth Street near Decoursey Avenue in this *c.* 1915 image. From left to right are Frank Carroll, who owned a bar next to Latonia Bakery; Levina Carroll, known as "Grandma Poopah," a Native American; cousin Arvo; family dog Trixie; and William Carroll with his wife, Mary, and their only daughter, Levina. William had been an important jockey, but he suffered a serious injury in a racetrack accident. The original Latonia Christian Church is in the background. (Courtesy of Mary Cecil.)

Two

THE RACETRACK

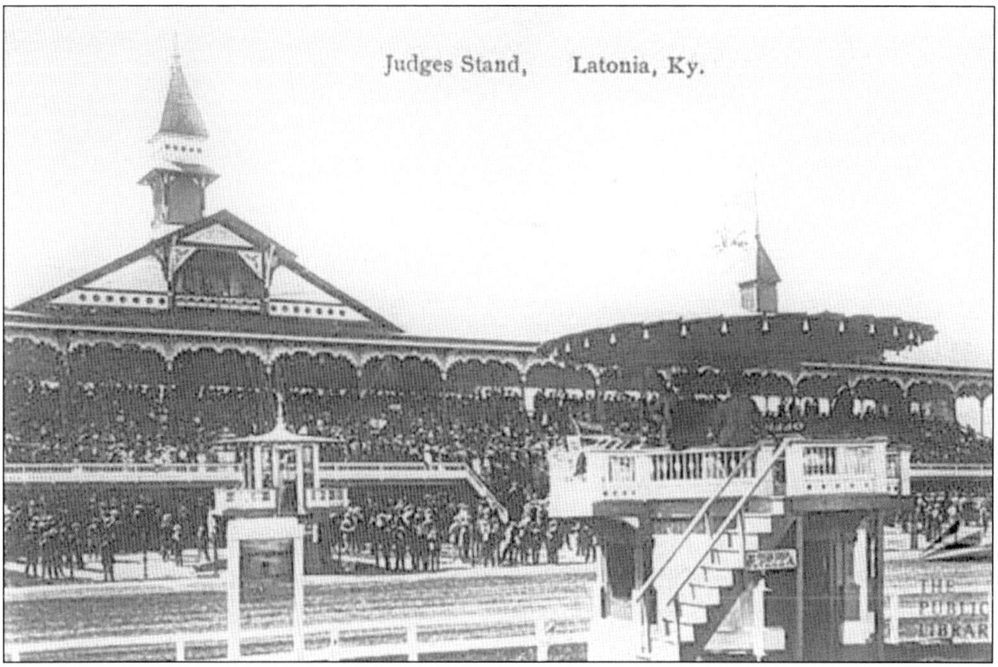

The Latonia Racetrack was opened in 1883 by the Latonia Agricultural and Stock Association, and it closed in 1939. During the interim, it enjoyed a colorful history and helped to build a town. It was, indisputably, one of the finest and most beautiful racetracks in the country during its heyday of the 1880s through the 1920s. It offered rich purses and quality stakes races that drew top horses, owners, trainers, and jockeys. Latonia held two yearly meets, spring-summer and late fall. Its premier race was the Latonia Derby, which, though not as old as the Kentucky Derby, for a time paid a higher purse. Among top horses that ran at Latonia were Kentucky Derby winners Leonatus, Old Rosebud, Exterminator, Zev, and In Memoriam. Top jockeys such as Isaac Murphy, Roscoe Goose, Mack Garner, Johnny McCabe, Johnny Loftus, and Eddie Arcaro rode there. For the town, its namesake, it created prosperity and drew celebrities and huge crowds every racing season. During its peak, the racetrack drew more than 100,000 visitors annually. It put Latonia on the map, nationwide. (Courtesy of www.nkyviews.com.)

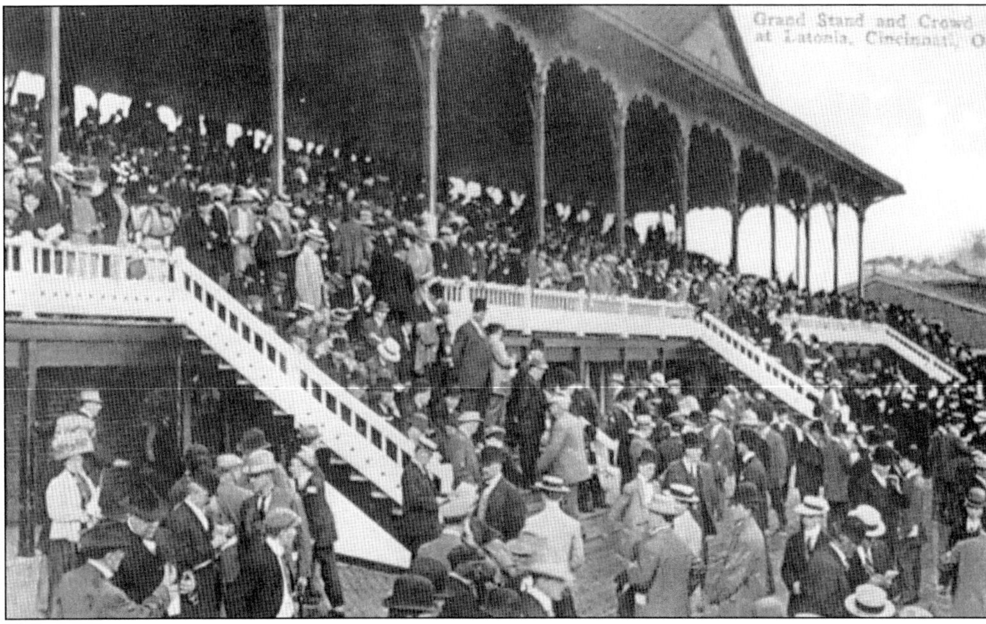

Latonia Racetrack's opening day, which was on July 9, 1883, drew a crowd estimated at 8,000 and was covered by the *New York Times*. The crowd arrived by carriage, wagon, on horseback, or on foot. Notice that this postcard located the racetrack in Cincinnati, Ohio. Cincinnati, of course, was the much larger and better-known city. Northern Kentucky's struggle for identity went on even then. (Courtesy of www.nkyviews.com.)

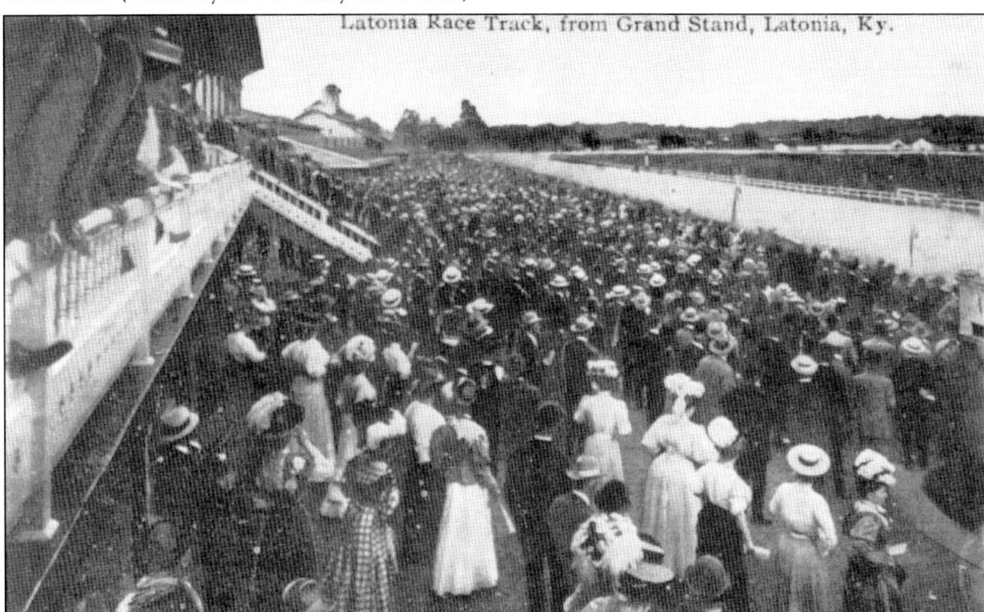

Season after season, the crowds came. Residents rented their homes and moved into their basements to profit from the influx of racetrack people. Businesses flourished, especially saloons; yet, Latonia Racetrack was as proper—and popular—a place for women as it was for men. It was the place to see and be seen. Most people dressed their best, as shown by the grand hats of these Edwardian ladies, in this *c.* 1909 image. (Courtesy of the author's collection.)

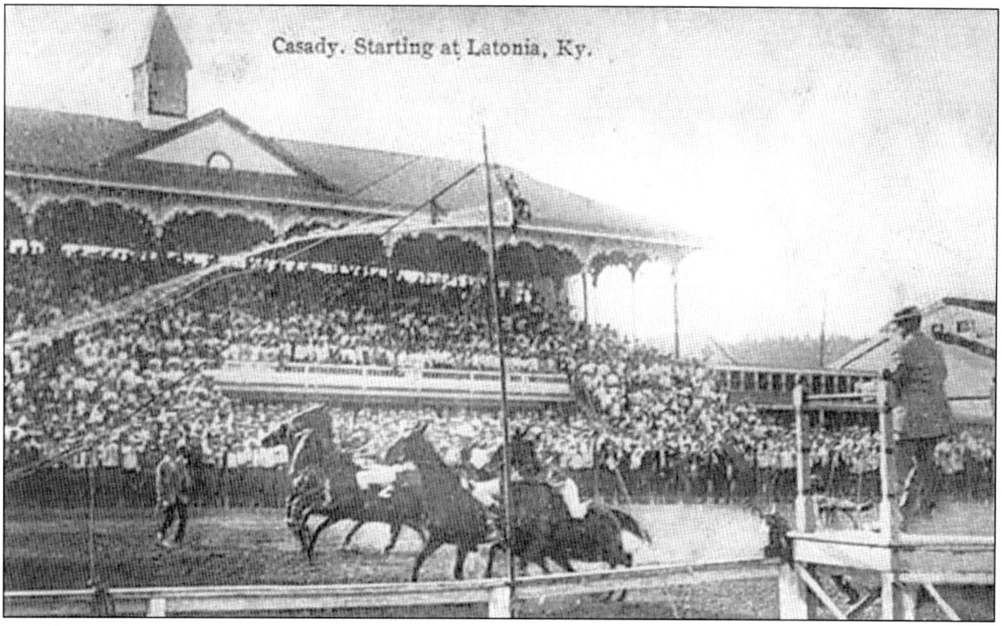

A talented starter was a real asset before the 1930s invention of the starting gate, and Marshall "Mars" Cassidy was one such star. In the early days, the horses were simply lined up and then broke at the discharge of the starter's pistol. The starter's job was to ensure that the horses remained calm and that each got a fair start. Cassidy was the first starter to use a barrier to start a race. (Courtesy of www.nkyviews.com.)

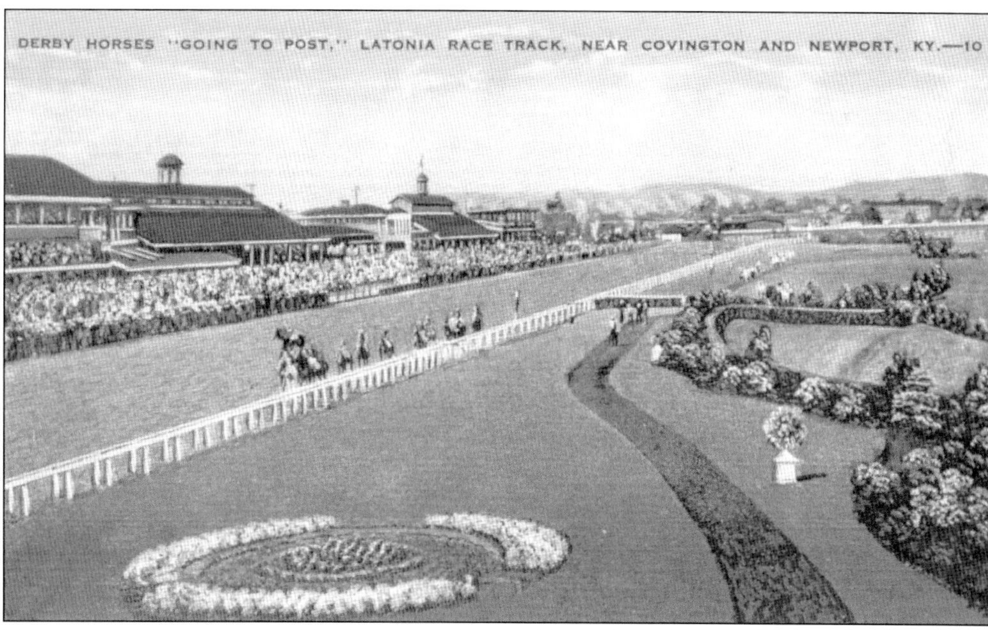

This postcard shows the track's landscaping. The infield was planted with formal beds and included a lake. James T. McGibben of Cynthiana, Kentucky, was the first president of the racetrack association that was made up of horsemen, businessmen, and officials from Northern and Central Kentucky. They purchased 109 acres in Milldale from John Taylor who was the son of Gen. James Taylor, who had extensive land holdings in the area. (Courtesy of the author's collection.)

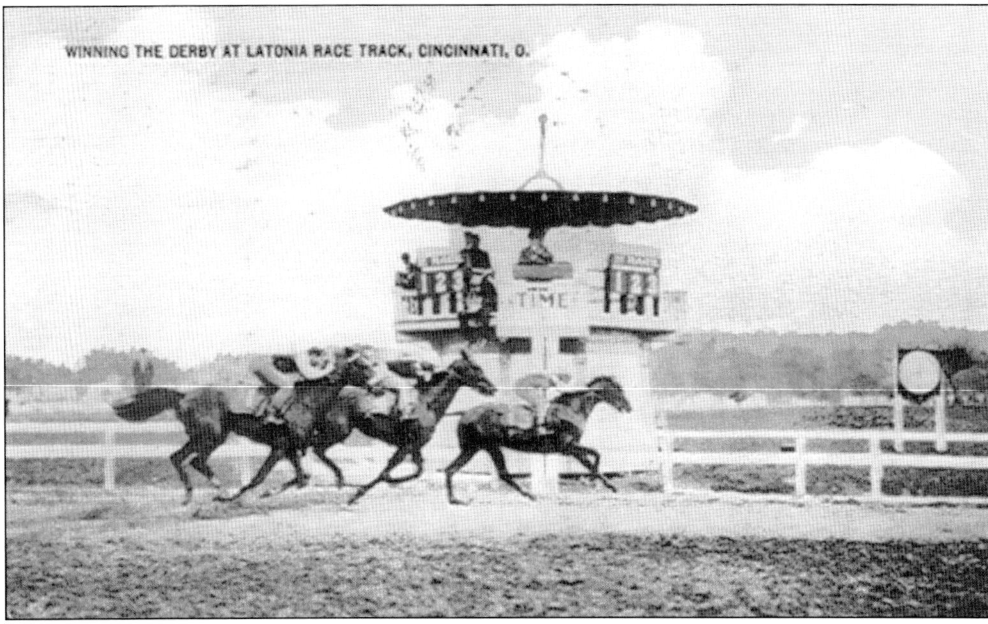

Horses cross the finish line in the Latonia Derby, passing the original judges' stand. It stood there so the judges could have a clear view of the order of finish. This was especially important in the days before the "photo finish." The decision of the judges was final. The Latonia Derby was a mile and a half long and like the Belmont Stakes today, was a grueling contest. (Courtesy of www.nkyviews.com.)

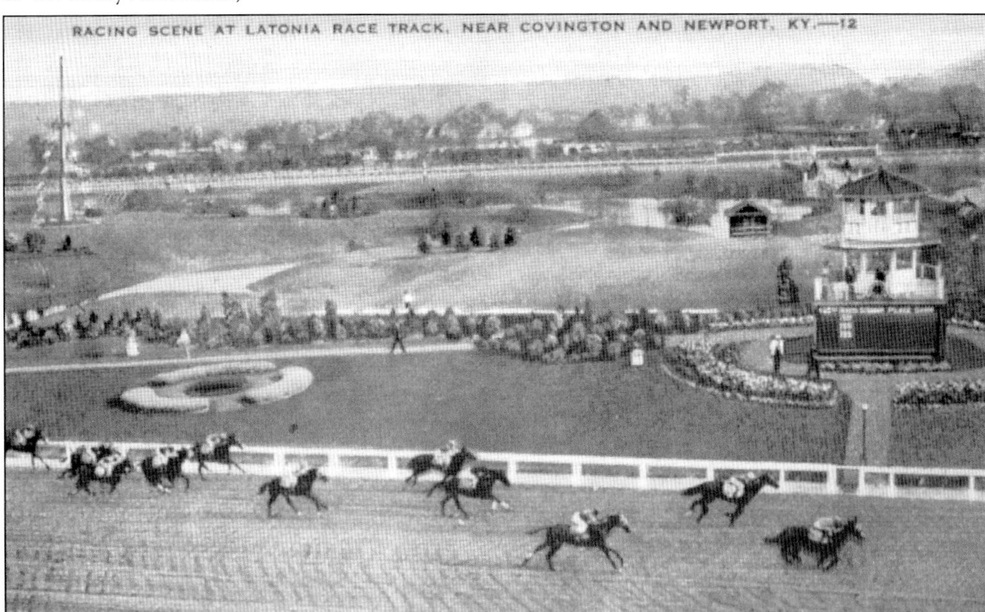

This postcard shows a broader view of the racetrack grounds in later years. Note the carefully manicured planting beds and the lake, visible beyond the hillock in the center. The old judges' stand had been replaced with a more substantial structure, and the grounds were expanded to 179 acres. The softly rolling Kenton County hills made a backdrop for the track, sometimes appearing in smoky silhouette like distant mountains. (Courtesy of the author's collection.)

Isaac Murphy was the first jockey inducted into the Hall of Fame. He won 44 percent of his races, an astonishing record that has never been threatened. Murphy won the Kentucky Derby three times and the Latonia Derby five times. Before 1910, black jockeys were quite common. In 1875, in the first Kentucky Derby, 13 of the 15 jockeys were African American. But Jim Crow laws intensified segregation, and black jockeys disappeared. (Courtesy of the author's collection.)

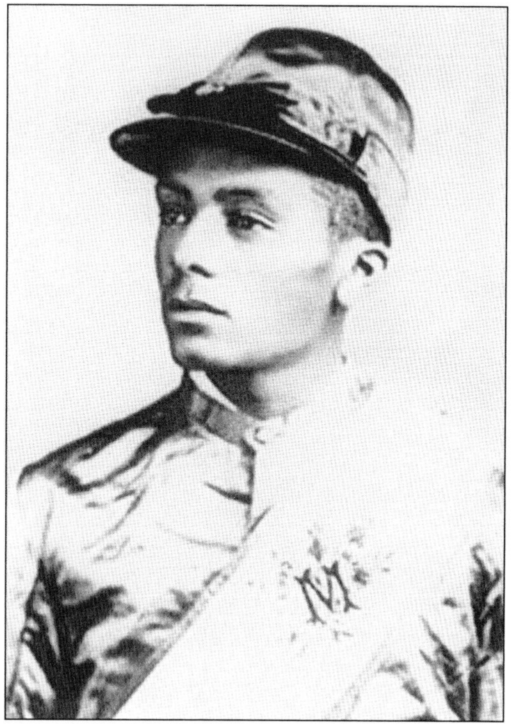

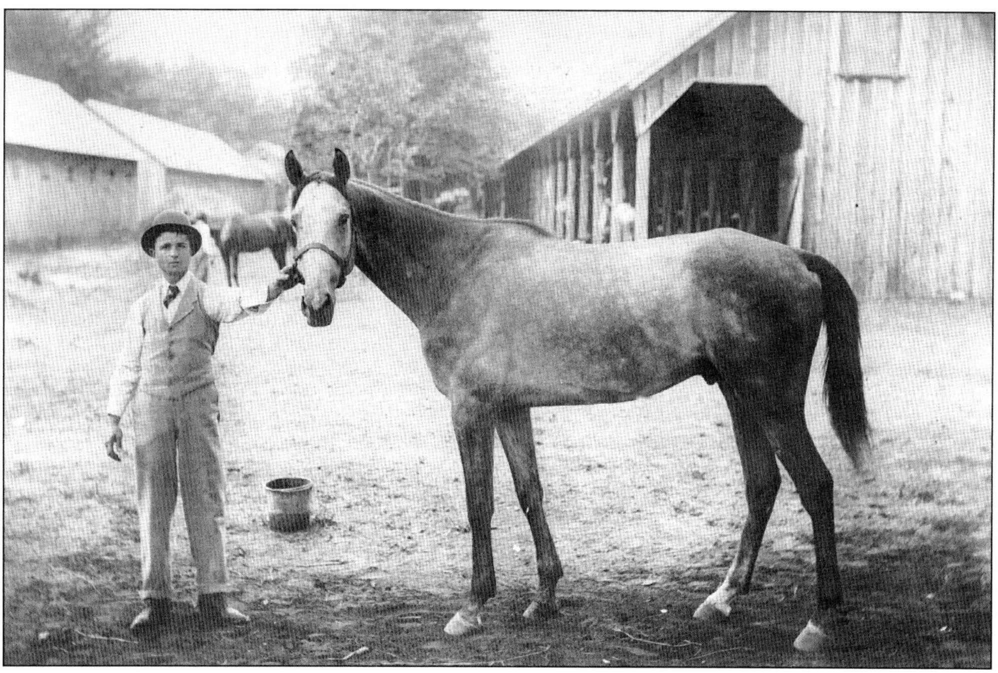

Billy Carroll, a well-known jockey and owner, holds one of his best horses, Lord Zeni, near the racetrack barns. When not following the racing circuit, the Carrolls lived at Southern and Eugenia Avenues. They stabled their horses at home in the sparsely populated area. Carroll's racing accident ended his riding career, but he continued to train and race his own horses successfully. (Courtesy of Mary Cecil.)

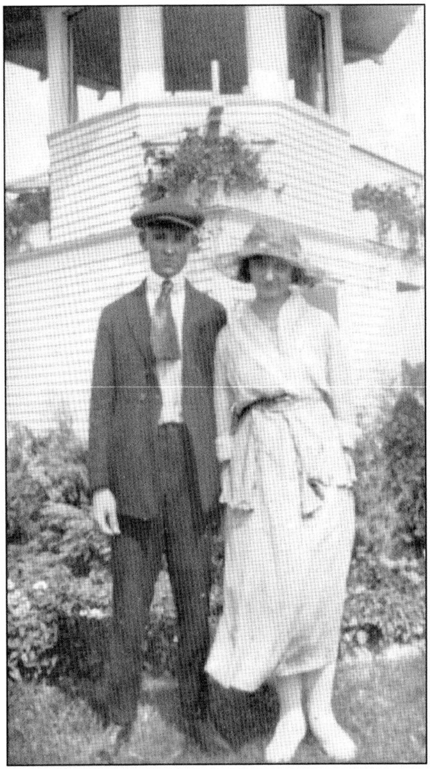

John and Edna Straley Kupper enjoy a day at the races. Ladies always wore hats when dressed up, and Edna looks lovely as a summer day. Anyone could feel like royalty at the magical racetrack. In 1905, however, "Princess" Alice Roosevelt, daughter of then president Teddy Roosevelt, visited the track with her future husband, Nicholas Longworth. It was a social pinnacle for Latonia that was long remembered. (Courtesy of Virginia Kupper Kaufman.)

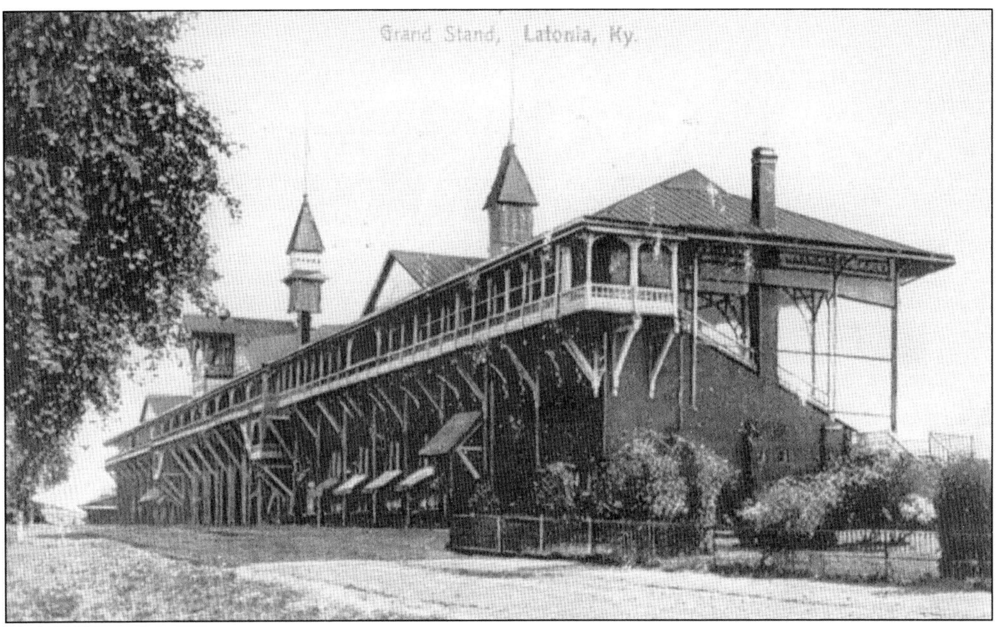

This is a 1907 view of the rear of the grandstand. Behind the grandstand was the paddock where horses were saddled for the post parade. Like backstage at a theater, racing fans could see the horses up close in the paddock and sense how they were feeling before their performance. The paddock still stands, though walls have been added to what was once an open, roofed area. (Courtesy of www.nkyviews.com.)

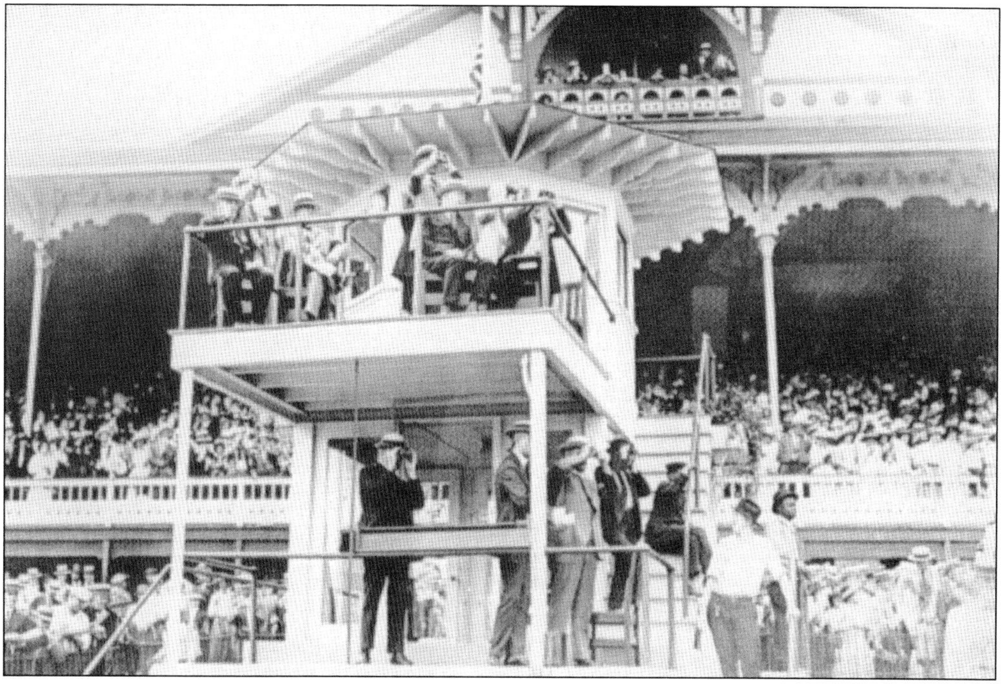

Here is another view of the judges' stand, with the grandstand behind it. Notice the ornamental fretwork and gingerbread trim adorning the graceful architectural lines. A kind of social distinction prevailed between the grandstand and the clubhouse, with the clubhouse offering a luxurious atmosphere and more amenities. However, both exhibited an unusual degree of desegregation in an era when most public facilites had areas designated as "white only" or "colored." (Courtesy of www.nkyviews.com.)

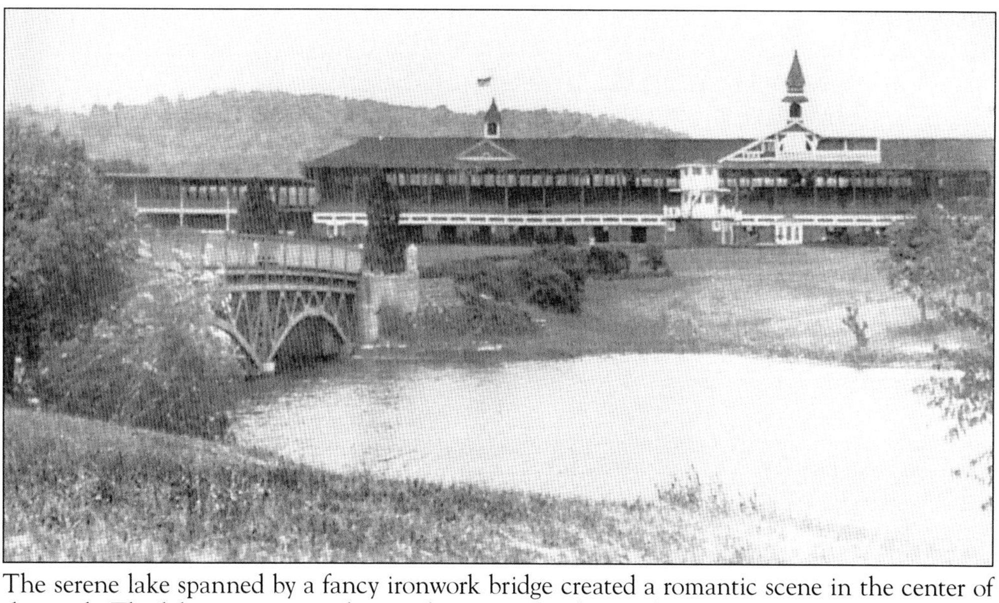

The serene lake spanned by a fancy ironwork bridge created a romantic scene in the center of the track. The lake was man-made, not that it was hard to strike water anywhere in Latonia, as any homeowner in pursuit of a dry basement will attest. After the track closed, there was many a Latonia kid who sneaked in for a swim or a bit of fishing. (Courtesy of the author's collection.)

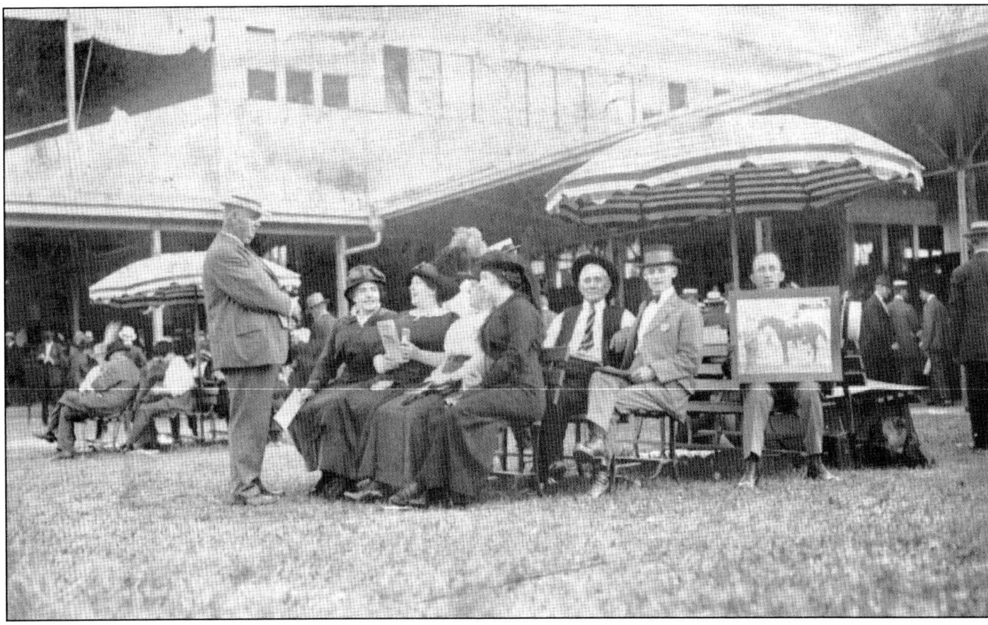

Under the umbrella, from left to right, are Henry Luzader (left) and his son-in-law, John "Bub" May (center). May owned a number of good racehorses, including High Ball. One is displayed by the friend at their right. May and his wife, Annie, built a large brick house on the west side of Latonia near her family. However, most of the time they followed the races around the country. (Courtesy of the author's collection.)

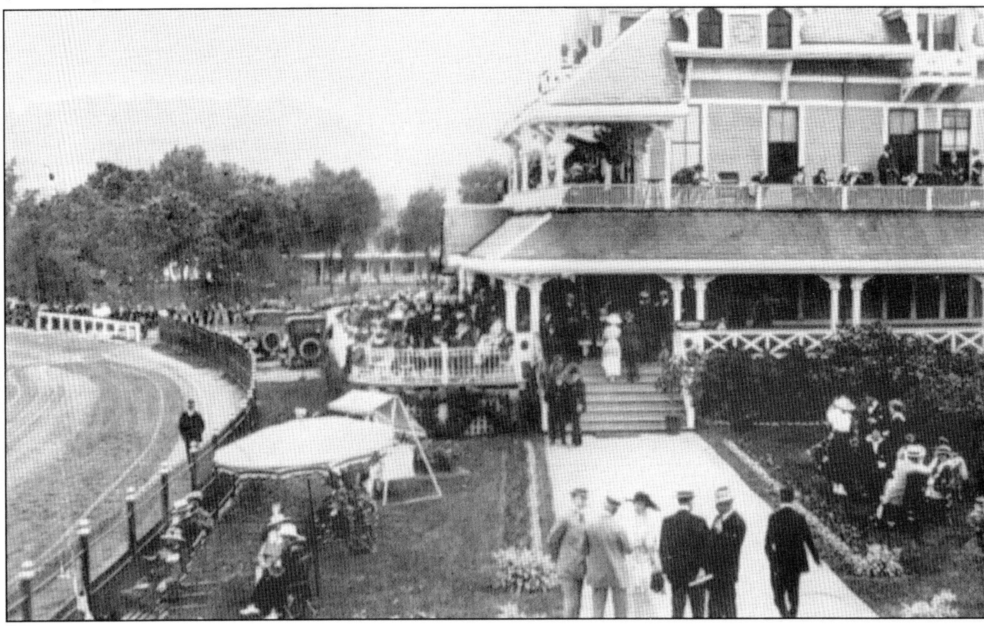

The clubhouse was an impressive piece of Victorian architecture. It offered shelter on spacious porches and had richly appointed interiors and surfaces detailed with carving and fancy millwork. Here, for a price, could be found refreshment befitting elegant ladies or hard Kentucky bourbon for horsemen, politicians, and businessmen. They socialized, flirted, made deals, and even occasionally watched the horses. (Courtesy of www.nkyviews.com.)

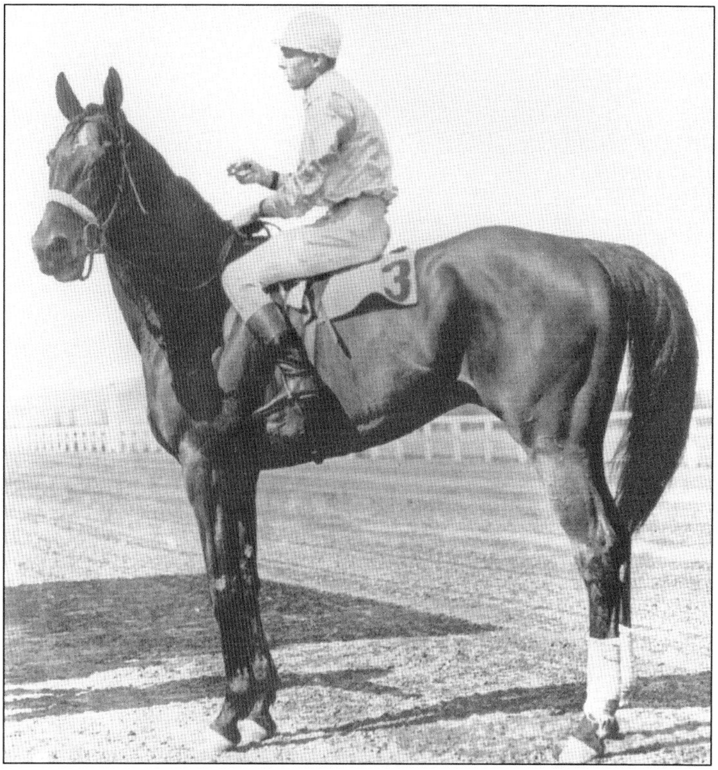

Johnny McCabe is astride Old Rosebud, the horse he rode to victory in the 1914 Kentucky Derby. Both competed in Latonia often. McCabe was in town long enough to woo a young lady he'd hoped to marry. Alas, she turned him down. Old Rosebud had local adventures, too. As part of his training, he was hitched to a sulky and, according to folk story, pulled it around the streets of Latonia. (Courtesy of the author's collection.)

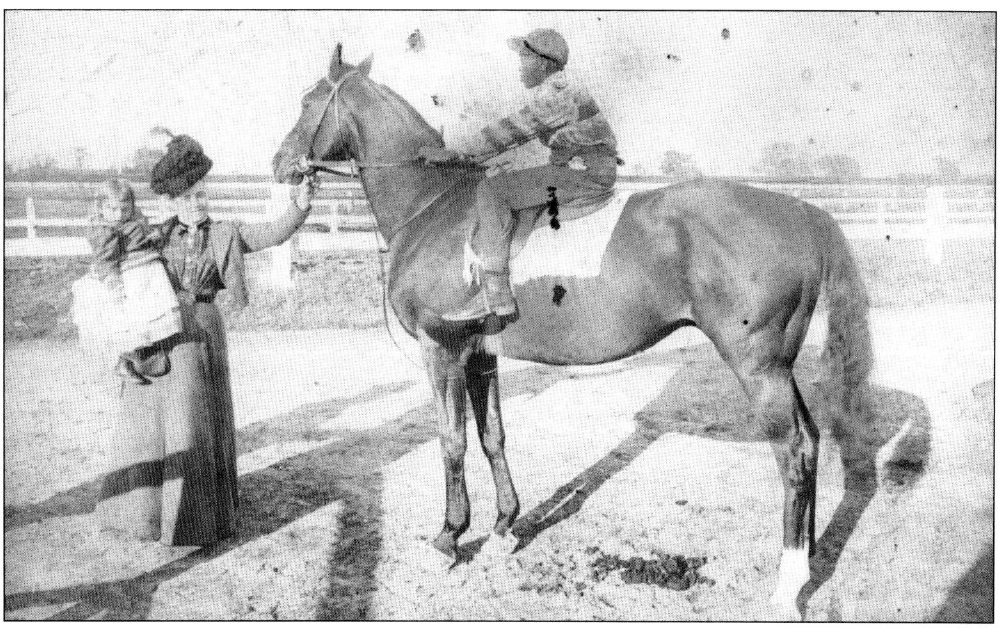

Mary Carroll, wife of owner, trainer, and jockey Billy Carroll, holds their only daughter, Levina, in one arm and one of their horses with the other. This may be their filly named Levina C, in honor of their little girl. Mrs. C. E. Durnell of California, the first woman to own a Kentucky Derby winner, Elwood in 1904, raced her horses at Latonia. This exercise boy is unidentified. (Courtesy of Mary Cecil.)

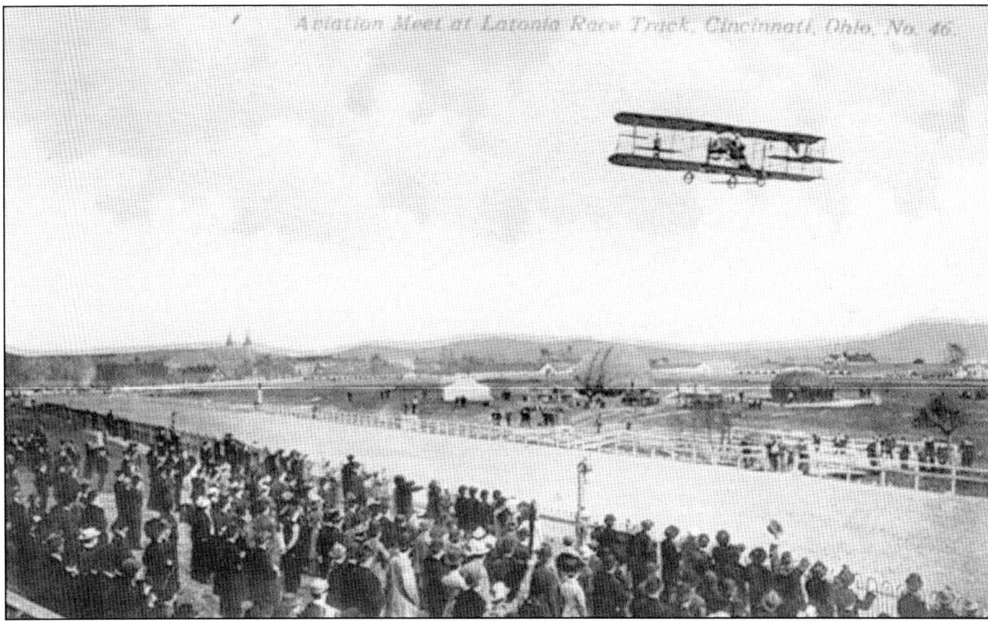

After 1900, the racetrack became a venue for events other than horseracing. In 1909, an aviation meet was held there. Its highlight was a race between famous aviator Glenn Curtiss and Charles Willard. The meet was part of an effort to make Cincinnati the site of the 1910 international air meet. Cincinnati lost out to Los Angeles, but Curtiss won the race. (Courtesy of www.nkyviews.com.)

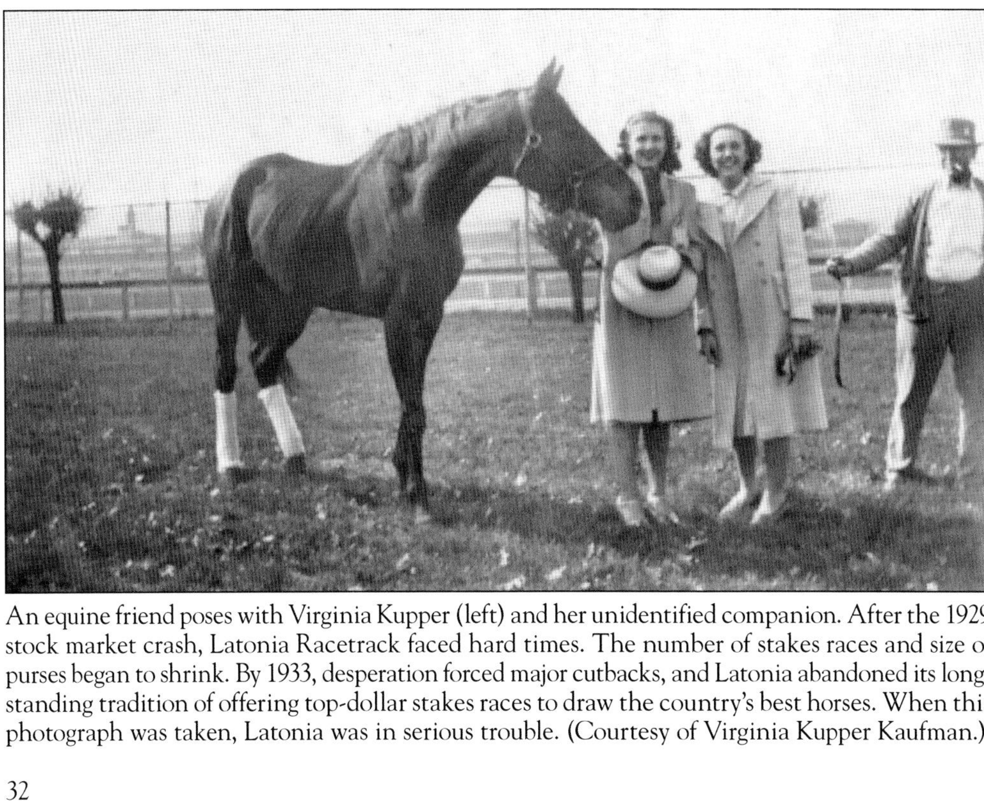

An equine friend poses with Virginia Kupper (left) and her unidentified companion. After the 1929 stock market crash, Latonia Racetrack faced hard times. The number of stakes races and size of purses began to shrink. By 1933, desperation forced major cutbacks, and Latonia abandoned its long-standing tradition of offering top-dollar stakes races to draw the country's best horses. When this photograph was taken, Latonia was in serious trouble. (Courtesy of Virginia Kupper Kaufman.)

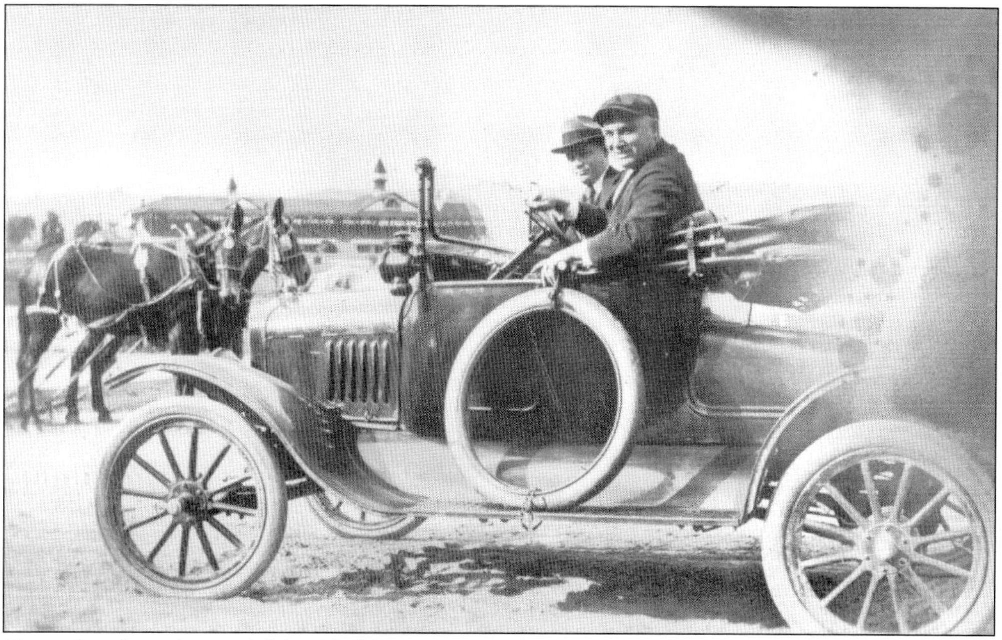

Harry Smith, right, and John "Bub" May cruise the grounds in Harry's "flivver." In the track's earliest days, transportation had been largely by streetcars drawn by mules like those facing Harry's automobile. By 1893, there were electric streetcars, and L&N railroad shuttles brought crowds from Cincinnati. By the 1920s and 1930s, automobile traffic on big racing days could be bumper to bumper for miles into Covington's streets. (Courtesy of the author's collection.)

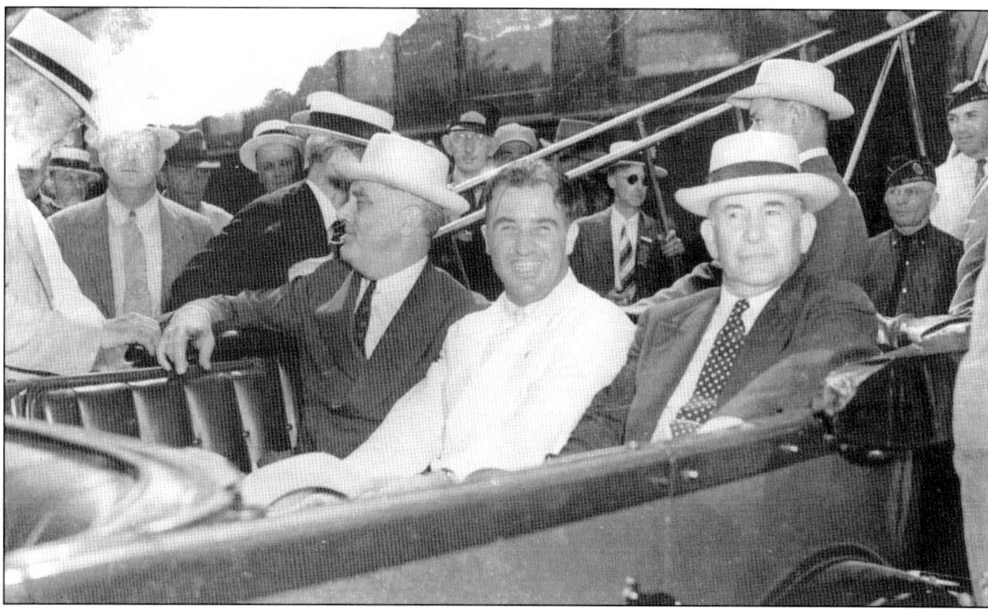

In 1938, President Roosevelt visited Latonia Racetrack while campaigning for U.S. senator Alben Barkley. Barkley's spotlight dimmed when opponent Kentucky governor "Happy" Chandler planted himself between Barkley and President Roosevelt in the touring car. Chandler grins broadly, while a solemn Barkley watches him from the corner of his eyes. Barkley had the last laugh though, defeating Chandler. (Courtesy Kenton County Public Library.)

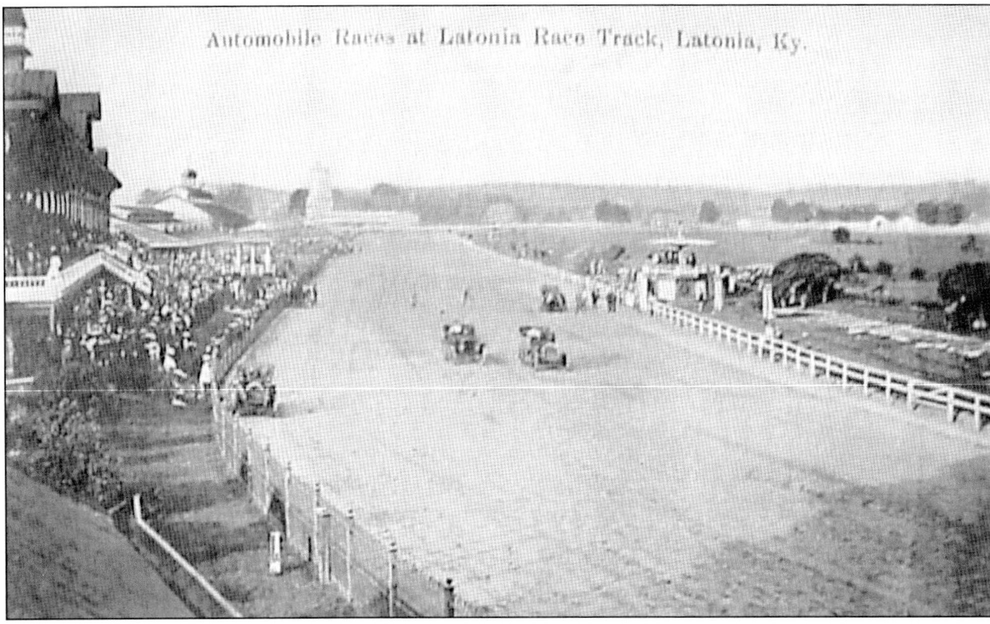

Automobile and motorcycle races were held at the track in later years. The world was changing around the elegant old dame of a racetrack. One by one, the major stables left. Major trainers, who were once the backbone of old Latonia, retired or died. Jockeys followed richer purses elsewhere. By the late 1930s, Latonia had become a second-rate track with dismal horses and puny purses. The writing was on the wall. (Courtesy of www.nkyviews.com.)

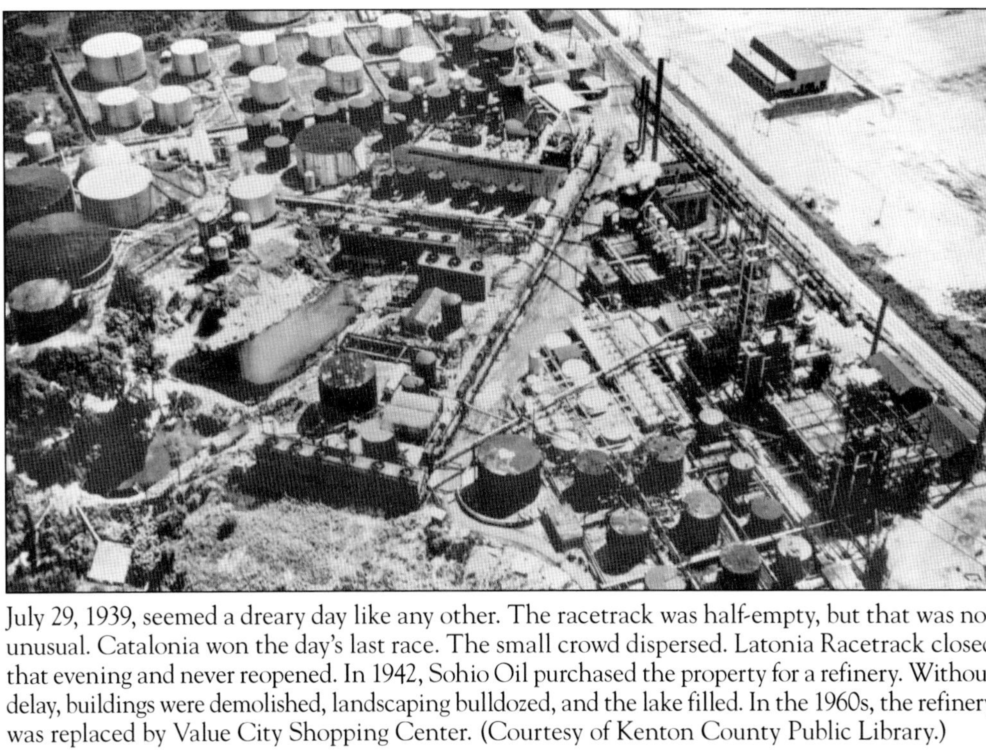

July 29, 1939, seemed a dreary day like any other. The racetrack was half-empty, but that was not unusual. Catalonia won the day's last race. The small crowd dispersed. Latonia Racetrack closed that evening and never reopened. In 1942, Sohio Oil purchased the property for a refinery. Without delay, buildings were demolished, landscaping bulldozed, and the lake filled. In the 1960s, the refinery was replaced by Value City Shopping Center. (Courtesy of Kenton County Public Library.)

Three

THE RAILROAD

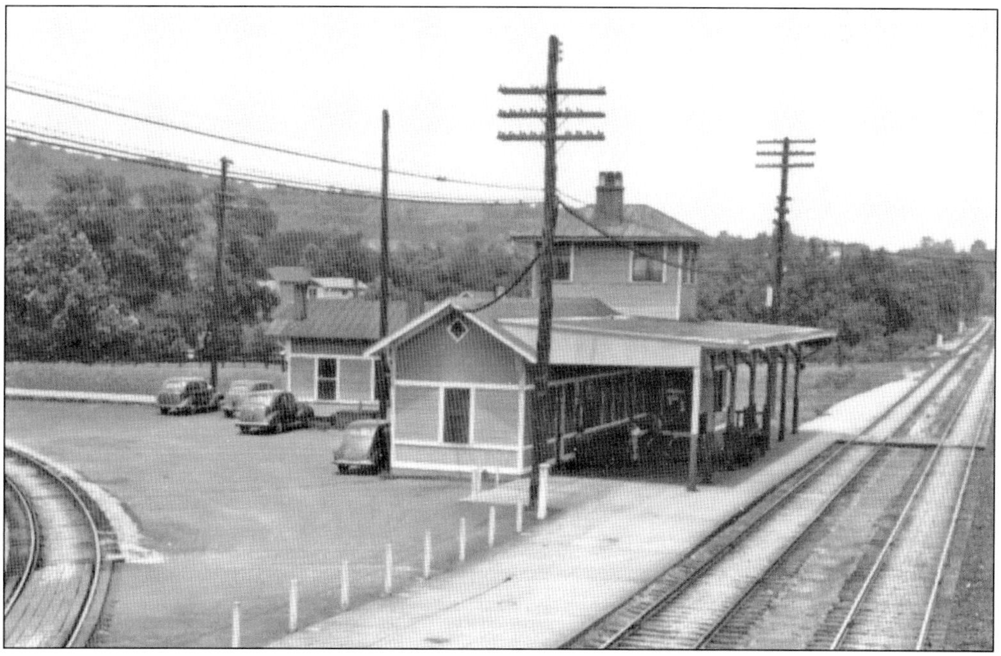

The Latonia Depot stood at the end of Park Avenue, north of Thirty-sixth Street, where several tracks met. This depot saw family visiting family, soldiers going to war or coming home, racetrack denizens, and coal company managers. The Louisville and Nashville (L&N) acquired the Kentucky Central in 1890, after having acquired the Louisville, Cincinnati, and Lexington line in 1881. This enabled the L&N to penetrate the eastern Kentucky coalfields. At that time, the L&N operated trains into three different passenger stations in Cincinnati's metropolitan area. To alleviate confusion, the company operated a connection train between Cincinnati's Central Union Depot at Third and Plum Streets and the Latonia Depot. Over the years, though, passenger numbers dwindled until the station sat unused. Correctly sensing public outcry to save the depot, the railroad quietly razed the station in 1978. (Courtesy L&N Railroad Company Collection, University of Louisville Archives and Records Center, Louisville, Kentucky.)

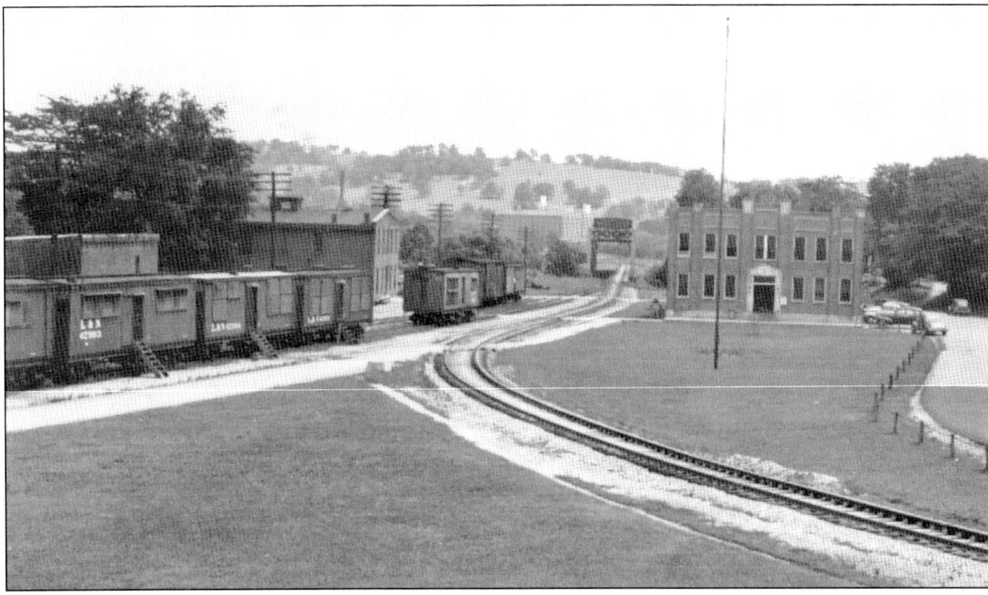

This is looking east from the depot where two rail lines intersected, making the location favorable for industry. It offered access to the Licking River and to Campbell County via a rail trestle (seen to the left of the flagpole). Before 1900, a distillery and mill were here and nearby was a pickle factory. Remaining buildings were used for railroad storage and office space. (Courtesy L&N Railroad Company Collection, University of Louisville Archives and Records Center, Louisville, Kentucky.)

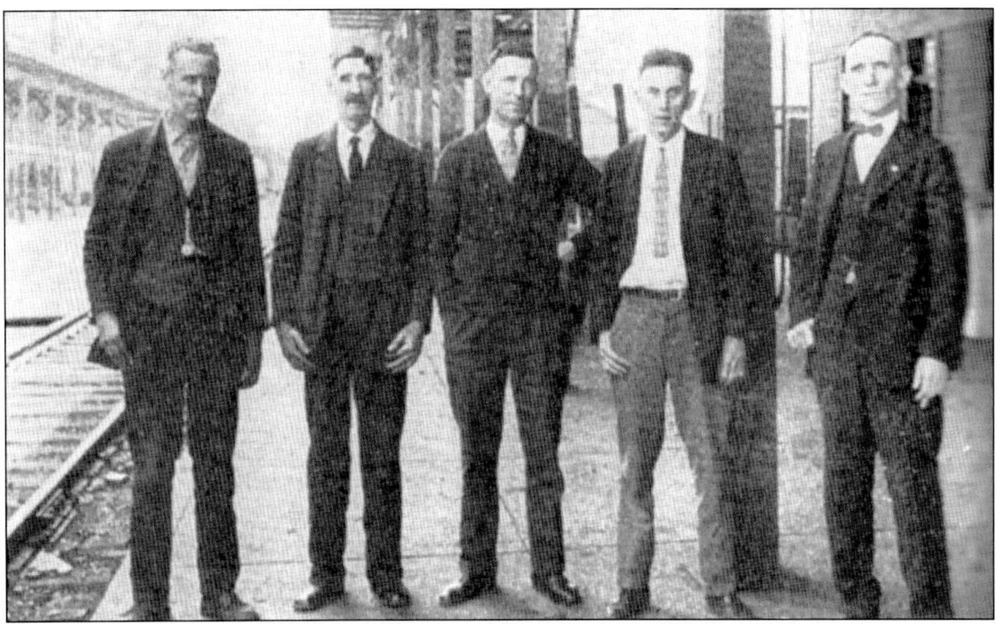

Latonia Depot staff poses in 1927. From left to right are J. E. Poll and S. E. Peniston, baggage masters responsible for handling baggage; A. H. Aulick, telegraph operator; J. G. Schorr, ticket clerk; and Charley A. Mulvey, stationmaster, who oversaw depot operations. In 1885, the L&N carried 4,328,383 passengers. The year 1920 was peak time for passenger service with 17,418,093, surpassing even the busy years of World War II. (Courtesy of www.nkyviews.com.)

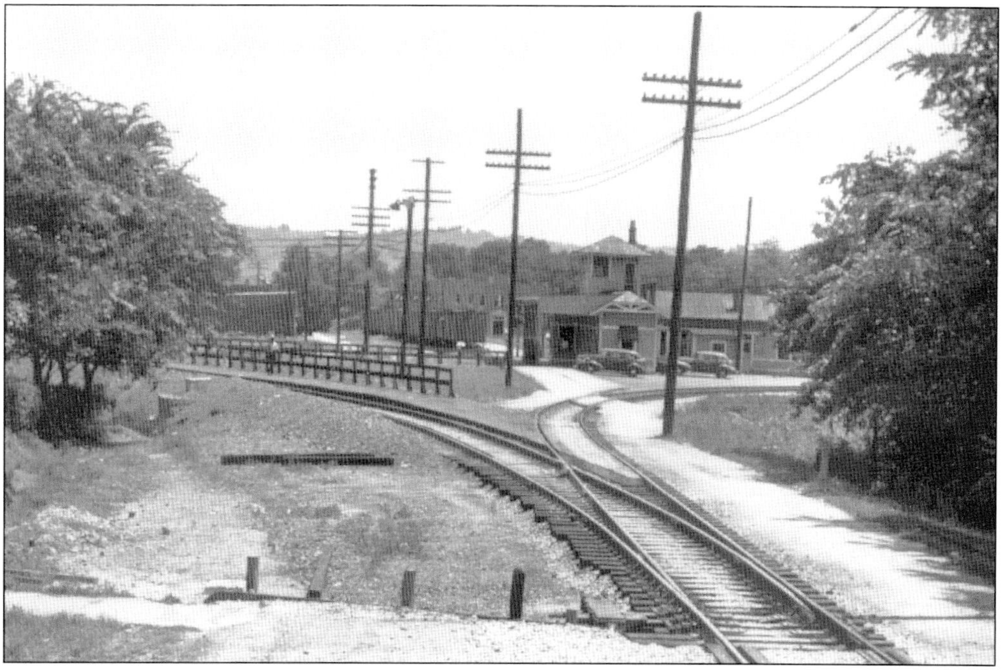

This looks from the west toward the depot in 1941. These tracks travel west to cross Decoursey Avenue heading into Latonia yard. Waiting for trains that periodically block the streets is a fact of life in Latonia. When the Caroline Street Underpass was completed in 1931, there was a parade, band music, and dancing in the streets—literally. (Courtesy L&N Railroad Company Collection, and University of Louisville Archives and Records Center, Louisville, Kentucky.)

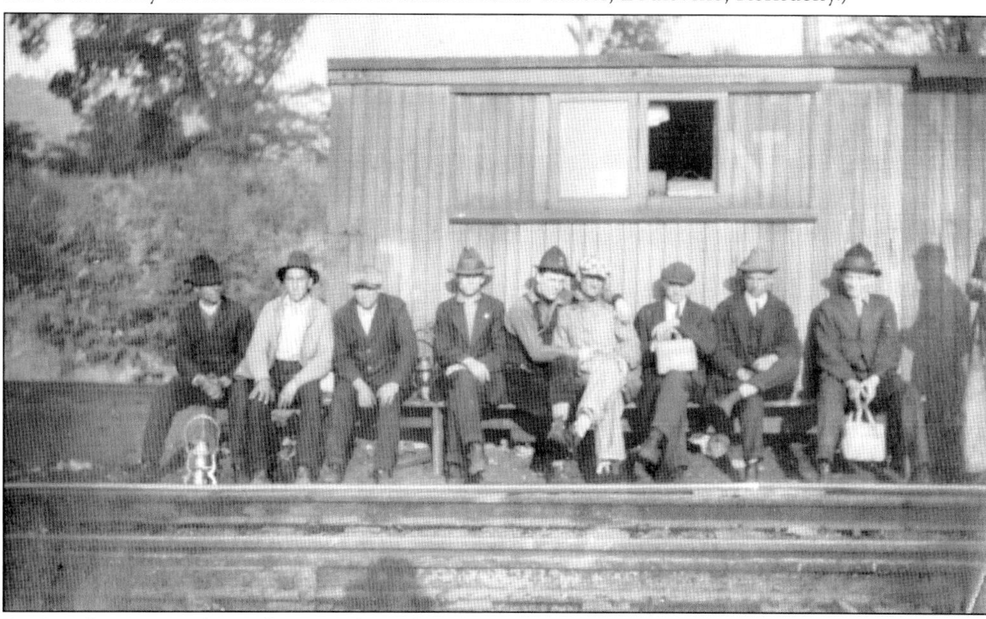

Railroaders await the "Chippy," slang for a prostitute. A small train took the men back from Decoursey yards to Forty-fifth Street and Huntington Avenue, then they could walk or catch a streetcar home. It was known as the Chippy because it picked up railroad men. (Photograph by Ray Kochersberger; courtesy of Mary Cecil.)

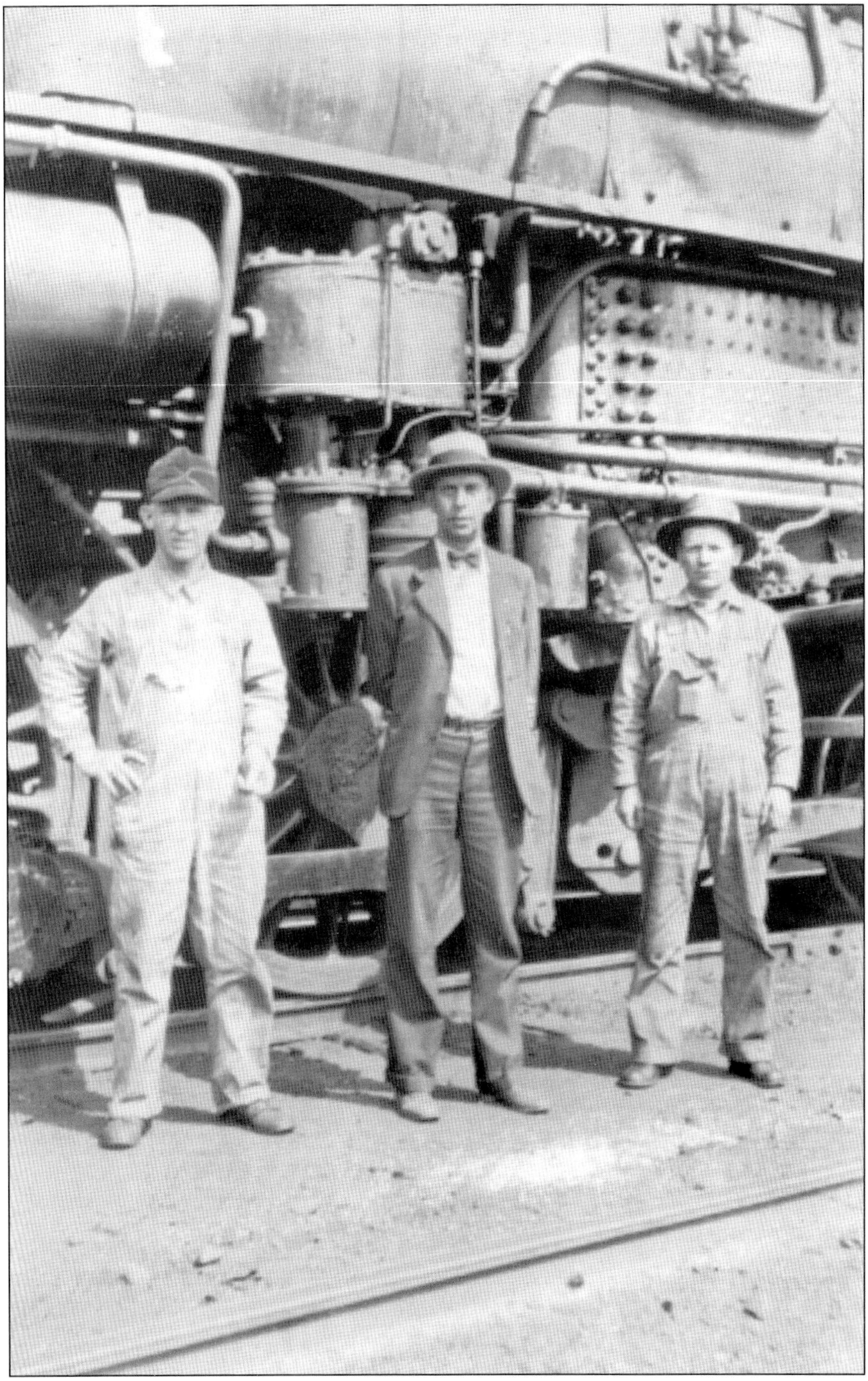

Charles Gillham (center), yardmaster at Decoursey yards, stands with two unidentified crewmembers, probably an engineer and fireman, around 1912. The locomotive looming behind them dwarfs them all. A crew of a least two was required to operate a steam locomotive: One, the engineer, was responsible for controlling the locomotive, and the other, the fireman, was responsible for the fire, steam pressure, and water. (Courtesy of the author's collection.)

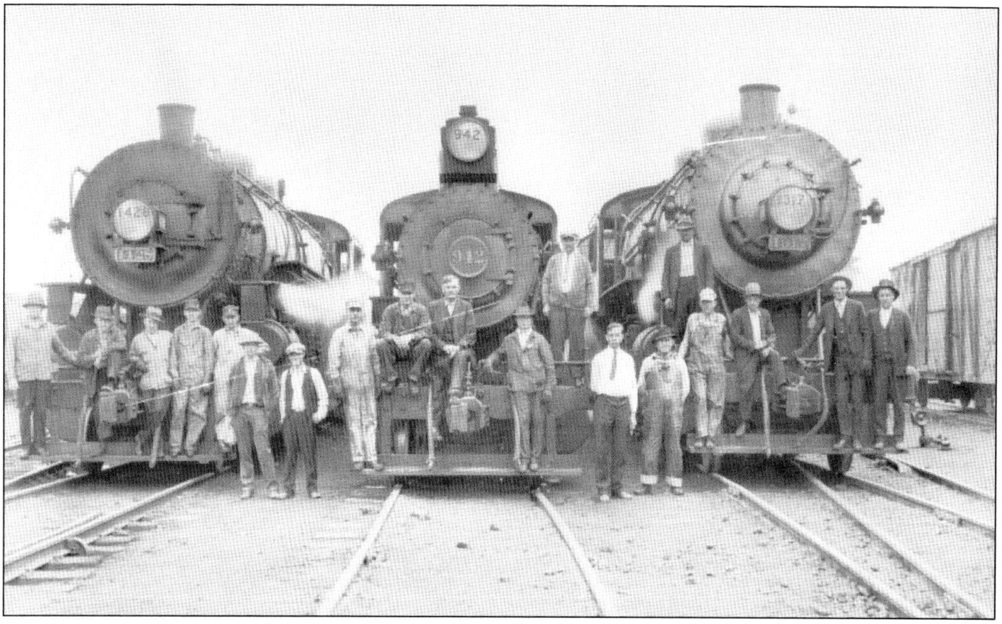

A Decoursey yards crew poses with their trains around 1920. Yardmaster Charley Gillham is wearing the white shirt and tie. Sixth from left is Joe Gibson, and the rest are unidentified. Railroad work was extremely dangerous, especially in earlier days. Hand coupling, riding atop cars, and working near scalding steam were only a few risks. Gillham took the danger to his men seriously and emphasized safe practices in the yards. (Courtesy of the author's collection.)

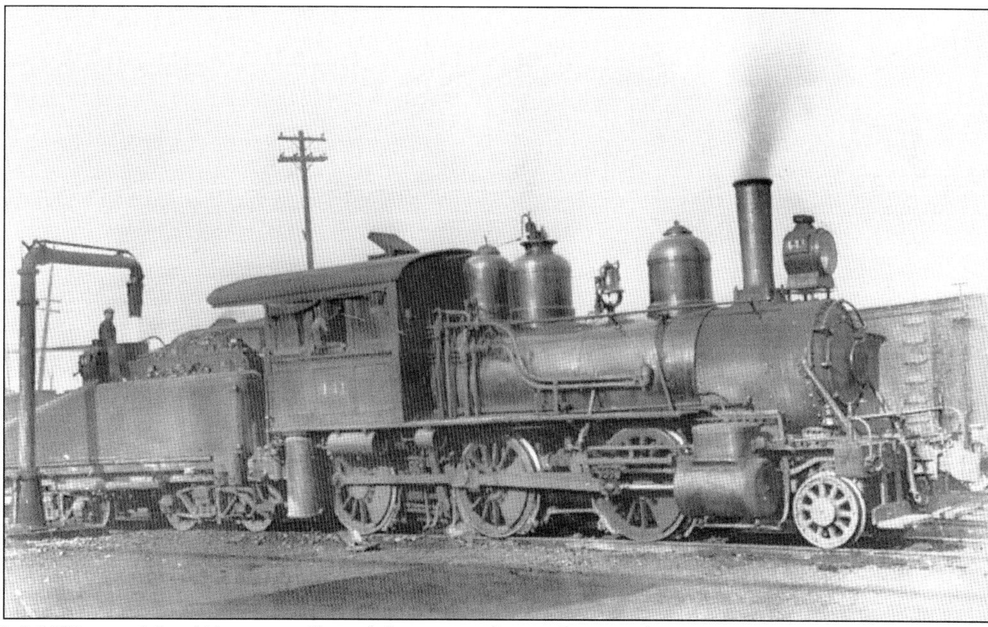

L&N Engine No. 441 stops at Rosedale station, located in southeastern Latonia, in 1913. Latonia had annexed Rosedale in 1904. Although the principles of steam locomotive operation are simple, something in its presence, dark and powerful like a great snorting beast, draws a deeply rooted response. Yet this dark animal was like part of the family, choo-chooing along past backyards and laundry on the line. (Courtesy of www.nkyviews.com.)

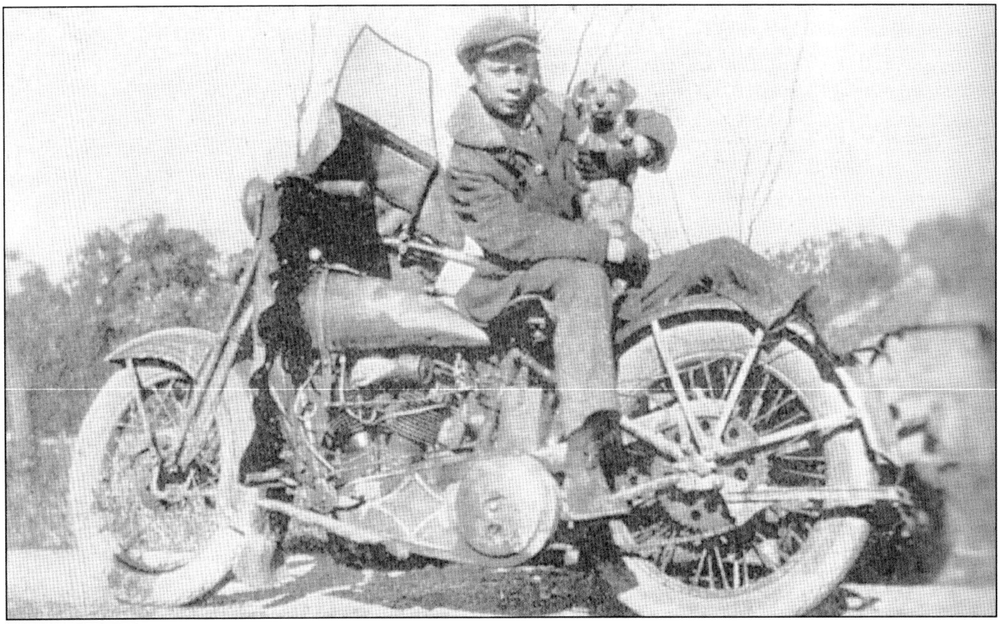

James E. Miller, photographed with his prize pup around 1927, was a motorcycle messenger at Decoursey yards. At 17, his job was to deliver important papers and to call men to work. Many employees had no home telephones, so when the company needed them to come in for a special shift, the messenger or "call boy" would go to their house to tell them to report for work. (Courtesy of www.nkyviews.com.)

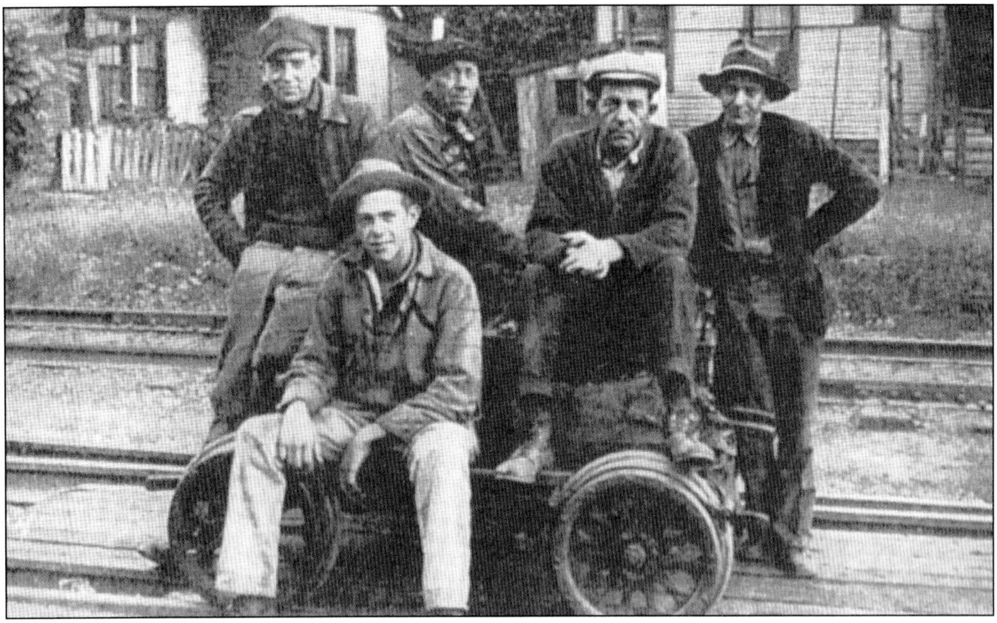

Latonia signalmen pose on a small truck. Signalmen maintained signals for hot box detectors, dragging-equipment detectors, railroad crossings, and, in earlier days, telegraph lines. Before electrical signals, railroad lanterns were used. The lantern's glass was tinted, so it would glow with colored light. Each color had a meaning. The signalman waved the lantern, and the approaching train would see the moving light and know what to do. (Courtesy of www.nkyviews.com.)

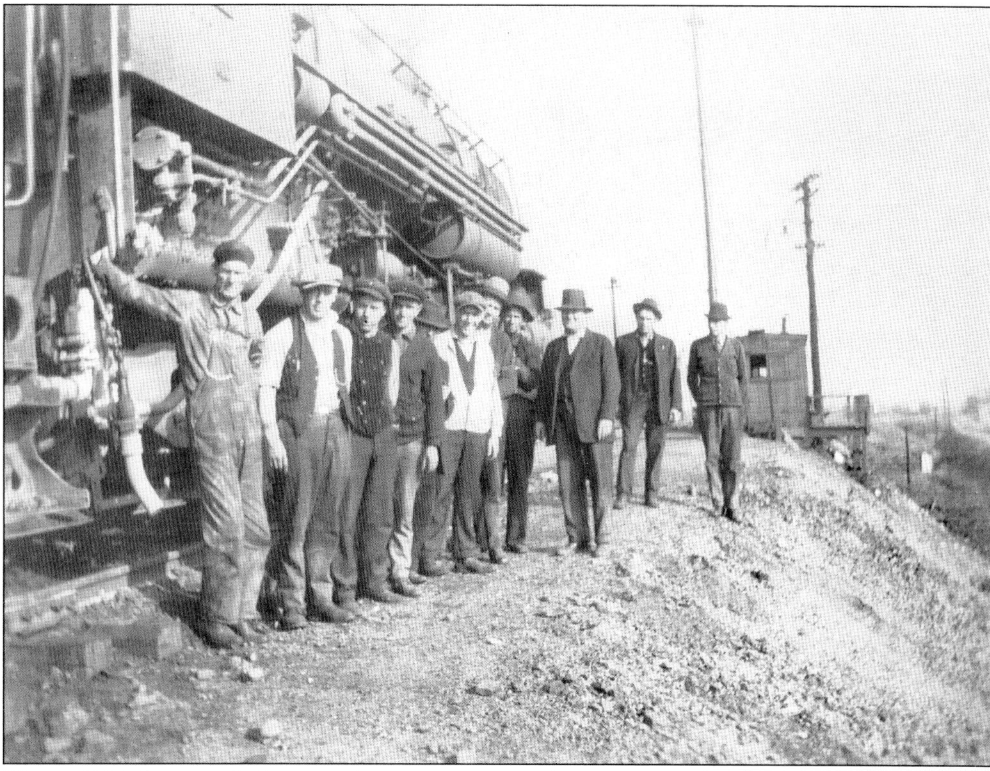

This c. 1925 photograph features a locomotive crew at Decoursey yards. The unidentified engineer is at left. Third from right is switchman Walter Smith. Railroad workers were subject to layoffs, as economic conditions caused the volume of freight to fluctuate. The Depression caused massive layoffs. When Walter was laid off, he and his wife moved back to their respective family homes and waited until he found a job at the Crescent Dairy. (Courtesy of the author's collection.)

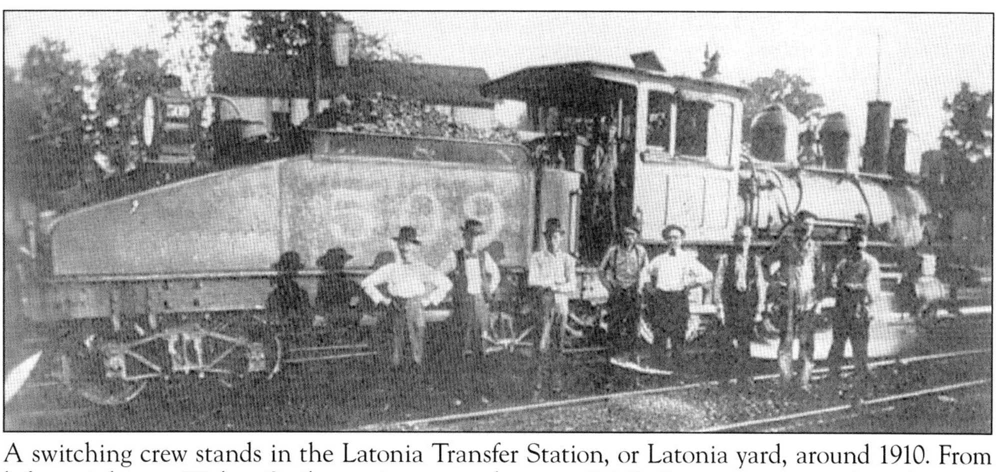

A switching crew stands in the Latonia Transfer Station, or Latonia yard, around 1910. From left to right are Walter Steibe, assistant yardmaster; W. E. Burgoyne, general yardmaster; Frank "Mull" Carlton, switchman; Fred "Mope" Kreis, switchman; Allan Fisher, manager of a Latonia hardware store; O. E. Hendrickson, yard foreman; unidentified; and William Adrian, engineer. The fireman on the engine is also unidentified. (Courtesy of www.nkyviews.com.)

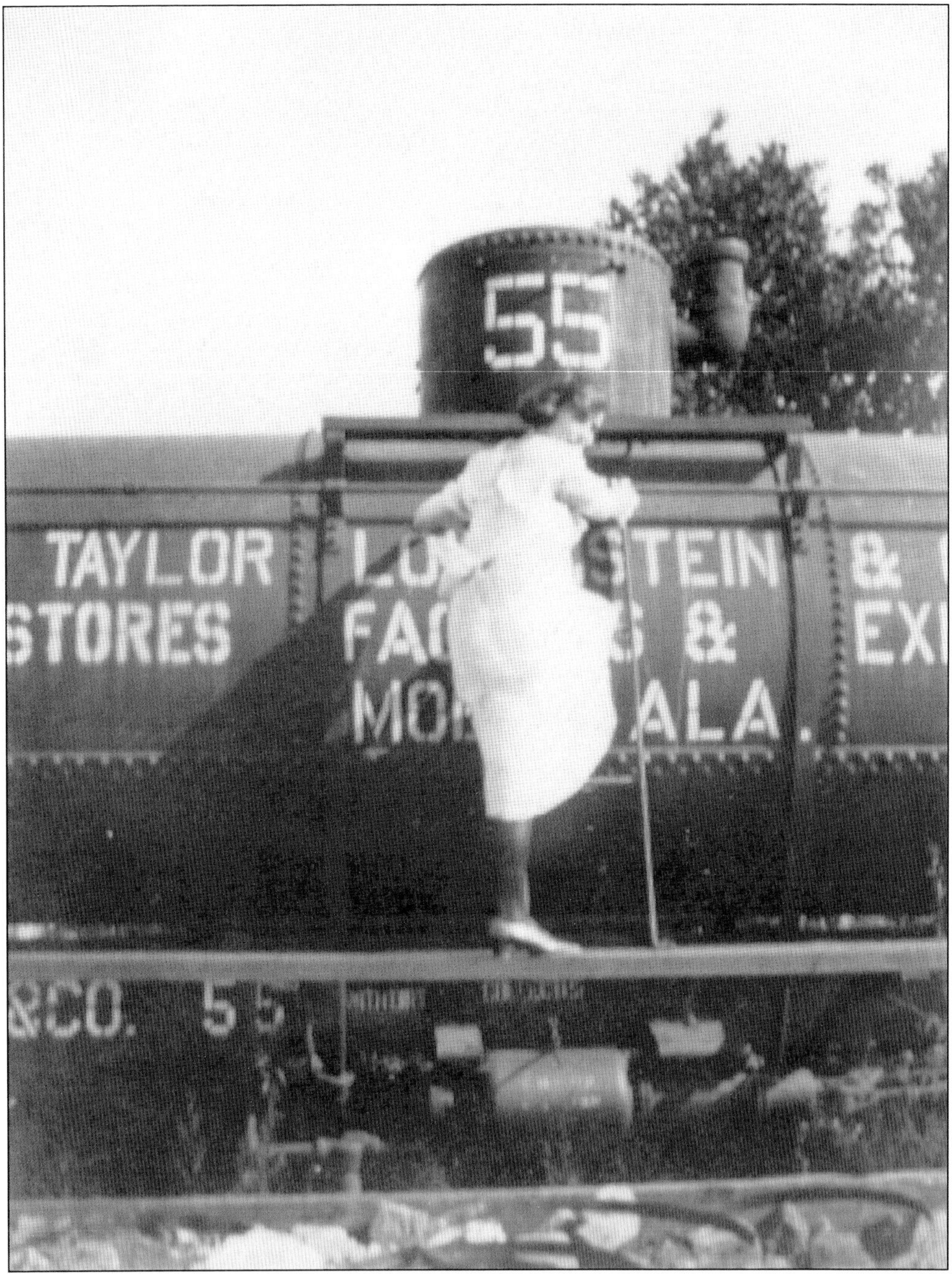

Edna Kupper was not jumping freight trains; she was only playing on the railroad tracks. This was probably at the Latonia Transfer Station, or Latonia yard, a hub of railroad activity. Seventeen tracks lay between the west side of town and Ritte's Corner, with only a cinder path across. Trains roared through, and cars were switched back and forth as trains were made up. It was called the "Big Crossing," and guards were stationed on each side to ensure the safety of pedestrians. The Greater Cincinnati Railway Museum is there now, and CSX still uses some tracks. (Courtesy of Virginia Kupper Kaufman.)

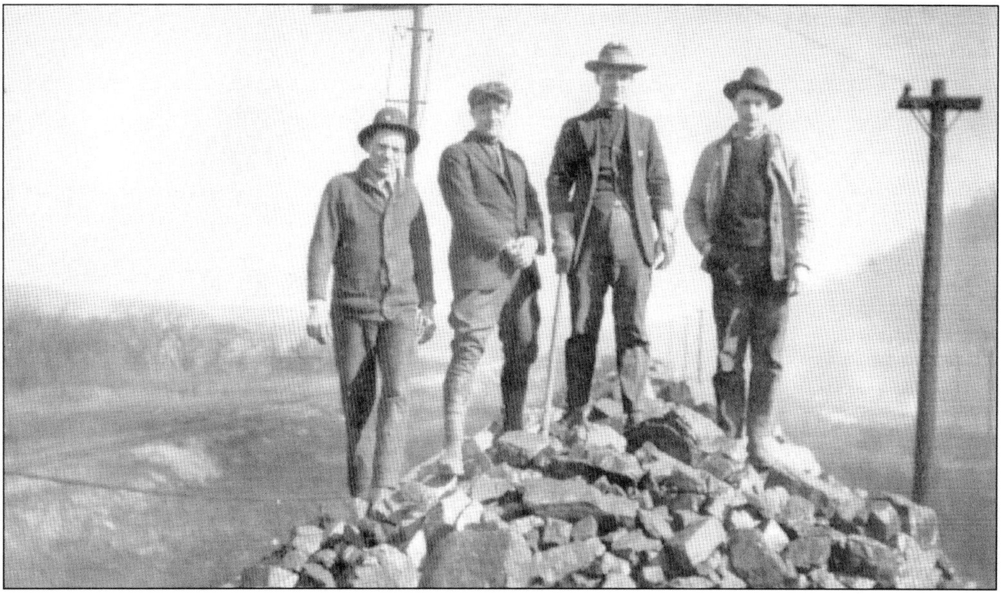

Yardmaster Ray Kochersberger (second from right) stands on a stone mound with three of his crew at Decoursey yards in this *c.* 1920s photograph. With the large number of railroad lines squeezing into Cincinnati freight facilities, downtown was a sea of freight cars. This compelled several railroads to move away from downtown, including the L&N, which constructed the Decoursey yards around 1910. (Courtesy of Mary Cecil.)

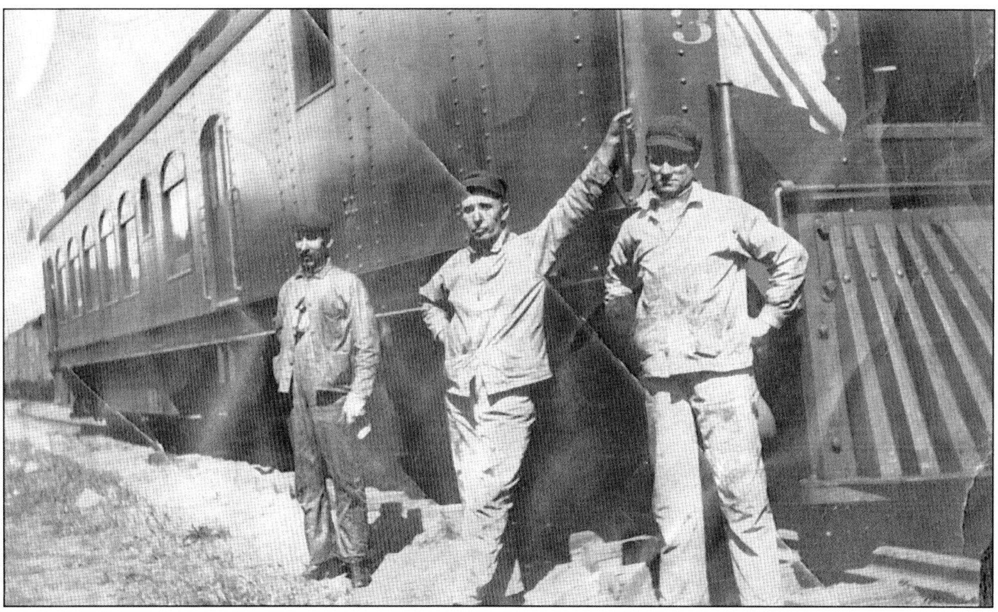

Engineer Ben Duke (right) and unidentified crew pose by their locomotive on the L&N Short Line in this *c.* 1925 photograph. Most engineers really loved driving those trains. L&N engineer Charlie Stichling said that no matter whether he got a call to go to work in the middle of the night, it was always "like Christmas morning" when it came to driving his locomotive. (Courtesy of the author's collection.)

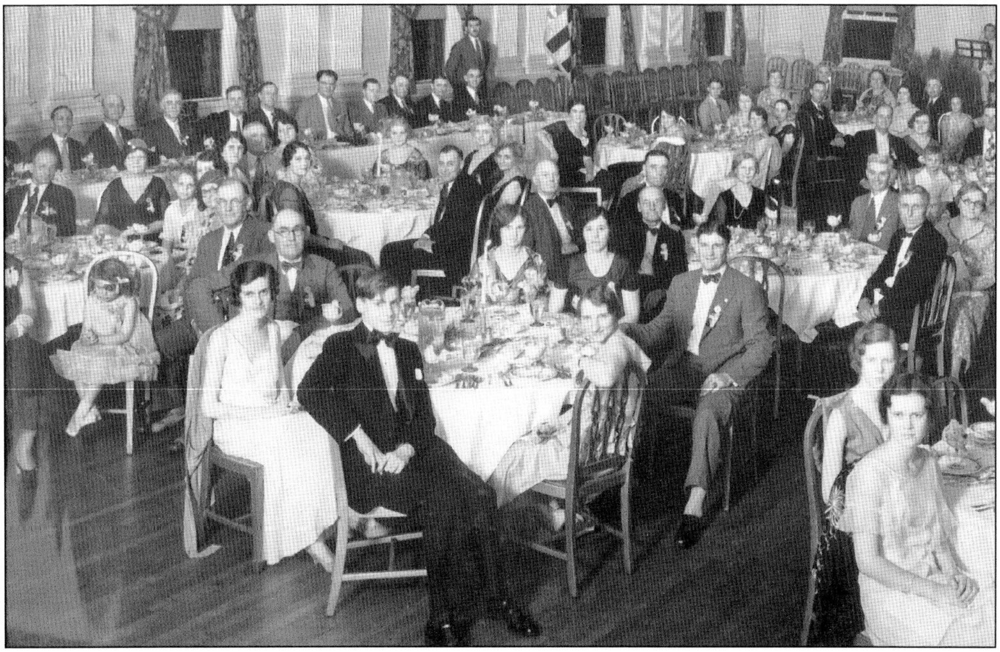

Diners at a yardmasters' convention are photographed around 1927. There were several yardmasters' associations that functioned as unions to protect the interests of yardmasters. Nearly each position in railroad work had its own union group, such as the Order of Railroad Telegraphers and the Brotherhood of Sleeping Car Porters. At the annual conventions, issues were presented and discussed. (Photograph by Ray Kochersberger; courtesy of Mary Cecil.)

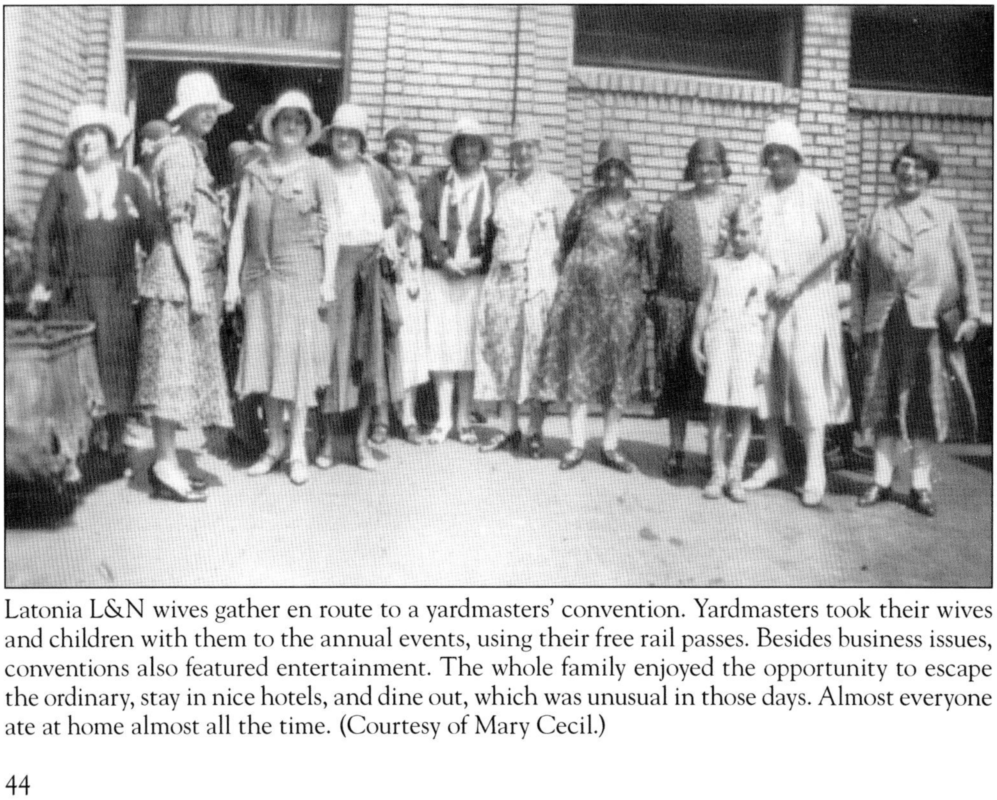

Latonia L&N wives gather en route to a yardmasters' convention. Yardmasters took their wives and children with them to the annual events, using their free rail passes. Besides business issues, conventions also featured entertainment. The whole family enjoyed the opportunity to escape the ordinary, stay in nice hotels, and dine out, which was unusual in those days. Almost everyone ate at home almost all the time. (Courtesy of Mary Cecil.)

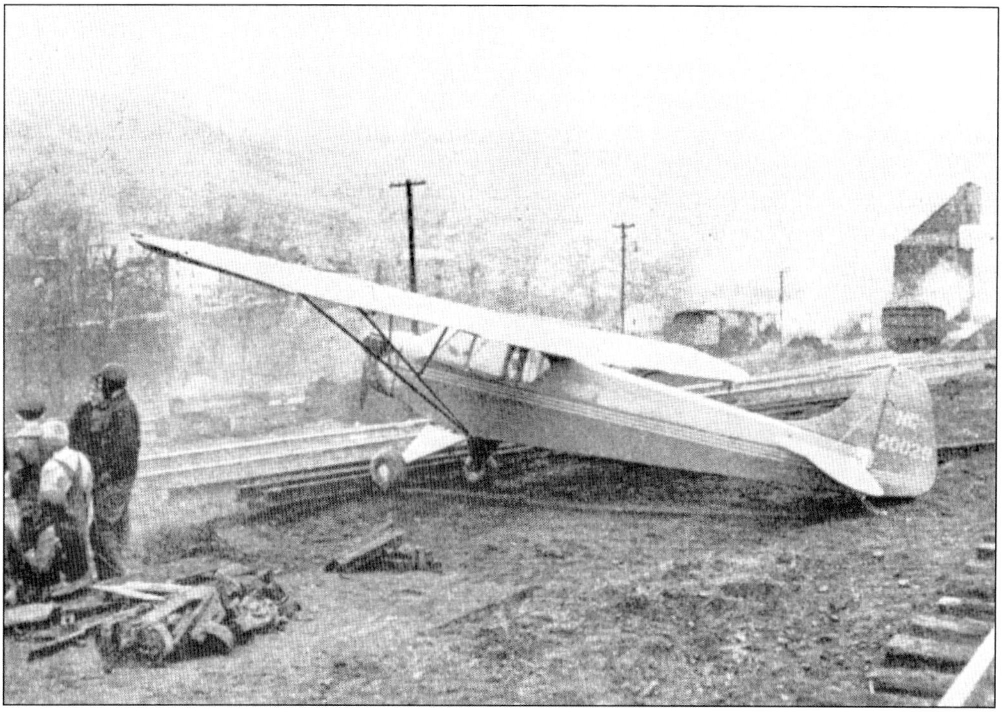

Employees at Decoursey yards could hardly believe their eyes when they saw a small cabin monoplane resting peacefully between the tracks. Its pilot, H. C. Morley of Cleveland, had set it down in the floodlighted yard during the night when he had run out of gas searching for Lunken Air Field. Suffering only minor damage, the airplane was repaired and is awaiting take off from its emergency airport. A Decoursey coal chute is in the background at right. On the right is a 1912 L&N Timetable. (Courtesy of www.nkyviews.com and Tim Hyde, Greater Cincinnati Railway Museum.)

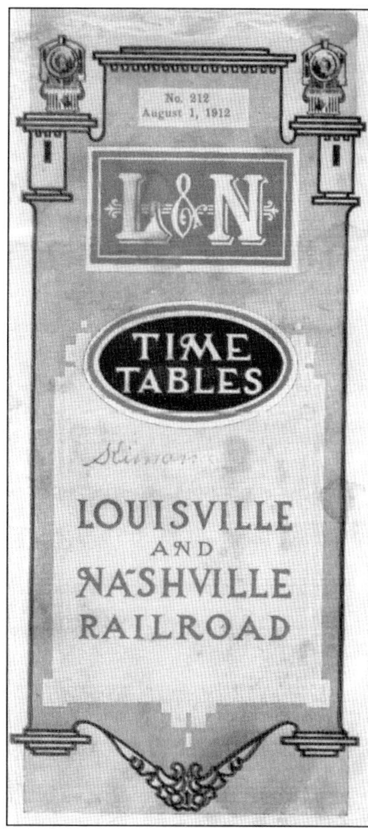

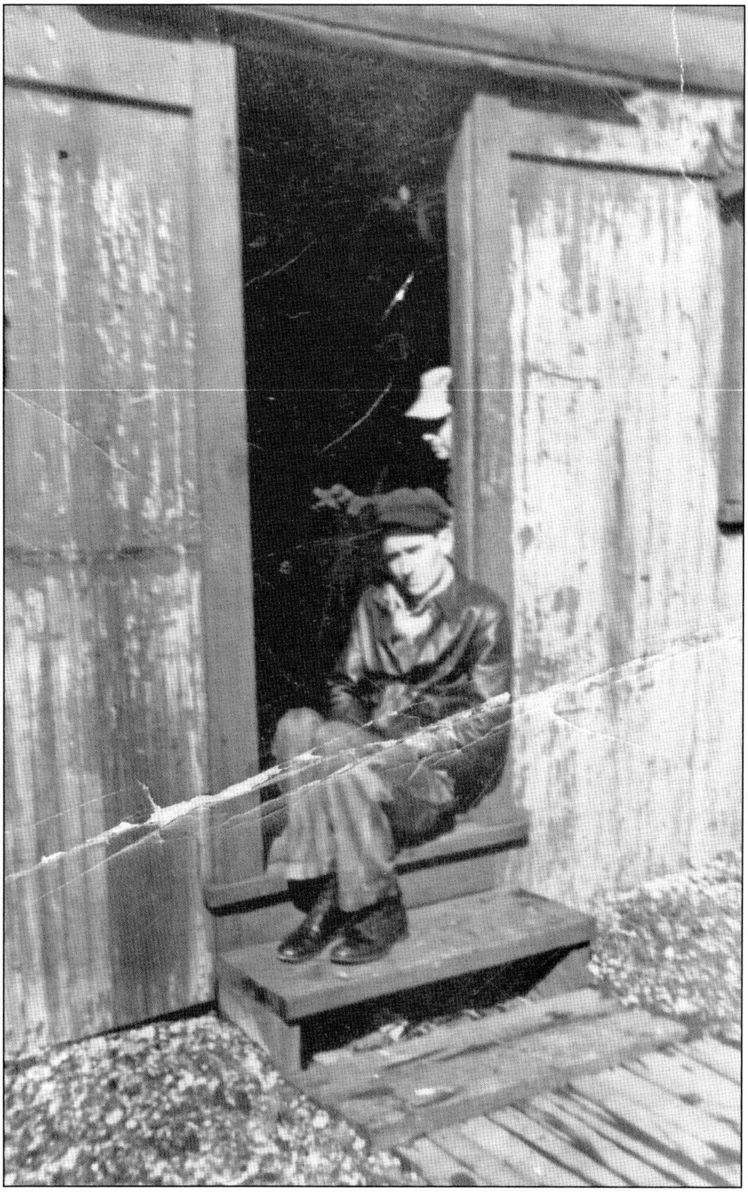

Diesel locomotives came to Decoursey yards in 1939 and began almost immediately to eclipse the steam engine. Diesels were lower maintenance, cleaner, easier to run, and more powerful. People exclaimed about the sleek, shiny diesels when they flew across the Latonia streets in the 1950s. Then there were fewer and fewer steam locomotives crossing those streets. The familiar wail of the steam whistle was now a barking air horn. In his book *Stations*, Michael Flanagan says, "We were there . . . when the last of the steam engines went pounding by on their way to Valhalla . . . It seemed . . . inconceivable that you would never hear or feel them, never smell them, never see them again." In this *c.* 1946 photograph, L&N worker Ernie Grissom sits in a shed at Decoursey yards after his discharge from the U.S. Navy. He looks as if he might be wondering what this new postwar world will hold. The last steam engine made its run to Decoursey in 1957. The Latonia depot was razed in 1978. The L&N was bought out in 1982. Their passing has not gone unnoticed. (Courtesy of Geoff Grissom.)

Four

RITTE'S CORNER

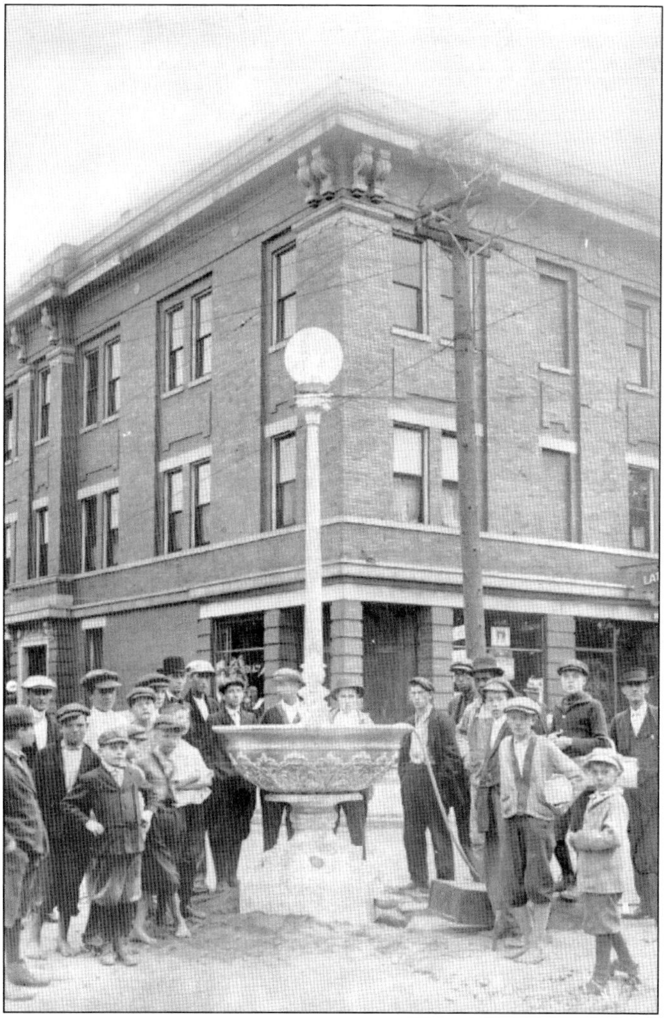

This is the old Ritte's Corner Fountain, which stood squarely in the middle of the five-way intersection. It was donated by Dr. R. E. Carlton to honor the first Latonia boy to go to World War I, who happened to be Walter (Bacon) Flake. Behind the fountain stands the Bird Building. The barefoot boy at left, closest to the fountain, is George Beuttel, and his brother Carl is the only barefoot boy at right. They are the baker's sons. Others present were named by Latonia historian Howard Litzler but were not identified. They are Heine Maxwell, an L&N switchman; Vincent Keller, superintendent of "Devou Fields" (Park); "Dutch" Flaege; Henry Tuptmann; Nick Thompson; Walter Ritte; Cecil Jones; George Childers, pitcher for Holy Cross Standards; "Slim" Wellbrock; and "Little Hard Tail" Webster, son of L&N yardmaster "Big Hard Tail." (Courtesy of Kenton County Public Library.)

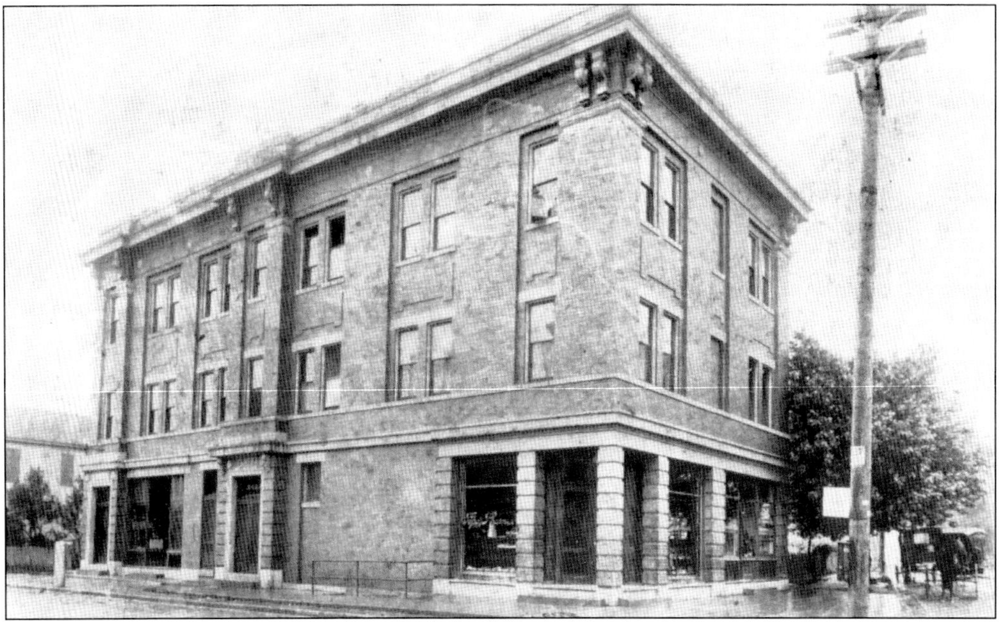

The Bird Building was constructed by Dr. R. Lee Bird around 1902. It had commercial space on the main floor as it does today; on the second floor were flats, and on the third floor were meeting halls. The Latonia Masonic Order and other benevolent organizations met there, and several churches got their starts there. In the 1940s, owner Dr. Lucas Lee remodeled the upper floors into apartments. Note the carriages at right. (Courtesy of the author's collection.)

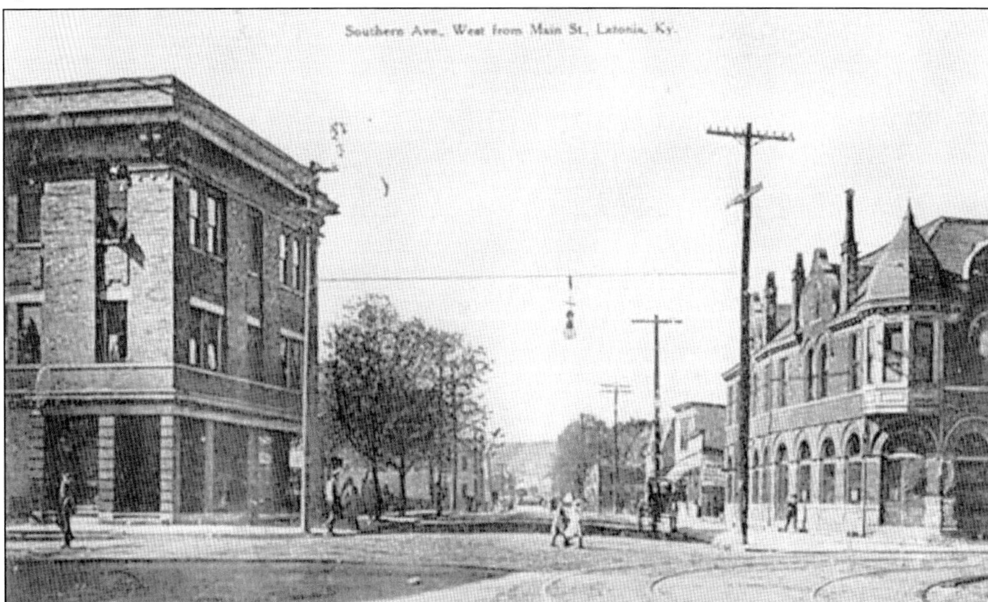

This c. 1915 photograph looks west toward the L&N's "Big Crossing." Notice there is no fountain yet. At left is Bird's Hall, where Pope's Pharmacy occupied the corner storefront for more than 40 years, followed by Schulte's Pharmacy for 36 years. The Latonia Deposit Bank started there. At right is the First National Bank of Latonia, which was also home to dentists' and doctors' offices and to Judge C. B. Schoborg's cobbler shop. (Courtesy of the author's collection.)

The First National Bank, built in 1903, featured marble counters and floors and polished wood and brass fixtures. The building still stands, its picturesque detail largely intact, though the bank and its accoutrements are gone. Among bank organizers were J. H. Kruse, Dr. R. E. Carlton, and J. T. Earle, bank president. On this site, around 1890, was the Draddy and Daven Feed Store. (Courtesy of Kenton County Public Library.)

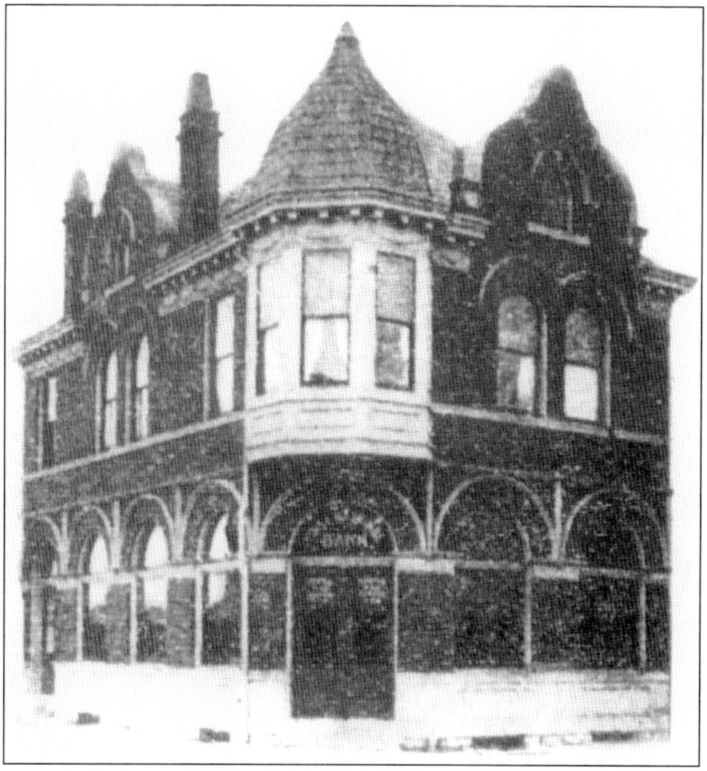

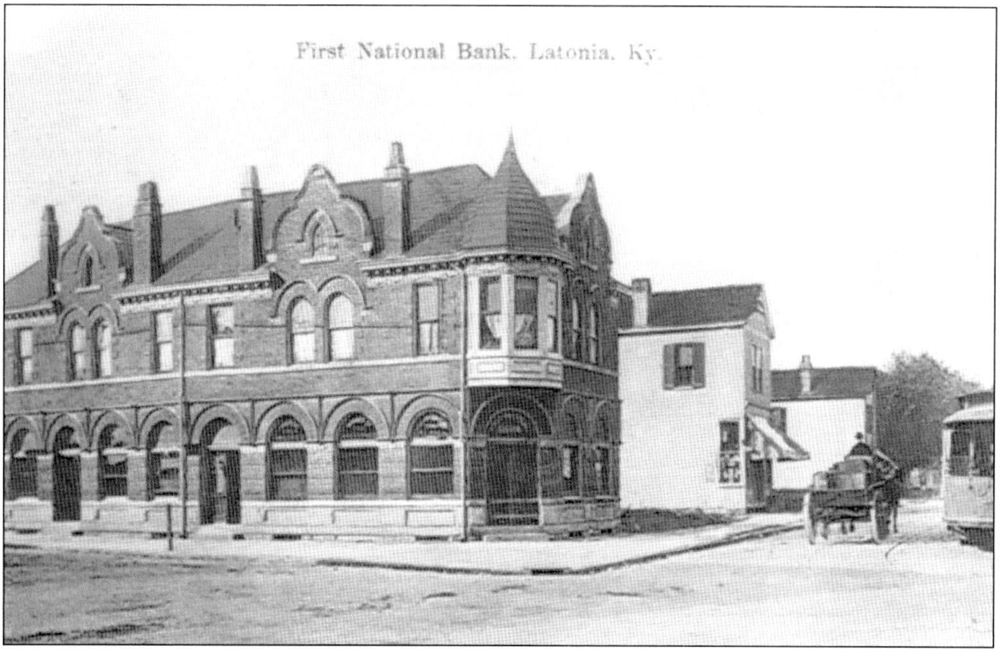

This is looking north up Decoursey Avenue. The First National Bank was enlarged just after completion to accommodate the Latonia post office, which had outgrown its old home. The third building down housed Harry Kleine's Latonia Sweet Shoppe. Notice the wagon passing the streetcar. (Courtesy of Kenton County Public Library.)

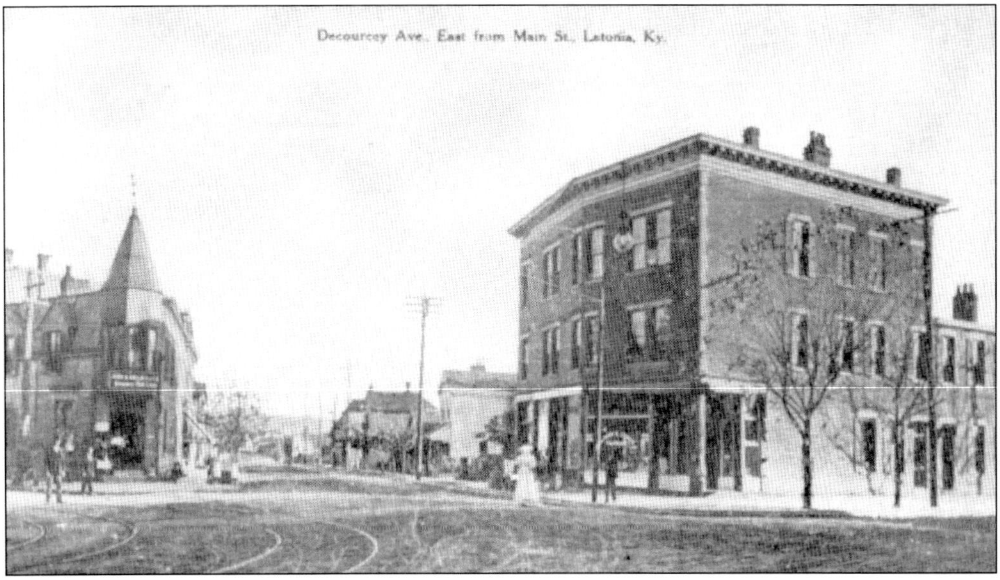

Here are two views of the same location, both looking southeast down Decoursey Avenue. To the right goes Main Street, which is now Winston Avenue. To the left of the flatiron building is Southern Avenue. The photograph above was taken around 1900, and the photograph below was taken around 1925. The wooden flatiron building with the tower held a dry-goods store and later housed R. R. Wegener's Dry Cleaning store on the ground floor and True and Walker's T&W Print Shop in the basement. The large building at right held Boeckley's Drug Store. The lower photograph shows construction on streetcar tracks. By this time, Oscar A. Boeckley had built his new brick flatiron building, but had not yet moved his store. Advertisements and activity are still visible in the windows of the old building. (Courtesy of Tom Martin and Kenton County Public Library.)

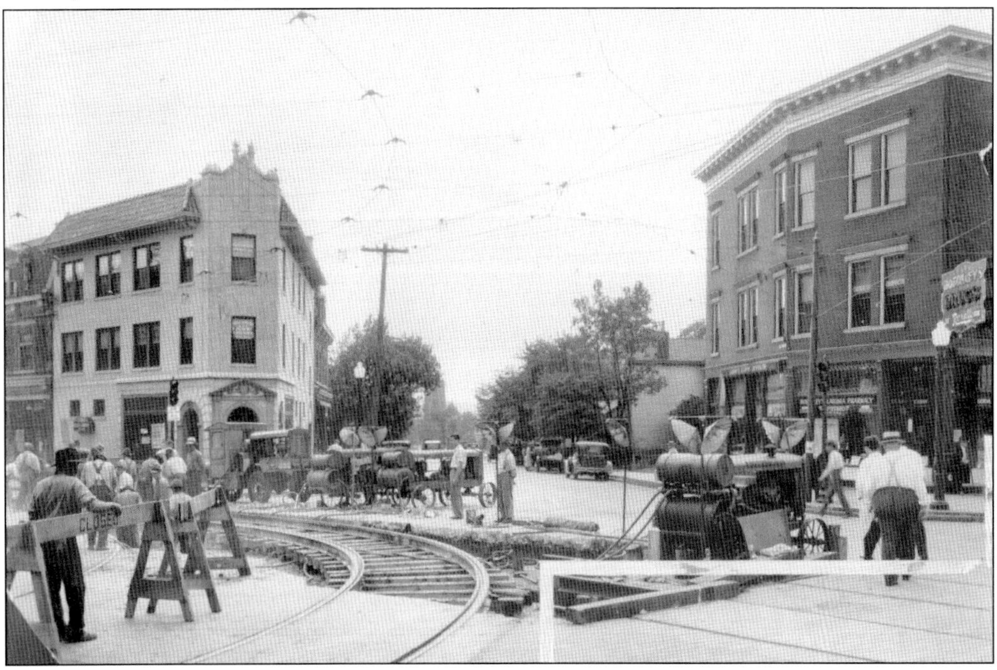

Oscar Boeckley sent invitations for the opening of his new building in 1928. He outfitted his new drugstore with the latest features, and the upper floors were apartments. In about 1941, Boeckley hired a young man named Harry Nieman, and, when Oscar retired, he took over. Harry owned Boeckley's for more than 30 years and was a Latonia institution. He retired in 1997 and is still missed. (Courtesy of Kenton County Public Library.)

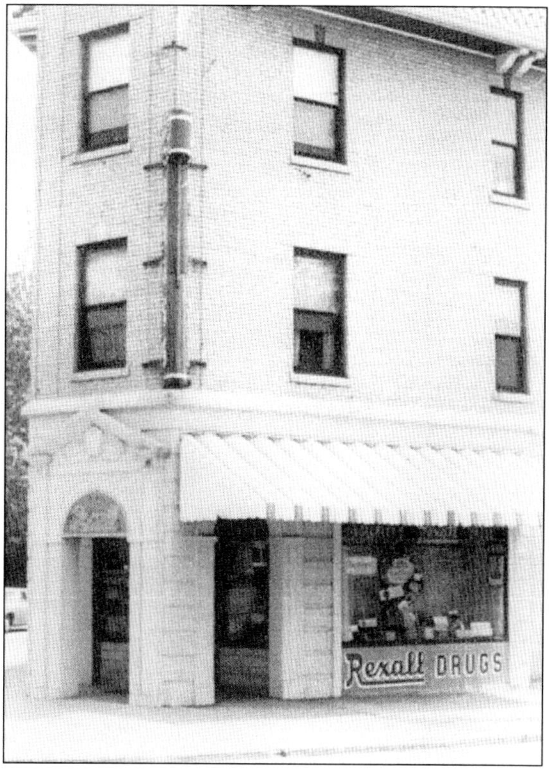

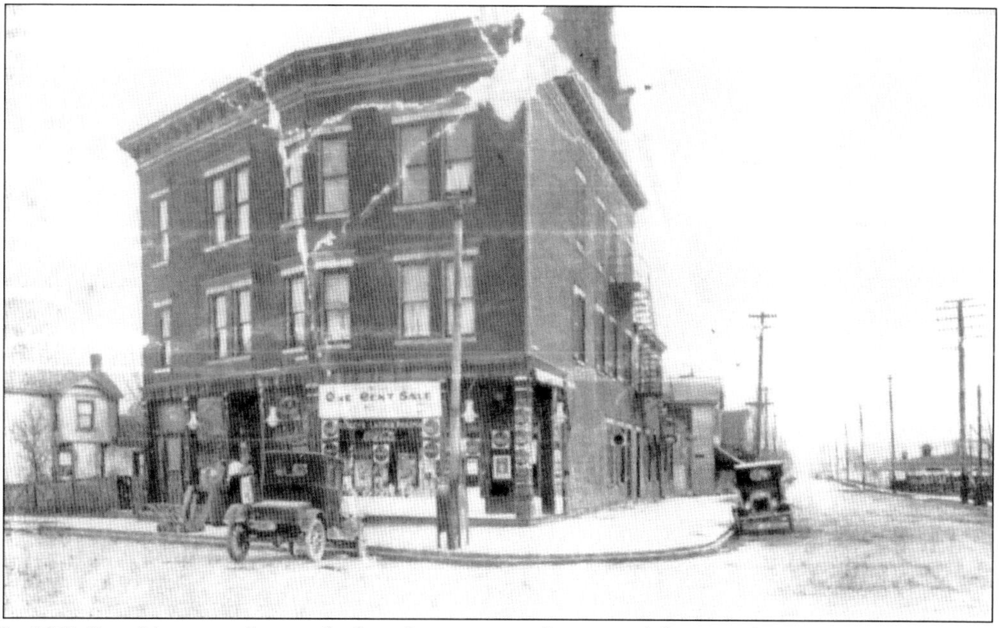

In 1917, Boeckley rented space for his pharmacy on the ground floor, with Evans Jewelers on the left. Apartments were upstairs, and Ryan Brothers Saloon was in back. Besides filling prescriptions, Boeckley's supplied liniment for racehorses. Later Joe Landwehr's Hardware Store occupied the space. The building was razed for parking in the 1970s. The Korean War Memorial Plaza is there now and was dedicated in 2004. (Courtesy of Kenton County Public Library.)

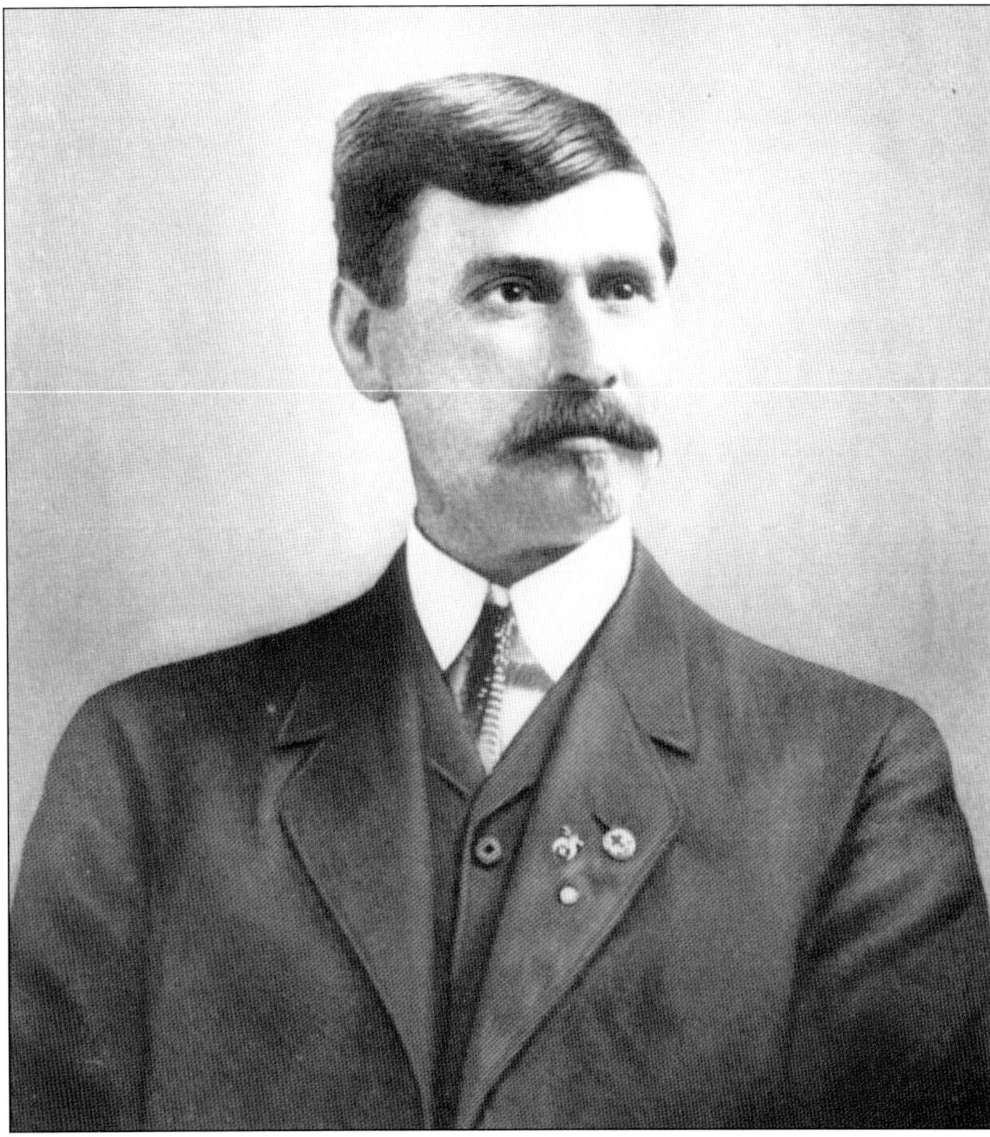

Dr. R. E. Carlton was a prominent physician and founder/president of the Latonia-Covington Anti-Tuberculosis Society. Beginning in 1908, it was Northern Kentucky's first anti-tuberculosis organization. A long-time goal of his was realized in 1937 when the old Pest House on Kyle's Lane became a TB sanatorium. Carlton died in 1944. That same year, Kentucky authorized $5 million for five new TB sanatoriums. Notice the Masonic pin on his lapel. (Courtesy of Kenton County Public Library.)

Dr. Fenton "Doc" Adams was probably the best-known doctor in Latonia. He owned pearl-handled pistols and a Reo Flying Cloud automobile, and he was larger-than-life. He drank. Still, many Latonians said they would rather go to a drunken Doc Adams than to any other sober doctor. (Courtesy of Cliff Adams.)

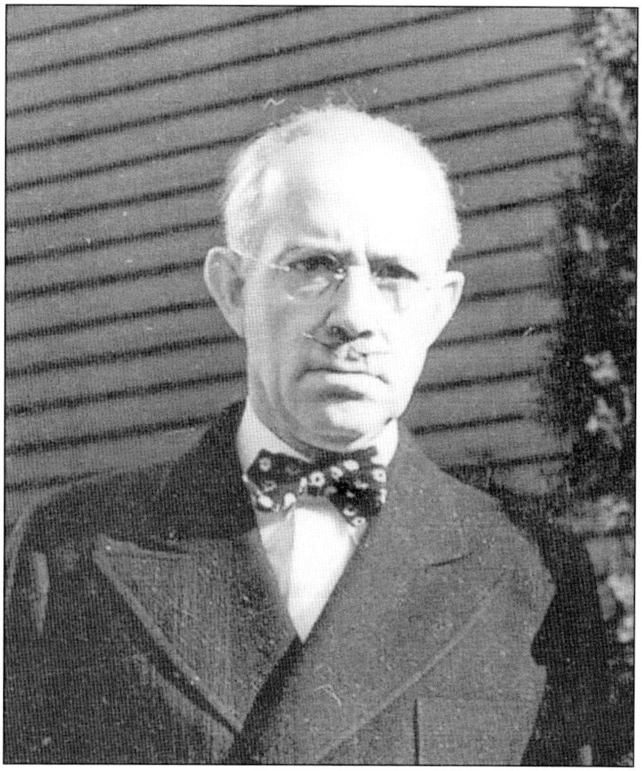

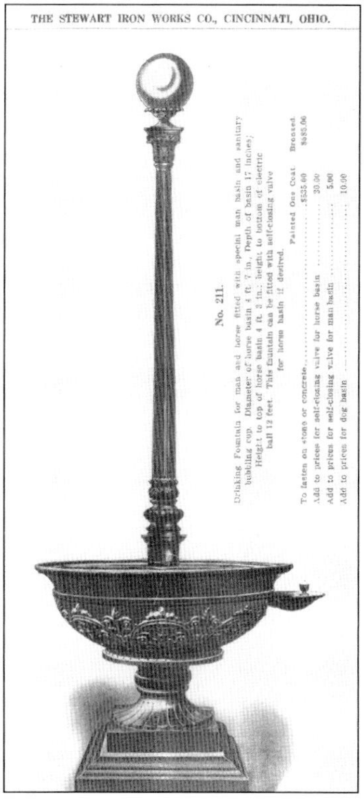

This fountain stood in the middle of Ritte's Corner (see page 47). Doc Adams and his Reo automobile were a dangerous combination, and before long, he hit the fountain. It was repaired, but Doc got it again. It was repaired and moved. After Doc went up on the sidewalk and got it the third time, the fountain was history. Some said the third time was just a matter of principle with Doc. The fountain illustration is from the Stewart Ironworks' catalog from about 1918. (Courtesy of the author's collection.)

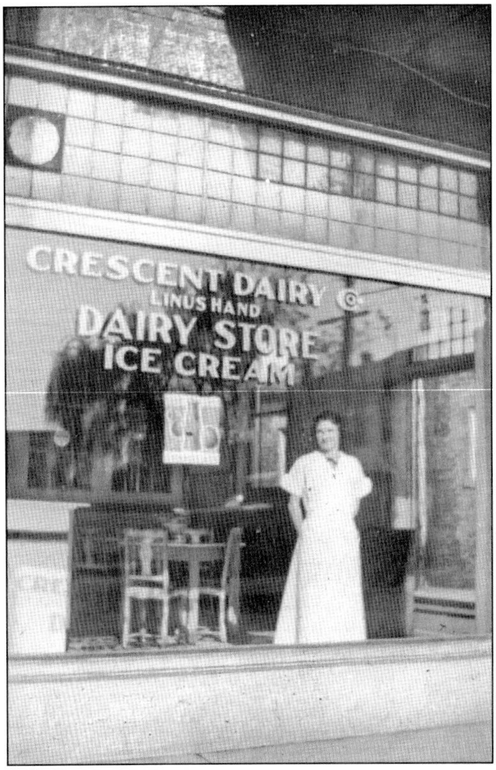

Owned by Linus Hand, Crescent Dairy was on Southern Avenue behind the First National Bank. Pictured here is Janet Smith, ice cream dipper, wearing her clean white uniform, thus communicating to the customer that the shop was clean and sanitary. During World War II, Janet married Benny Duke. They moved to a still-very-rural Taylor Mill, where they lived together happily for over 50 years. (Courtesy of the author's collection.)

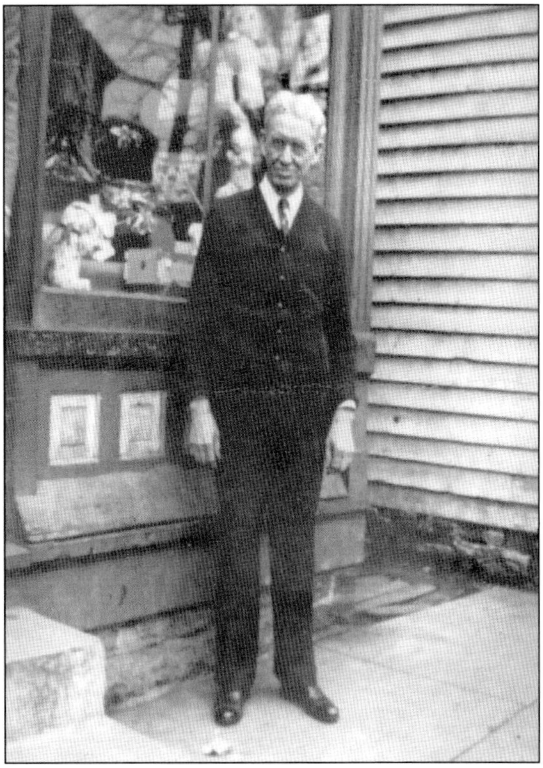

Thomas Martin stands before the original Johnny's Toy Store in this c. 1943 photograph. His son, Bill, worked at Miss Mary's candy store on Decoursey Avenue. In 1939, he bought it and added toys. World War II intervened. Bill served three years in the South Pacific in the U.S. Army Air Corps. Bill's father and sister kept the store going, but everyone assumed it belonged to Bill's well-known brother John. The name stuck. (Courtesy of Tom Martin.)

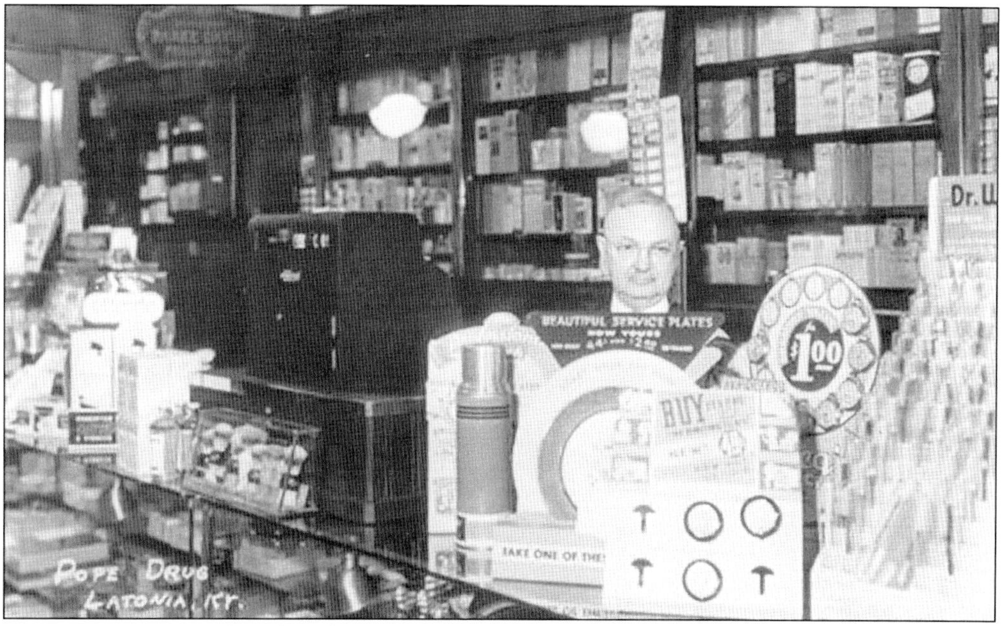

Forrest A. Pope stands in his pharmacy in the Bird Building. He opened his first Latonia drug store in 1897, three years after Dr. Bird began pharmaceutical sales. Pope and his wife, Lillian, built a home on Park Drive, and attended St. Stephen's Episcopal Church, where they have a commemorative stained glass window. After his death in 1941, Lillian ran the pharmacy until 1946. (Courtesy of the Kenton County Public Library.)

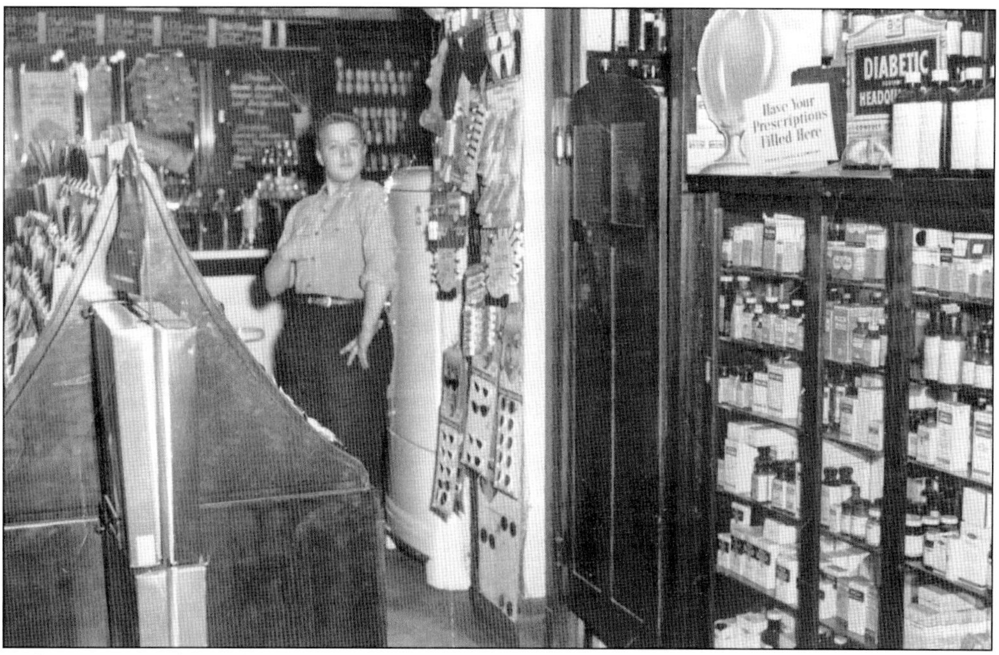

Eighteen-year-old Jim Skyrm was a soda jerk at Schulte's Drug Store, which replaced Pope's in the Bird Building. The Schultes bought the place in 1946 from Lillian Pope and were there until the early 1980s. Here Jim mugs for a friend who snapped this photograph in 1949. Jim's childhood in Latonia is a subject dear to him, as is the case with many. (Courtesy of Jim Skyrm.)

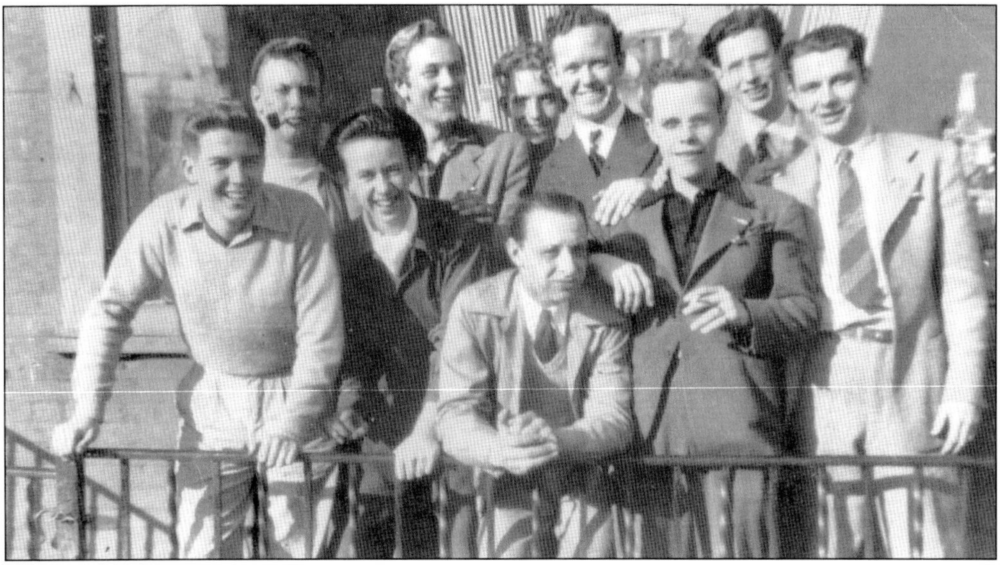

These young people are enjoying themselves, just hanging out at Ritte's Corner, in 1942. From left to right are (first row) Bob Bamberger, Bob Hessling (wearing hat), Bunny Meyers, Allen Born, and Bob Regan; (second row) Larry Gregory (pipe), Bernie Hellman, Bill Jones, Earl Egan, and Stew Selby. All too soon, the men would be drafted or would enlist to serve in World War II. (Courtesy of Bob Regan.)

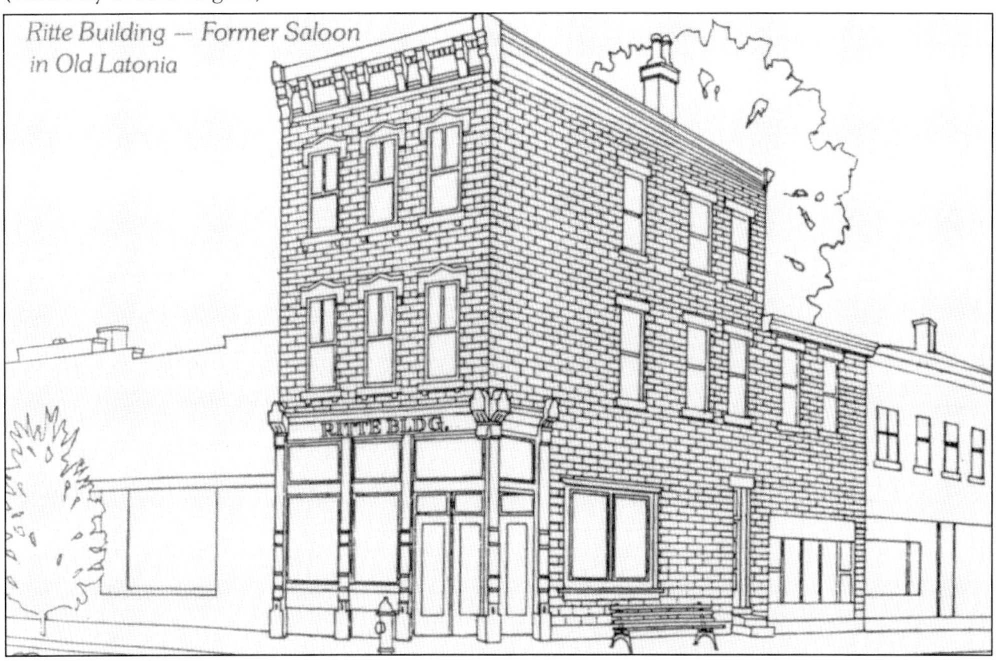

The Ritte Building housed Weber's Saloon from 1890 through 1899, then Henry Ritte's Saloon until its demise in 1927. During Prohibition, beginning in 1918, saloons switched to soft drinks, but it was not the same. Henry and his son, Walter, built the single-story building adjoining the saloon (at left) as a bowling alley and billiard parlor. In the 1890s, Henry Ritte had a beer garden on Decoursey Avenue between Thirty-third and Thirty-fourth Streets. (Drawing by and courtesy of Charles Gillham.)

Five

CHURCHES

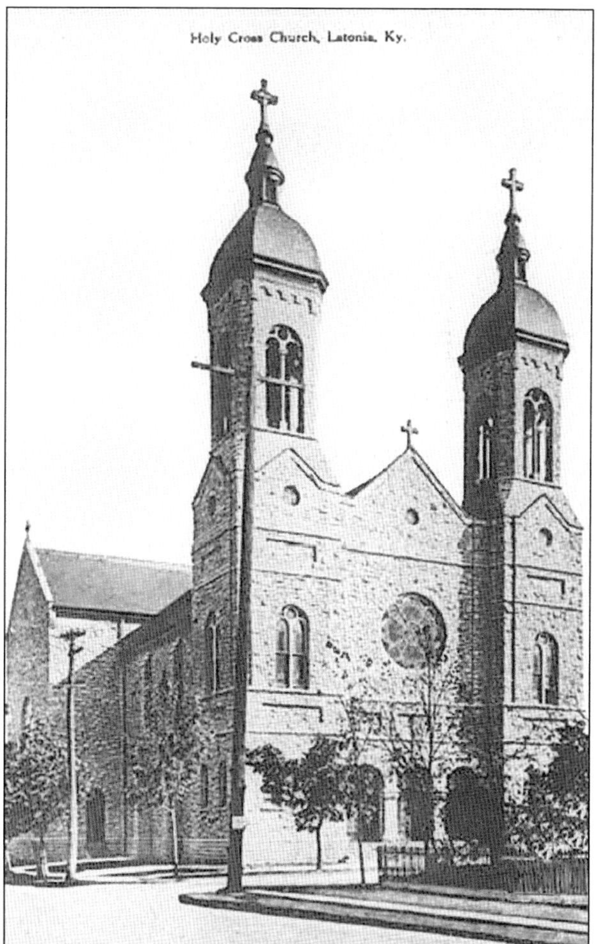

Churches have always been an important part of Latonia, and Holy Cross Church is among the oldest. This Romanesque stone church, dedicated in 1908, was the second home to the Holy Cross congregation. The twin spires, reaching 100 feet from the ground, are landmarks in Latonia. The sound of the bell or chimes is familiar to everyone. This beautiful and imposing building can seat 950 worshippers. (Courtesy of www.nkyviews.com.)

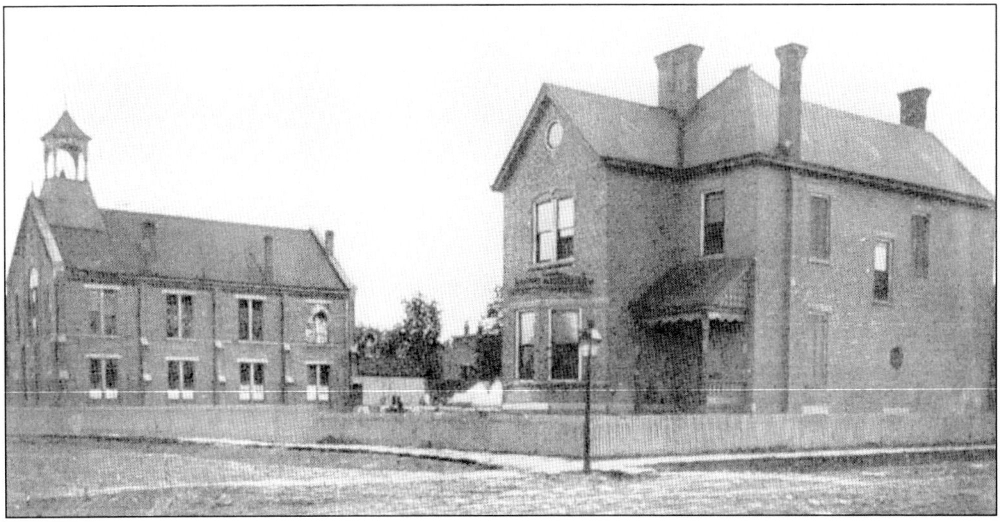

In 1887, Catholic families, mostly German-American, began discussion with Bishop Maes about establishing a church and school in Milldale. A site was found on the west side of Longworth Street (now Church) between Southern Avenue and Franklin Street (now Thirty-sixth Street), across the street from the current church. The first mass was celebrated on Christmas in 1890, though the church was unfinished. The sanctuary was on the second floor, and the lower floor housed the elementary school and teaching nuns. However, by 1903, they needed more space. After the new church was built, the old one was gutted for use as a school and auditorium. Above left is the first church and school, completed in 1891, and above right is the first parsonage that followed in 1892. Below are the dedicated volunteers of the Church Cleaning Brigade in this c. 1900 photograph. (Courtesy of www.nkyviews.com and Jim Feldman.)

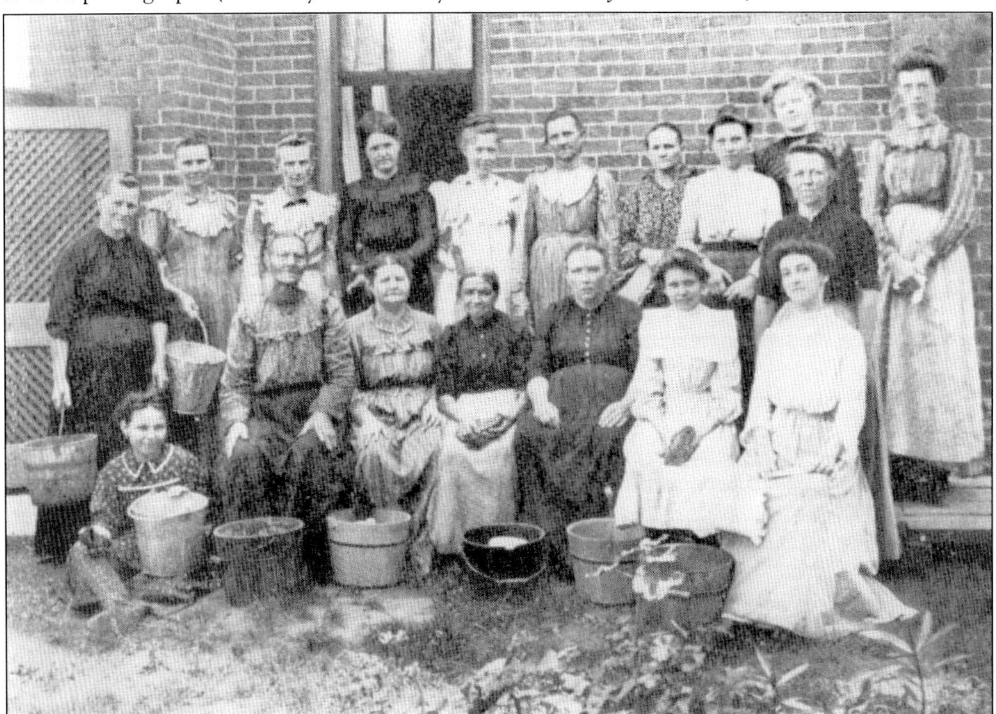

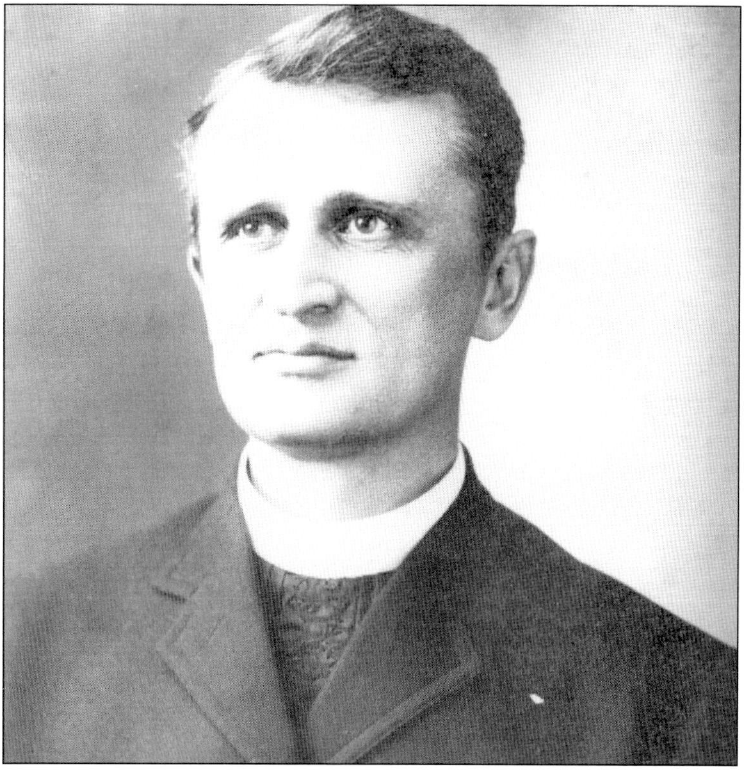

Father Reiter became pastor in 1898 and stayed 34 years. During his tenure, the new church was built, a new elementary school was built in 1914, and a high school was built in 1930. However, the high school created debt, and the Depression loomed. Latonia Deposit Bank held parish savings, and in 1931, it failed. Concern over these financial problems was too much for the beloved priest. In February 1932, he died. (Courtesy of the author's collection.)

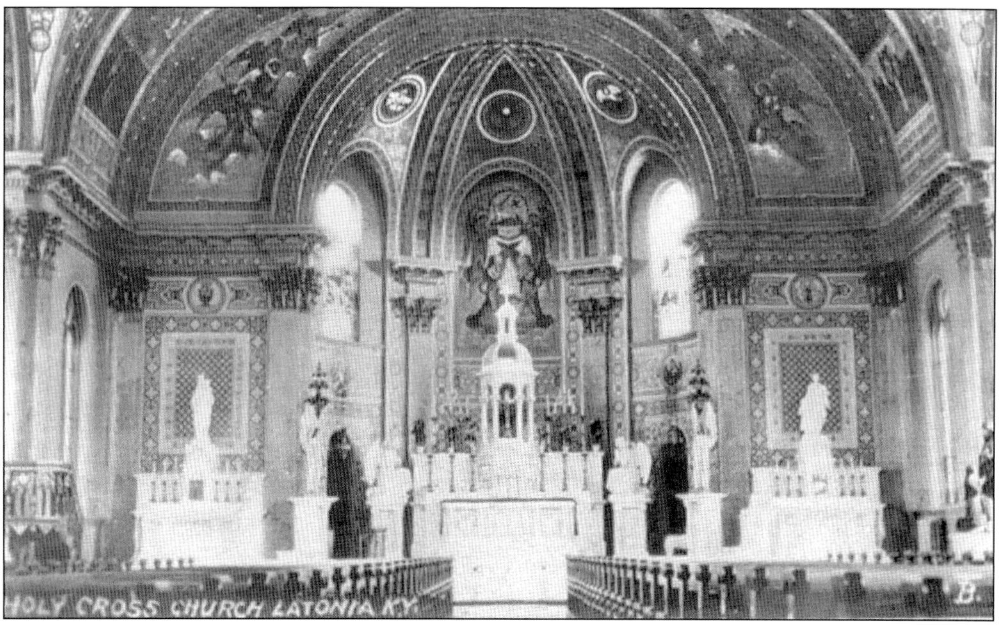

The original interior of the current church bore rich ornamentation. Major redecoration came in 1951 including marble walls and new stained glass windows. In 1989, planners for the centennial celebration decided to paint the church in light colors. Painting and other changes were underway in 1990, when fire seriously damaged the interior, leaving a large hole in the ceiling. Rehabilitation after the fire brought further changes to the interior. (Courtesy of www.nkyviews.com.)

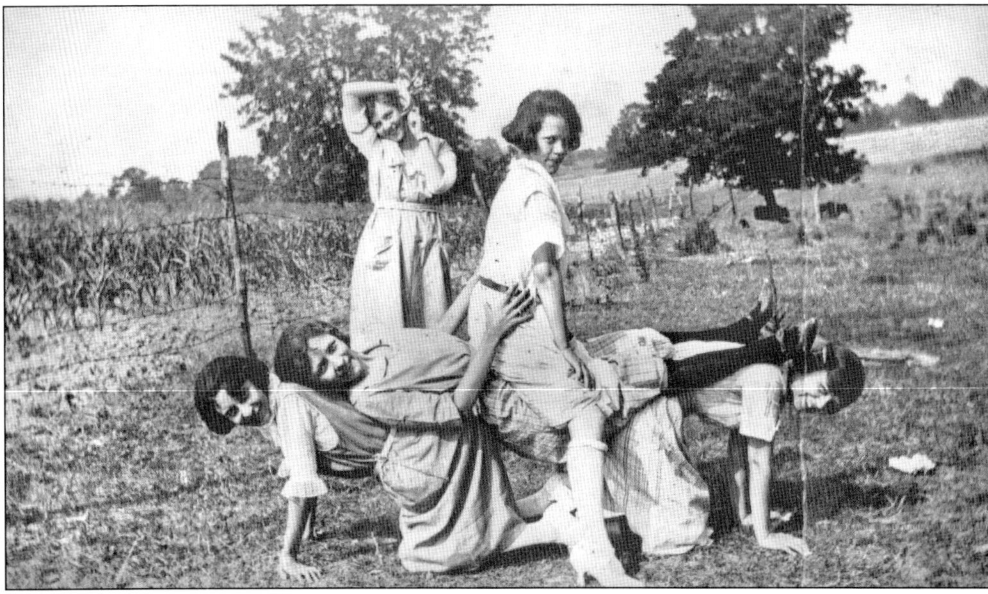

These young women enjoy hijinks for the camera at Holy Cross' Little Flower Camp in Locust, Kentucky, in June 1924. These girls are unidentified, but some of the campers were Loretta Heithaus (Lietzenmayer); Cyril Faust; Lee, Adelaide, and Harry Rieselman; Ann Dewes; and Bea and Jack Flesch. (Courtesy of Karl Lietzenmayer.)

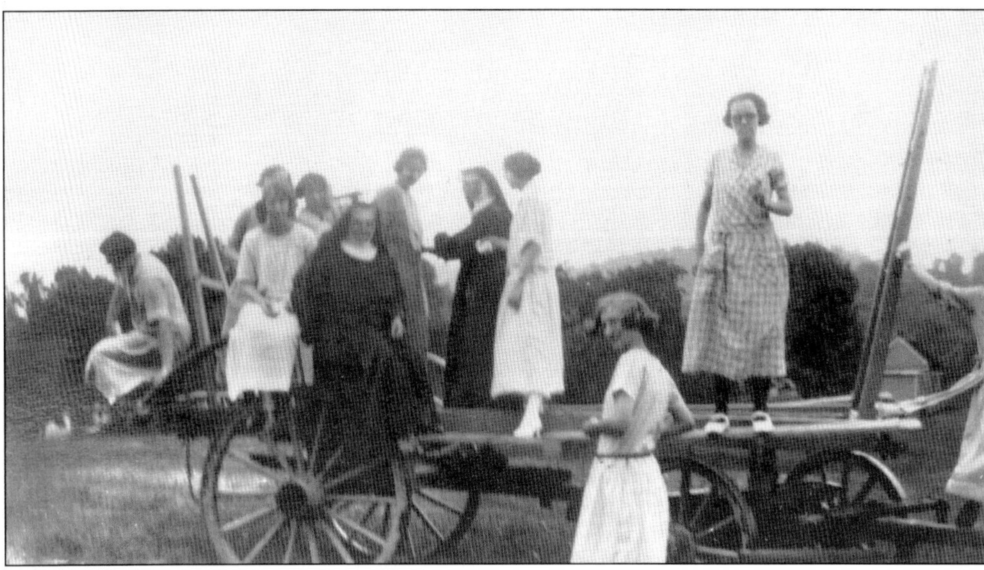

A Holy Cross picnic was held at Kollman's farm in the summer of 1924, which gave the girls and the sisters an opportunity to enjoy the country. The church also sponsored events for its young women such as a hike to Plainville, Ohio, in 1923. This must have given the girls a sense of freedom, since two of them were photographed daringly smoking cigarettes. (Courtesy of Karl Lietzenmeyer.)

In 1877, Benedictine Abbott Wimmer bought a winery on a hillside overlooking Milldale. He named it Monte Casino, and they supplied altar wine for the region. Prohibition was hard on the monks' winery, and, in 1922, they vacated the grounds. Their most famous building was this tiny stone chapel built by Brother Soltis around 1901. In 1965, the chapel was moved to Thomas More College, where it remains. (Photograph taken in 1934. Courtesy of Philip Zumdick.)

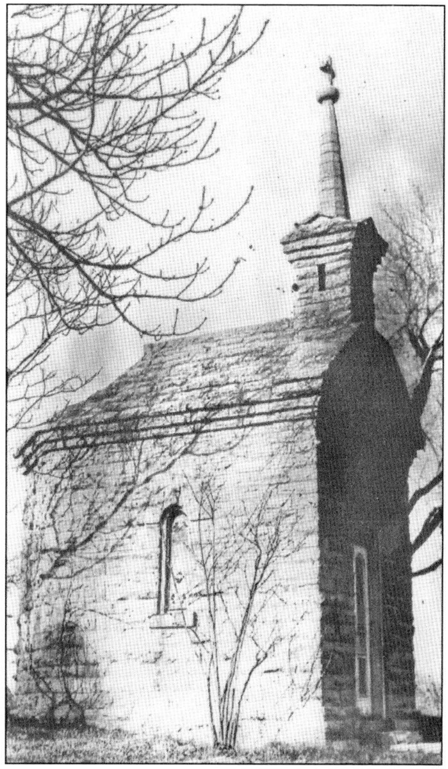

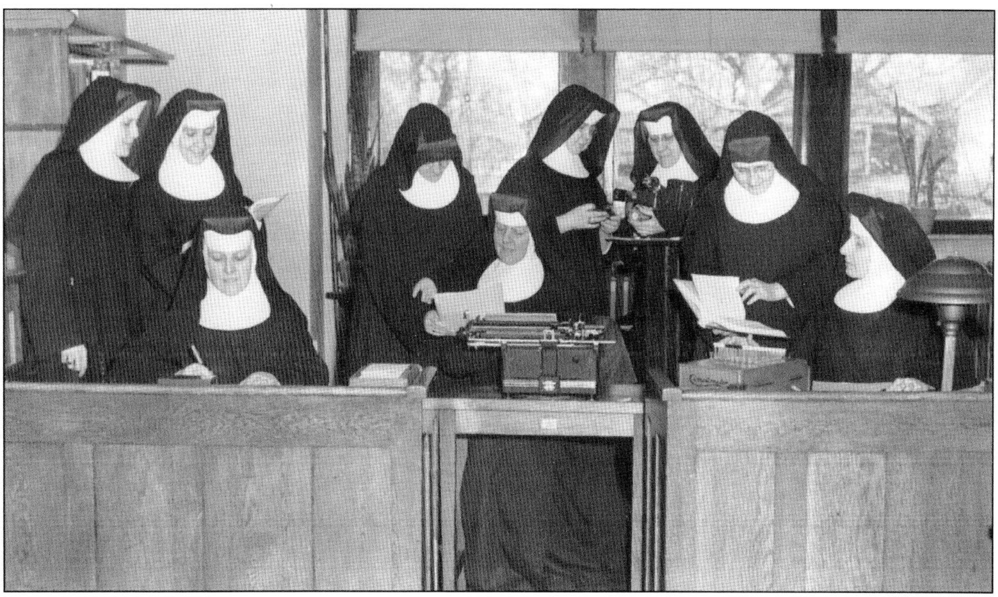

Some Benedictine nuns are at work in this *c.* 1940s photograph. Seated from left to right are Sister Judith, Sister Charlotte, and Sister Euphrasia. Standing from left to right are Sister Teresa, Sister Samuel, Sister Avila, Sister Frances, Sister Julitta, and Sister Mildred. Dr. Bird's house, located at Southern and Church, was demolished for construction of a modern nun's home, which was completed in 1941. They left in 1978, and Catholic Charities came in 1979. In 2002, they completed major remodeling. (Courtesy of Jim Feldman.)

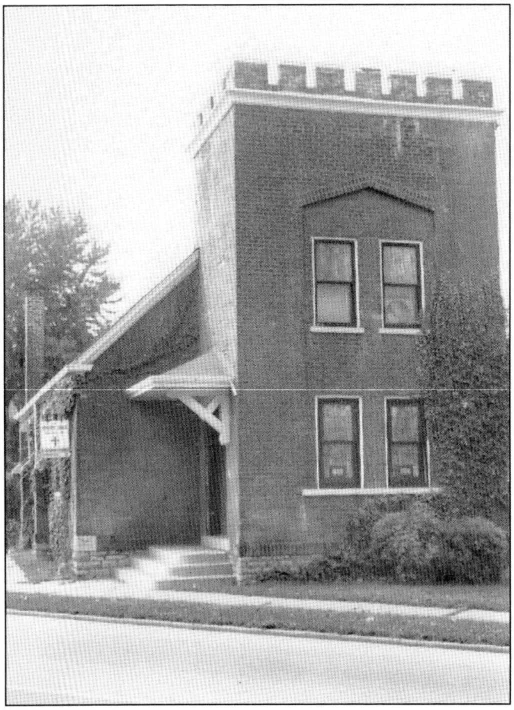

St. Stephens Episcopal Church was dedicated in 1911. In 1867, Covington's Trinity Episcopal built a mission at the southeast corner of Southern Avenue and Church Street. By 1890, they sold the chapel to Trinity Methodist Church. Their mission lay dormant until 1907 when it was reestablished and this Norman-style church built. All along, the small church had struggled financially, and in 2005 it closed. (Courtesy of Kenton County Public Library.)

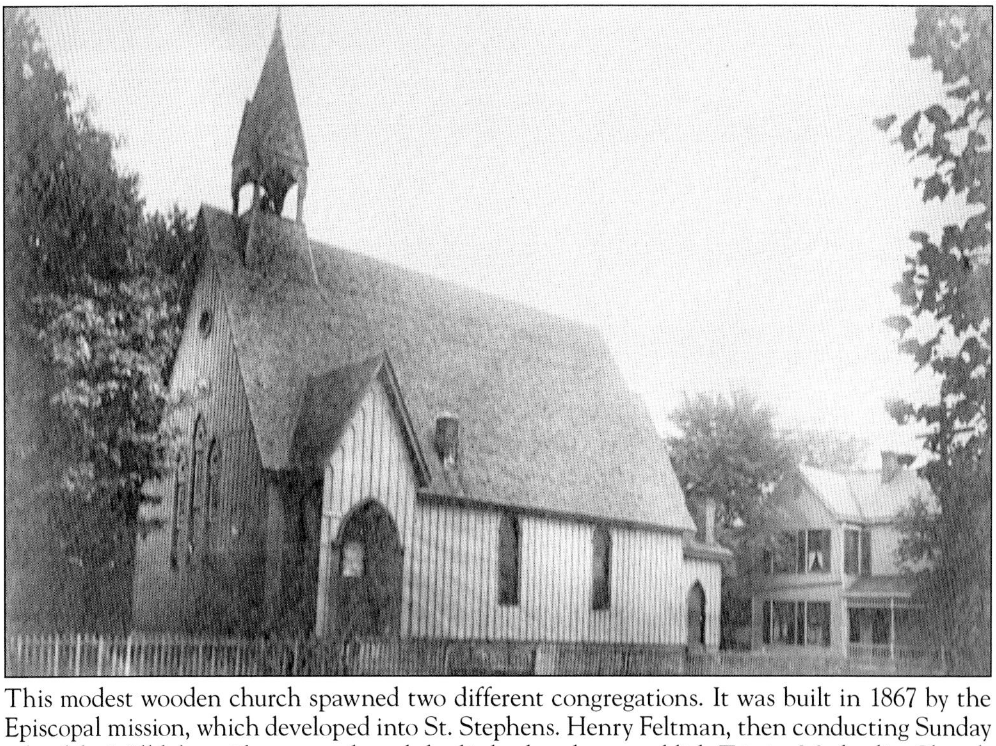

This modest wooden church spawned two different congregations. It was built in 1867 by the Episcopal mission, which developed into St. Stephens. Henry Feltman, then conducting Sunday school for Milldale residents, purchased the little church to establish Trinity Methodist Church in 1890. The congregation grew, and in 1910 they sold the building to Albert Dehlinger, who moved it for his new Delbee Theater. (Courtesy of Tom Martin.)

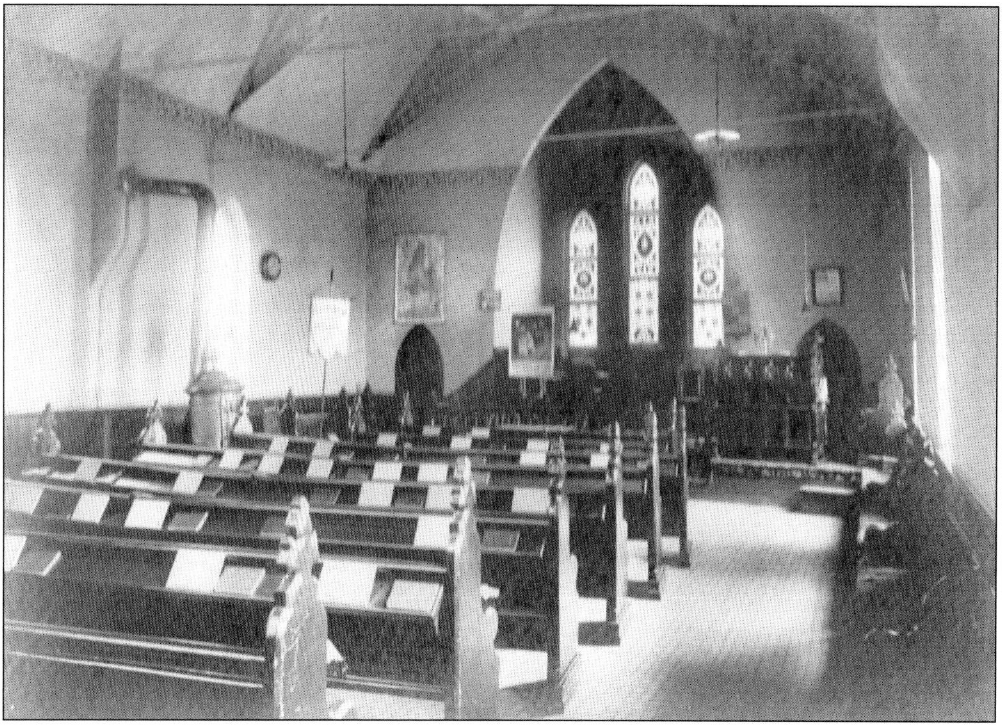

Trustees Feltman, George Mason, and W. B. Meyer kept the name Trinity, acknowledging its original owners. Rev. F. W. Harrop was the first pastor, serving until 1894 and from 1912–1915. These stained glass windows were removed before the building was moved and were installed in the new building where they remain today. (Courtesy of Trinity United Methodist Church.)

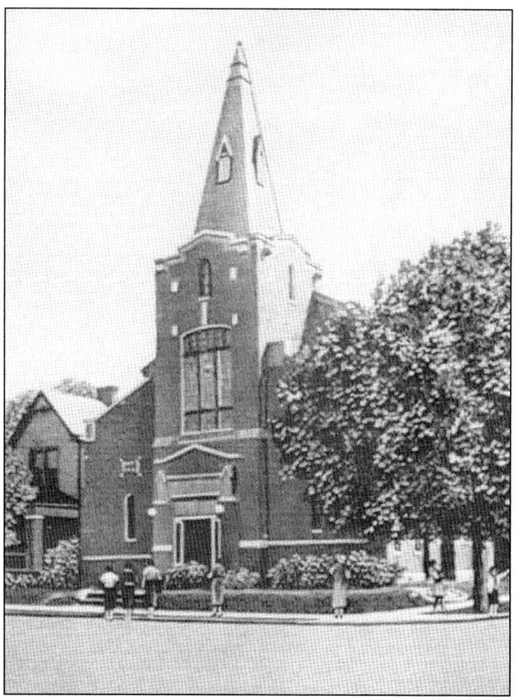

In 1910, construction began on Trinity United Methodist Church. It cost $25,000, but banker Henry Feltman not only donated $10,000 for construction costs, he matched all donations pledged by the congregation during the dedication. In 1930, a recreation hall was built replacing their old parsonage. Creative fund-raising was needed to meet payments during the Depression. They held dinners, donut sales, and a play called the *Womanless Wedding*. (Courtesy of www.nkyviews.com.)

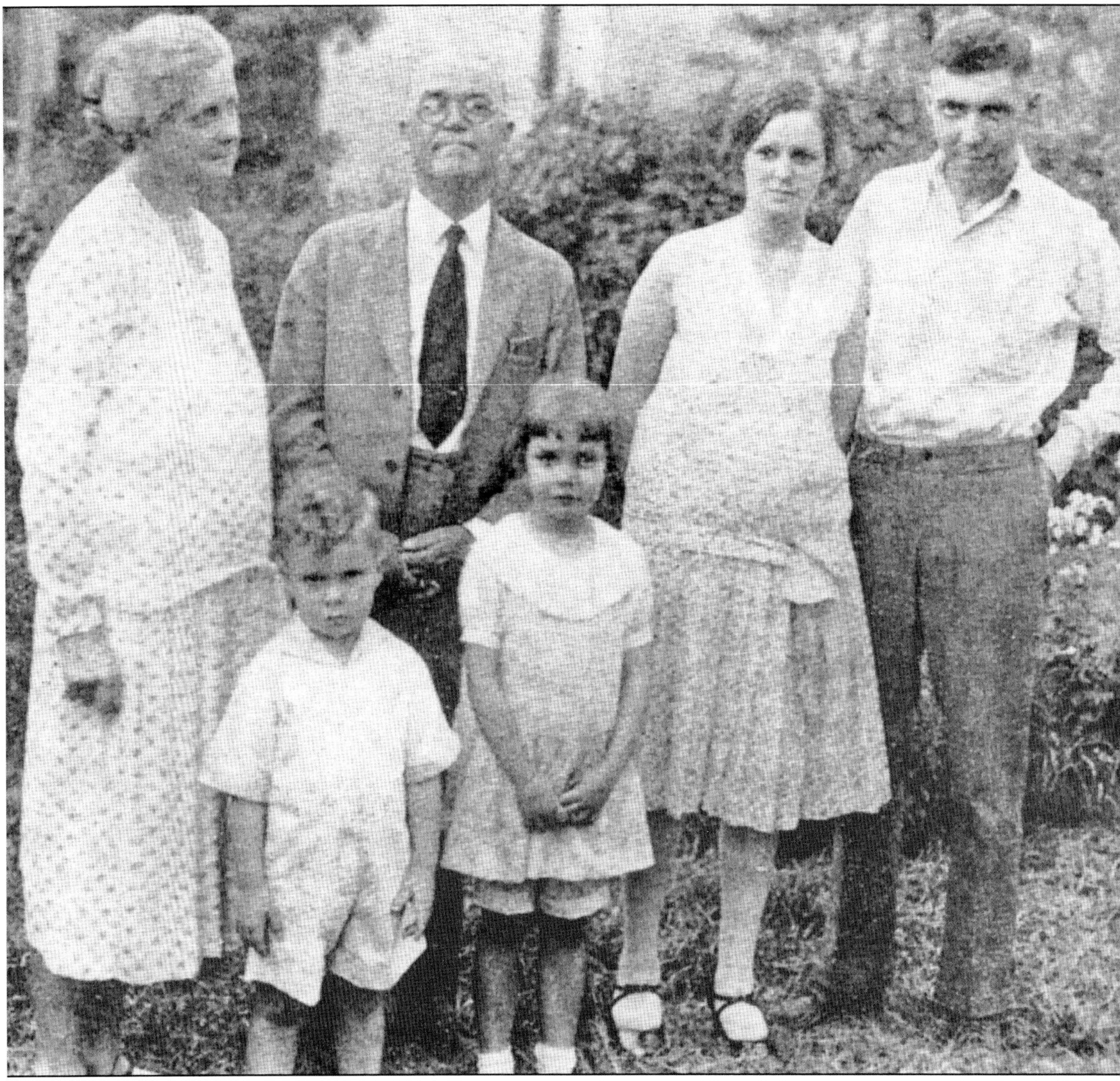

The congregation that would become Latonia Christian Church began meeting in Bird's Hall in 1898. In 1902, Harlan C. Runyon became pastor, and they built a chapel in 1906 on Thirty-sixth Street. With only 22 members, times were hard, but as Latonia grew, so did the church. The building grew, too—doubling in size. When even that became too small, they sold it to young Calvary Baptist in 1921. Undoubtedly, the power of Brother Runyon's personality was a feature in church growth. He was another of Latonia's long-tenured clergymen, who was known and respected beyond his own congregation. He served for 33 years and became an integral part of the community and was known as the "marrying and burying preacher." From left to right are Sister ? Runyon, grandson "Buddy," Brother Runyon, granddaughter Rebecca Jane, daughter-in-law ?, and son Hustin C. Runyon. (Courtesy of the author's collection.)

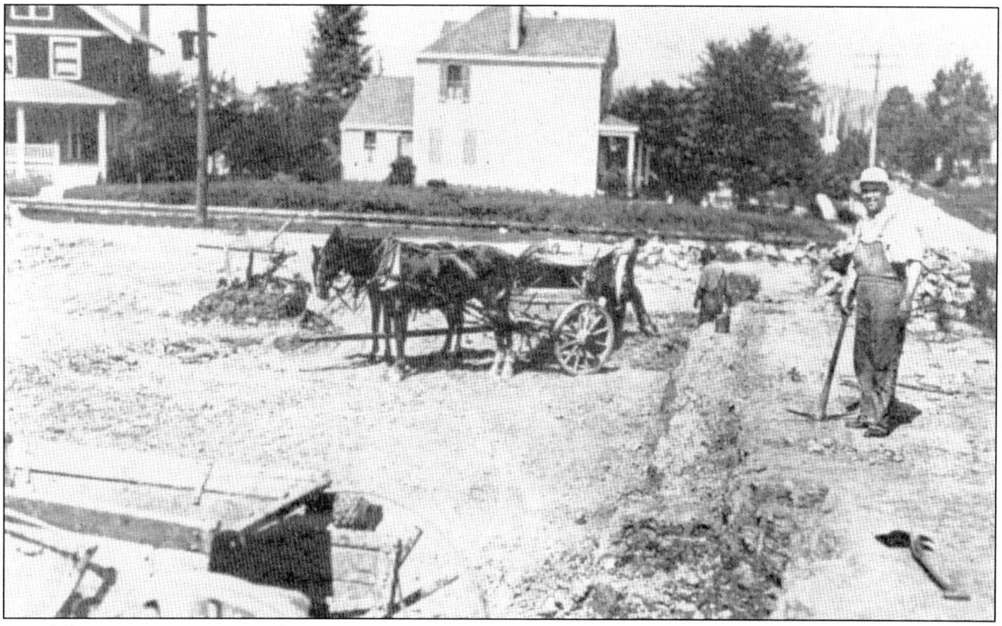

Work begins on Latonia Christian's new church at Thirty-ninth Street and Decoursey Avenue. It was dedicated in 1923. Reverend Runyon stands at right, in his overalls with pick in hand. After his death, a portion of the congregation split off and founded a new church in the old Latonia Deposit Bank near Ritte's Corner. In honor of their former pastor, they named it "Runyon Memorial," as it is known today. (Courtesy of the author's collection.)

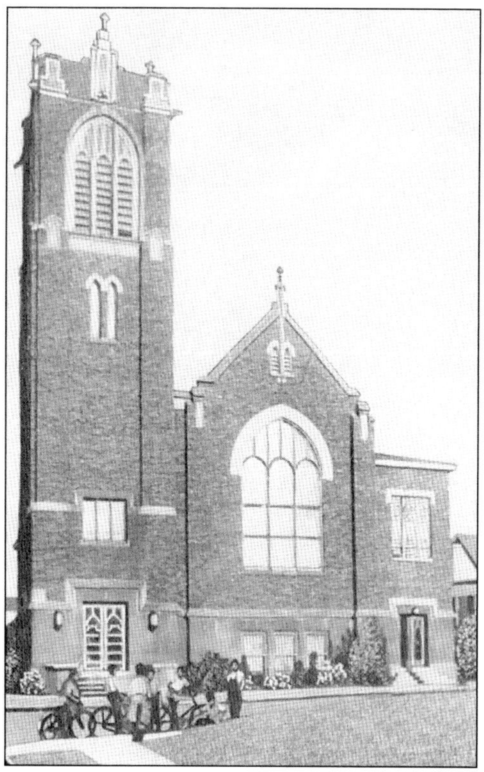

Latonia Christian Church is an active congregation today. In the 1920s, the church's Annual Street Bazaar held each September drew thousands from the region. Thirty-ninth Street was closed to traffic and filled with booths offering games, prizes, and novelties. Dressed in a gypsy costume, a Mrs. Schickner from St. Mark's Church told people's fortunes, but Reverend Runyon provided the biggest treat by carving elephants out of bars of Ivory Soap. (Courtesy of the author's collection.)

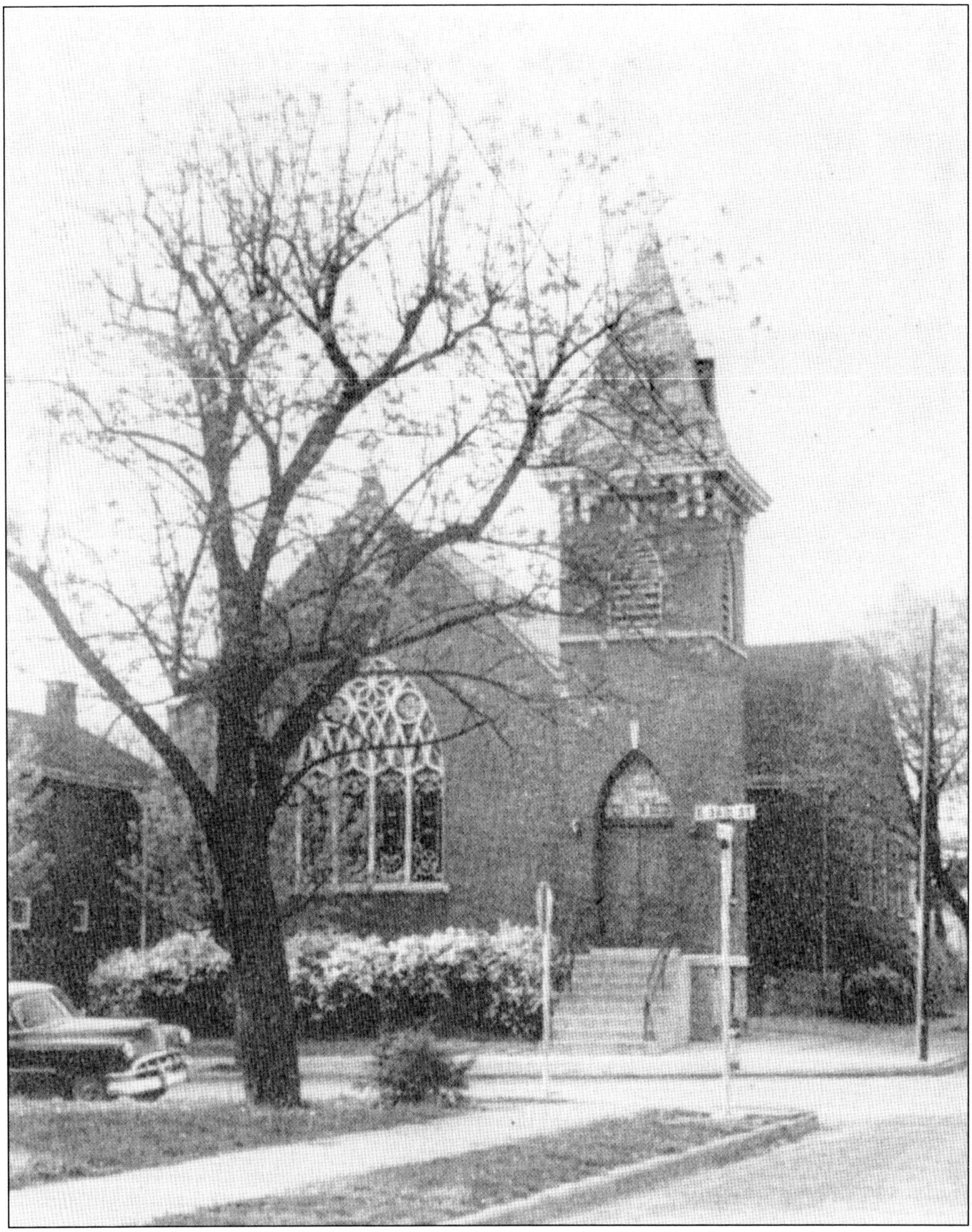

Here is St. Mark's Evangelical Church as it looked around 1950, already having had an addition (at right) to its original 1909 architecture. Rev. William Echelmeier initiated meetings in Bird's Hall in 1907. Echelmeier and the Ladies Aid Society of St. Mark's Church selected a site for the church building, choosing Golding Street (now Thirty-eighth) near Park Avenue. Then they selected the name, St. Mark, which was popular in Lutheran churches. In 1908, a church council was organized naming Henry Luzader as president. One year later, the church was complete. Some services were held in German until World War I. Major alterations were made to the building in 1956 to enlarge it. (Courtesy St. Mark United Church of Christ.)

Dorothy Scholl and Rev. Frank C. Scholl met and married at St. Mark's. Reverend Scholl, the church's fourth minister, came in 1919 and served until his death in the 1960s. His only departure was during World War II, when he served as U.S. Army Chaplain. Like Father Reiter and Reverend Runyon, Scholl's long tenure and warm personality made him a Latonia institution. (Courtesy of Lorna Harrell.)

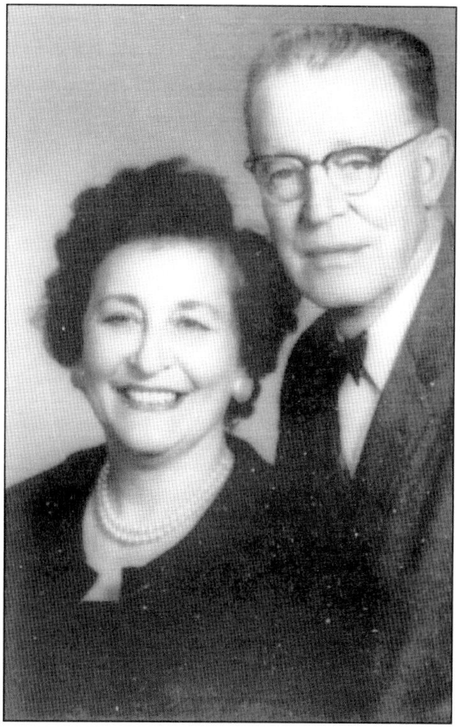

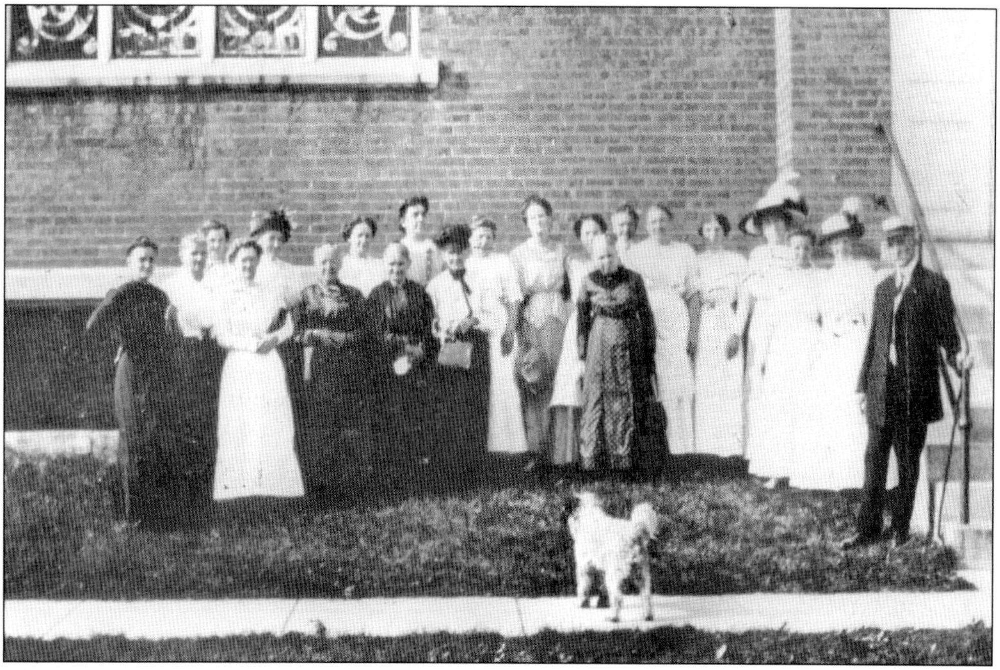

The Ladies Aid Society of St. Mark's Church poses with Reverend Echelmeier, the first pastor in this c. 1909 photograph. Eight ladies organized the group in 1907. The officers were Mrs. George Smith (Lizzie), president; Mrs. William Young (Anna), vice president; Mrs. Gustav Schickner, secretary; and Mrs. J. Granneman, treasurer. Lizzie Smith is fourth from left (white dress). (Courtesy of the author's collection.)

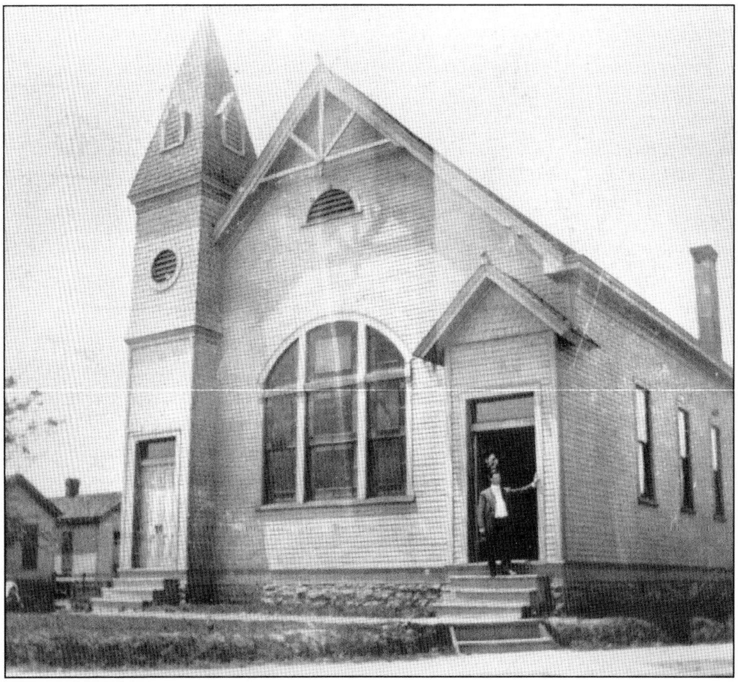

In the early 1890s, a Baptist mission group began meeting in the home of Mr. and Mrs. O. M. Johnson at Thirty-first and Rogers Streets. In 1896, the Milldale Baptist Mission was built at Golding and Pike Streets (now Thirty-eighth Street and Decoursey Avenue, respectively), and in 1900 it became the First Baptist Church of Latonia with the Reverend C. A. Earl as pastor. (Courtesy of Tom Martin.)

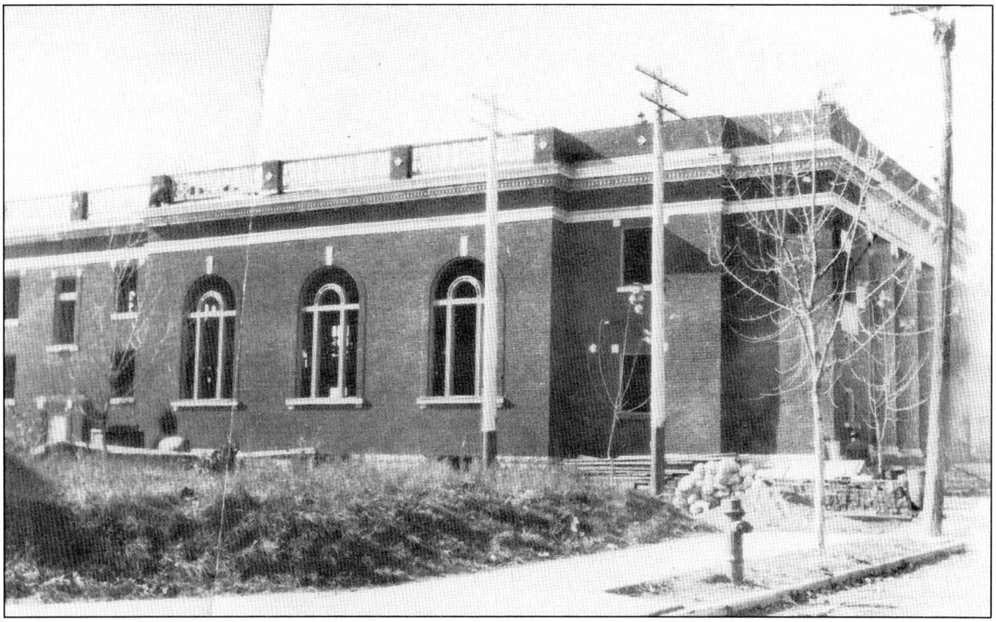

By 1913, growth called for a new church, which opened in 1917. Here the church construction nears completion. *The Hour of Power*, begun in 1941, became the nation's largest prayer meeting. The church continued to expand, began radio programming, and started two missions, which are now Rosedale Baptist and Ashland Avenue Baptist. Another offshoot became Calvary Baptist, which purchased Latonia Christian's old Thirty-sixth Street church in 1921. D. B. Eastep was pastor from 1927 until 1962—another exceptional term. A new church was built at Southern Avenue and Tibbats Street. In 1939, building continued, and Calvary Baptist has grown to nearly two blocks. (Courtesy of Betty McCoy and Latonia Baptist Church.)

Six

SCHOOLS AND CHILDREN

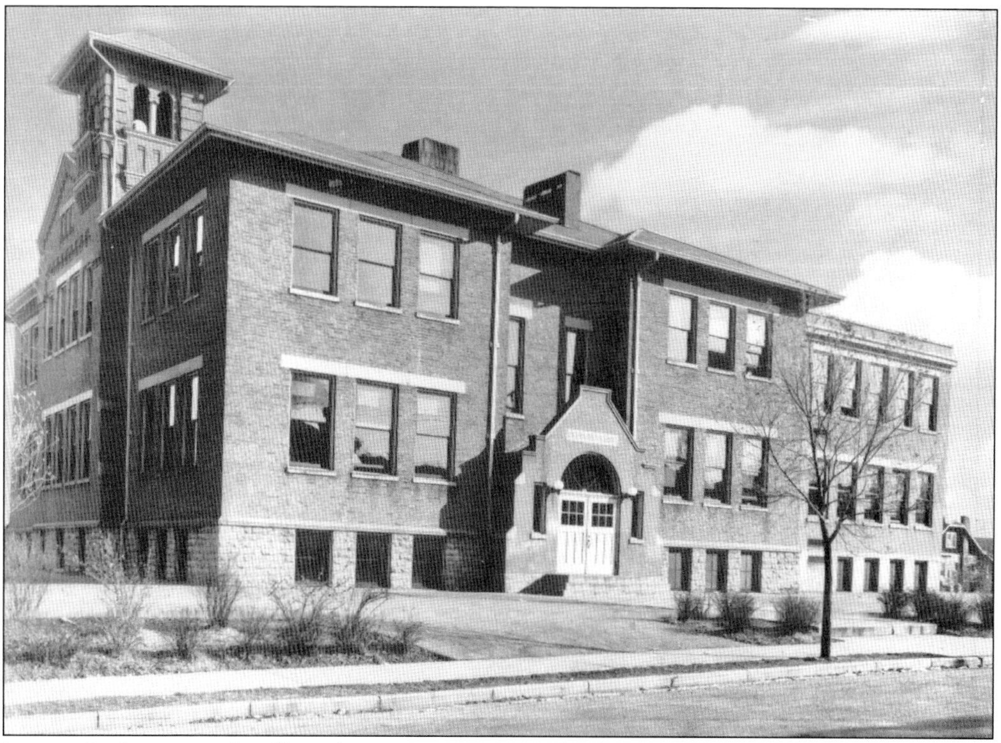

Latonia had its own school board to manage its four schools. It had three public schools for white children and had a "colored school," as it was commonly called. When Covington annexed Latonia in 1909, the Covington Board of Education simply took over Latonia's school board and assumed its debts. Additions were made to the three schools to create the larger ones needed. This original building pictured here was Latonia's Golding Street School, at Thirty-eighth and Locke Streets. After 1909, it became Eighth District Elementary, and Golding Street became Thirty-eighth Street. The building's two prominent rectangular wings connected by an inset and a doorway, seen in front, constituted the original school. The three Latonia schools were designed identically. The rest of the building, including the bell tower, was added when it became Eighth District Elementary. (Courtesy of Kenton County Public Library.)

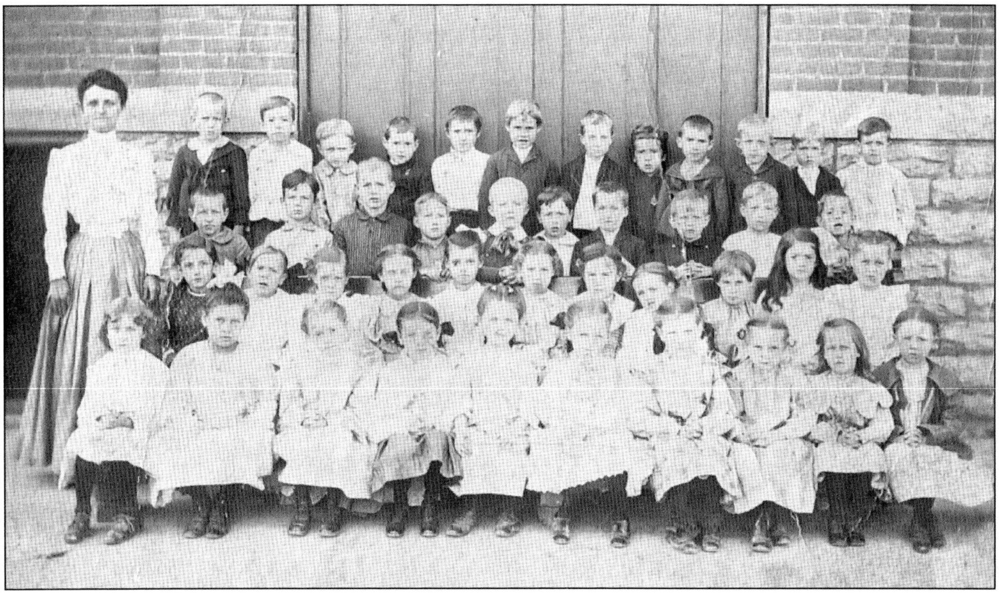

Here are two groups of schoolchildren posing in the doorway of Latonia's Golding Street School. Above, around 1900, the teacher stands at left. Kentucky law prevented female teachers from marrying, so they led circumspect lives, making meager livings and often boarding with students' families. Below, around 1907, a boy holds a slate reading "Latonia School Grade 2." Notice these children are all white. Milldale/Latonia's Colored School, started in 1883, was on Cherry Street near the racetrack and later moved to the corner of Kruse (now James) and Decoursey Avenues. One teacher taught all the elementary grades, and then students went to William Grant School on Seventh Street in Covington. After annexation, the school remained in use, but by 1913, Latonia's African American children were taken by streetcar to Covington's Lincoln Elementary School. (Courtesy of Tricia Dorman.)

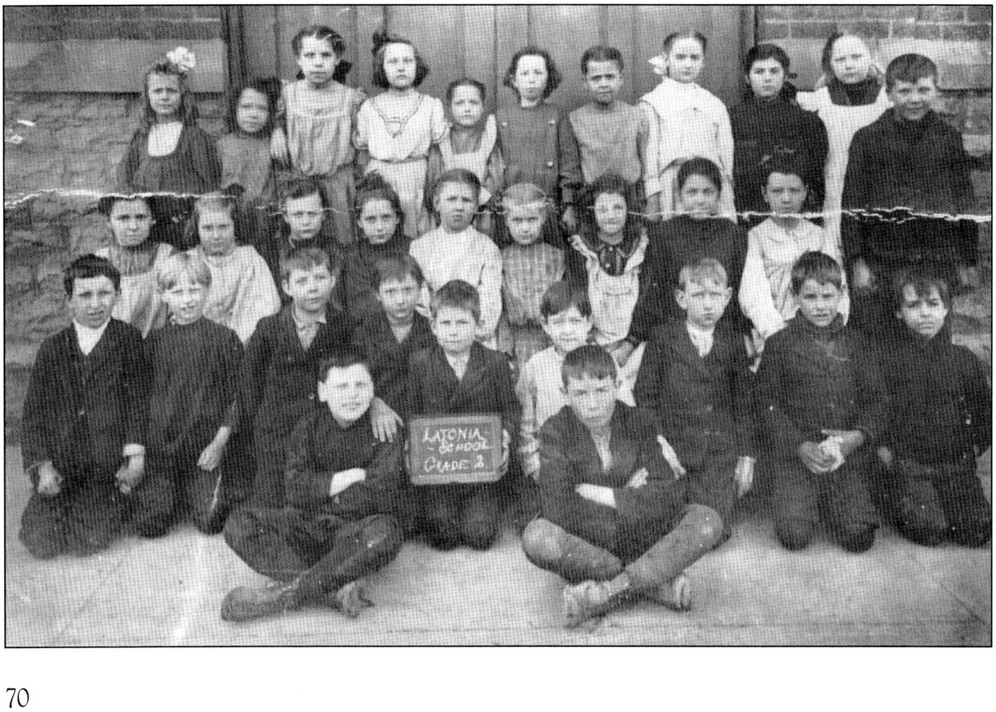

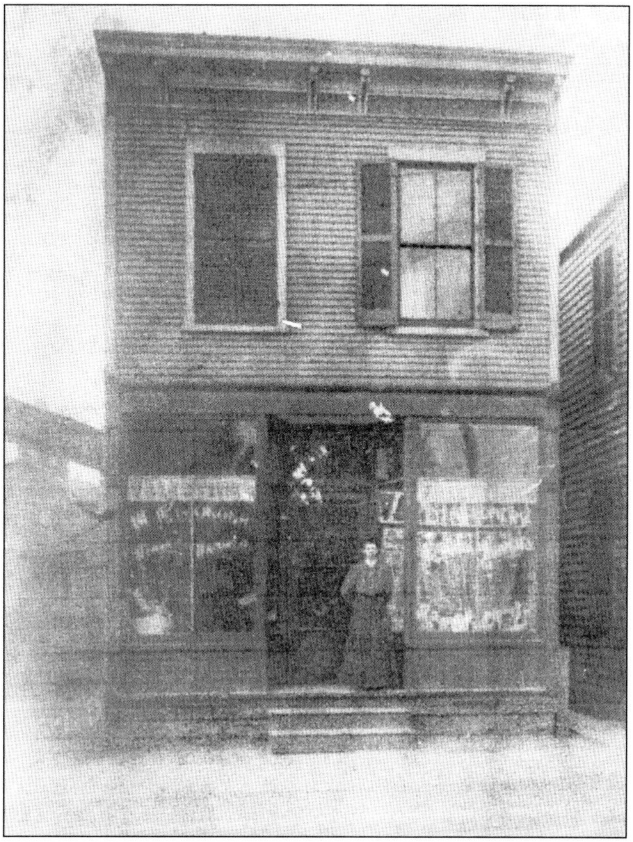

"Miss Mary" Ploeger stands in the doorway of her shop on Decoursey Avenue near Eighth District School. In her shop were all the things that schoolchildren wanted. She carried trinkets, toys, school supplies like Big Chief writing tablets and fat yellow pencils, and penny candy. She carried hard candy with different colored stripes, licorice, little tin pans filled with cream candy and its own tiny spoon, and little brown "potatoes" covered with cinnamon and brown sugar. The kindly Miss Mary was a big part of the attraction. Later Bill Martin took over her shop to open the first Johnny's Toy Store. Below is another class at Golding Street School featured in this *c.* 1904 photograph. Levina Carroll, daughter of jockey William Carroll, is seventh from right in the first row. (Courtesy of Mary Cecil.)

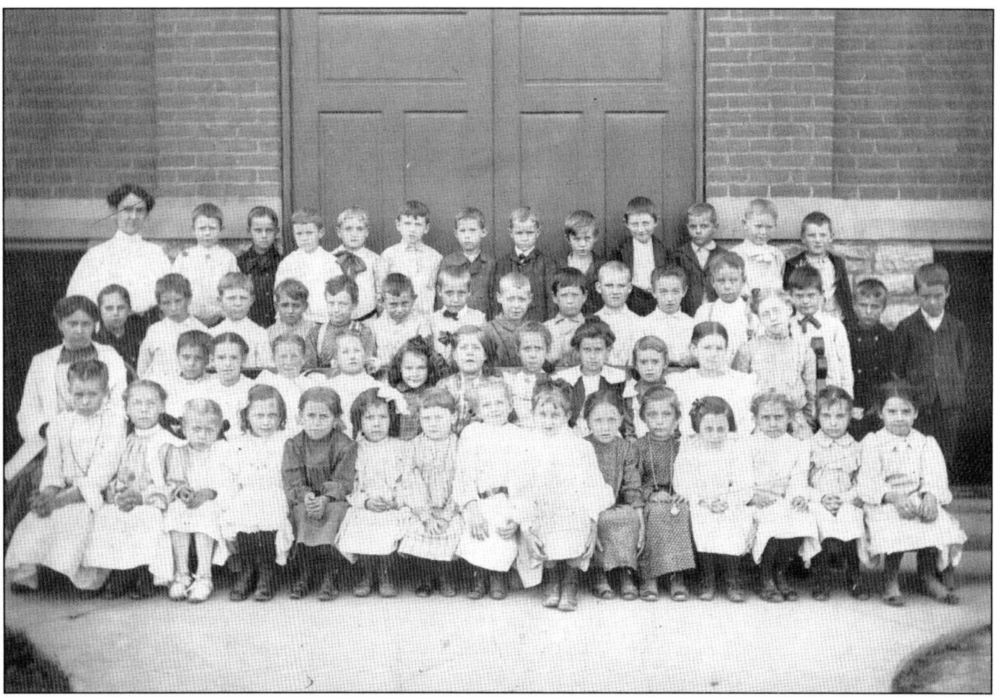

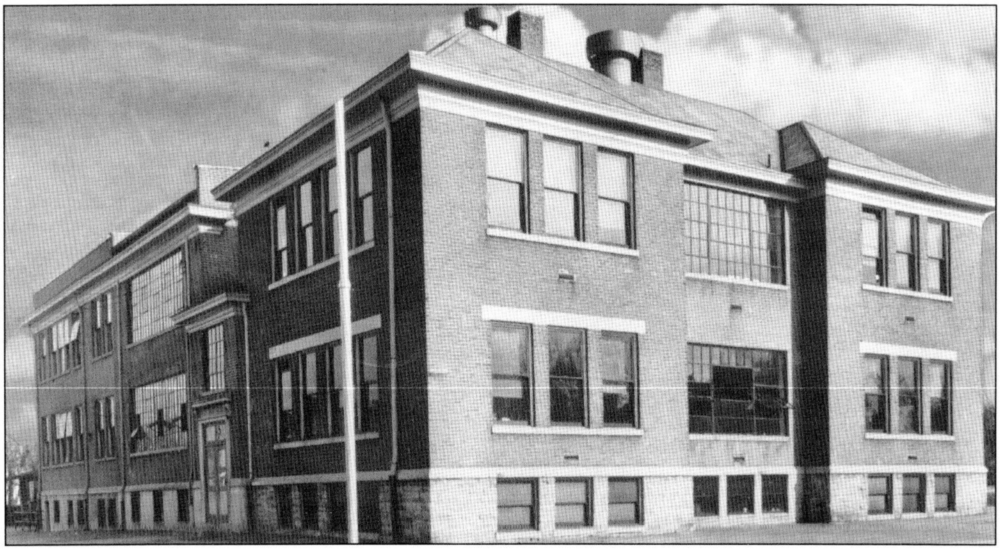

Ninth District Elementary stood at Thirty-third (originally Ferry) and Graff Streets, using the original two-room school behind it for some classes. In 1957, a new Ninth District school was built on Indiana Avenue. It occupies the site of the old Coppin mansion, which was razed to make room for the school that is still in use there today. The building pictured was demolished in the 1990s. (Courtesy of Kenton County Public Library.)

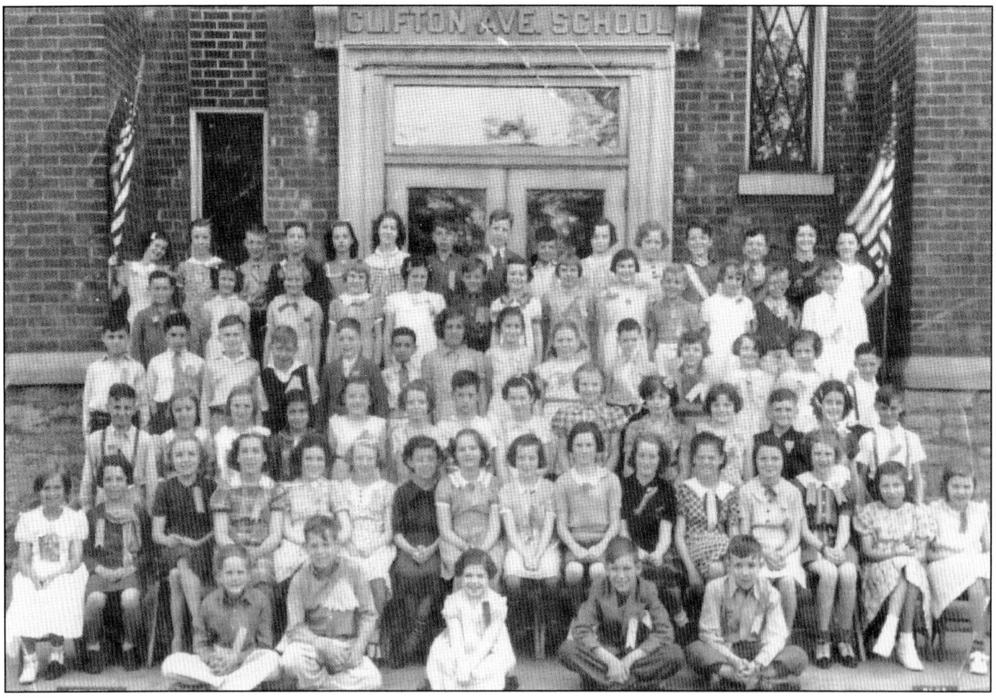

Tenth District School's fourth through sixth graders pose for Blue Ribbon Day in 1937. Blue Ribbon Day emphasized good physical health. Each child was examined by a nurse, and if his or her physical condition measured up, the child was pinned with a blue ribbon. "Clifton Ave. School" is inscribed above the door. The old school faced Clifton, and the addition faced Decoursey Avenue between Forty-fifth and Forty-sixth Streets. (Courtesy of Kenton County Public Library.)

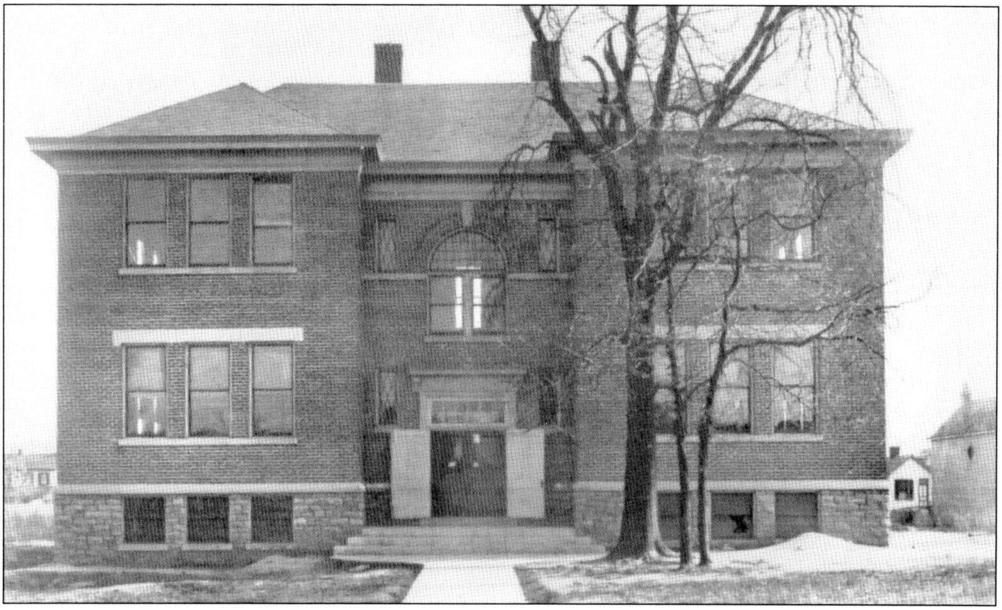

Latonia's Clifton Avenue School shows the standard Latonia school design of two wings connected by an inset. In remodeling each old Latonia school, Covington essentially attached another building to the back of the old one. Below is the addition attached to Clifton school after being remodeled as Tenth District, photographed in 1941. At first, Ninth and Tenth Districts had only grades one through four. Both schools were wired for electricity during construction about 1910, but the wiring was not connected nor light fixtures installed. The schools functioned without electricity for several months. In 1973, Latonia Elementary was built at Thirty-ninth Street and Huntington Avenue after several blocks of homes had been razed. The new school combined Eighth and Tenth Districts. Old Tenth District was demolished, and later Eighth District followed, in favor of high-rise apartments for seniors. (Courtesy of Kenton County Public Library.)

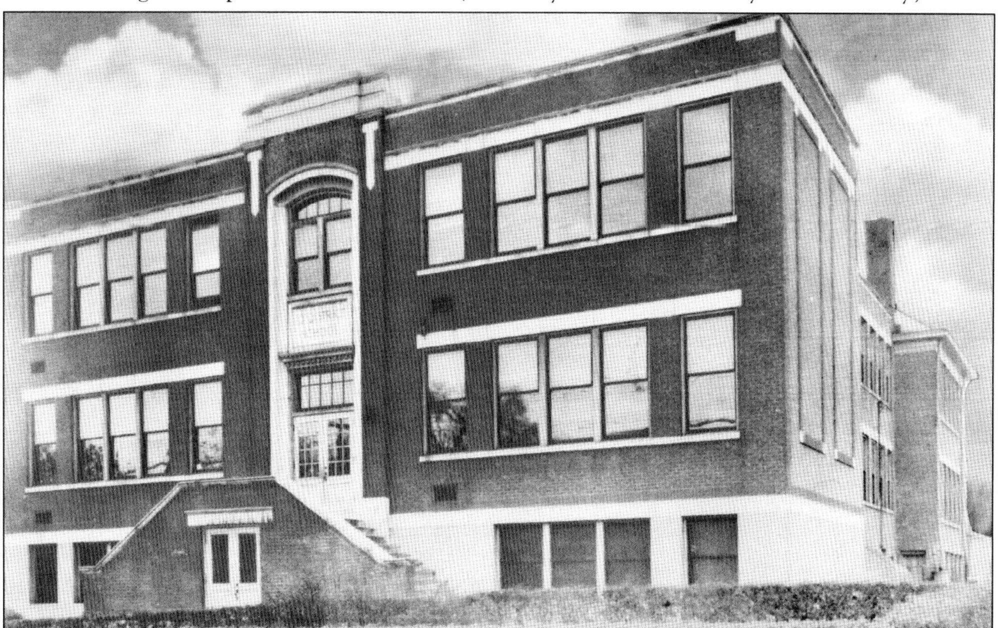

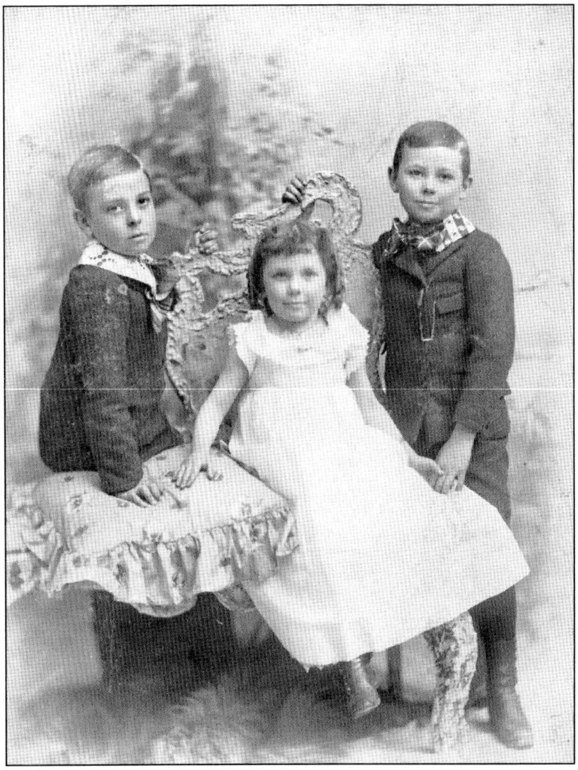

Charles Gillham, his sister Cokie, and older brother, Alfred, pose for a *c.* 1890 formal family portrait. The younger girl, Emma, was too young to join them. The Gillhams temporarily left Latonia for California in hopes that the warm climate would restore the failing health of their mother, Flavia. Sadly, it did not. They returned to Latonia, and she died in their Glenn Avenue home in 1904. (Courtesy of the author's collection.)

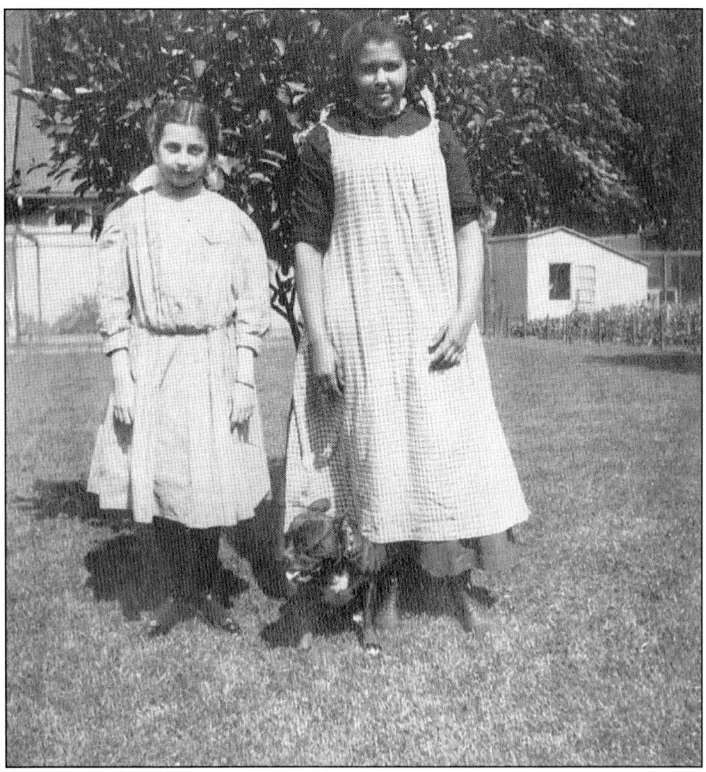

Levina Carroll (left), her unidentified friend, and a little dog are photographed around 1910. Levina lived on West Thirty-sixth Street, just past Decoursey Avenue. Her friend's parents, John and Lizzie, lived nearby on East Thirty-fifth Street. John, whose last name is unknown, worked at the First National Bank as a sort of "attending valet" for customers. He was well known and well liked in Latonia. (Courtesy of Mary Cecil.)

Richter Roe plays his drum, decked out in his World War I uniform. Richter did not have to go to war yet, though his Uncle Georgie did. Georgie's mother, Lizzie, put a Blue Star flag in her window, indicating she had a son at war. Immediately upon Georgie's homecoming at Latonia Depot, she tore the star out of the window and threw it away. (Photograph by George Roe; courtesy of the author's collection.)

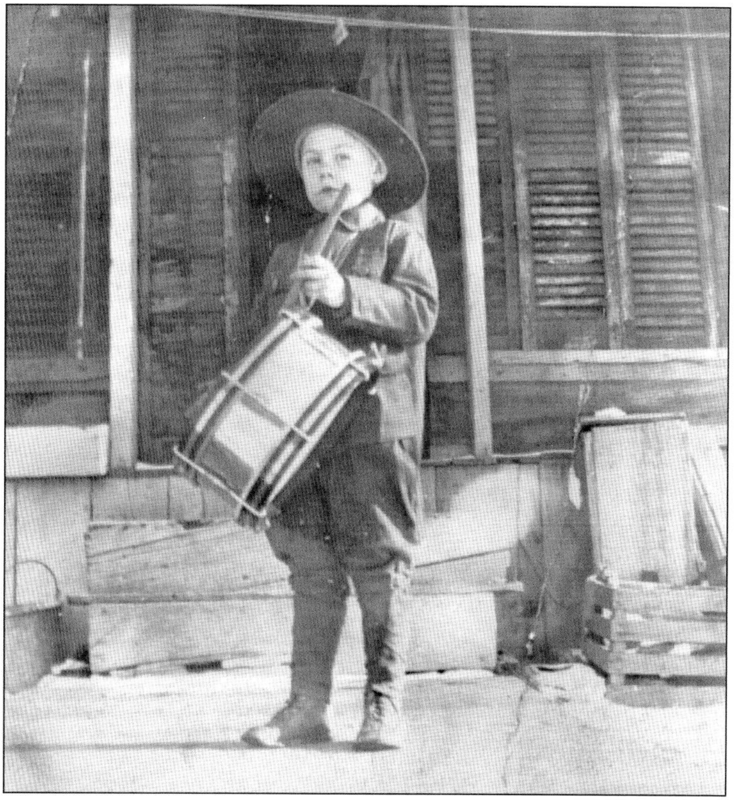

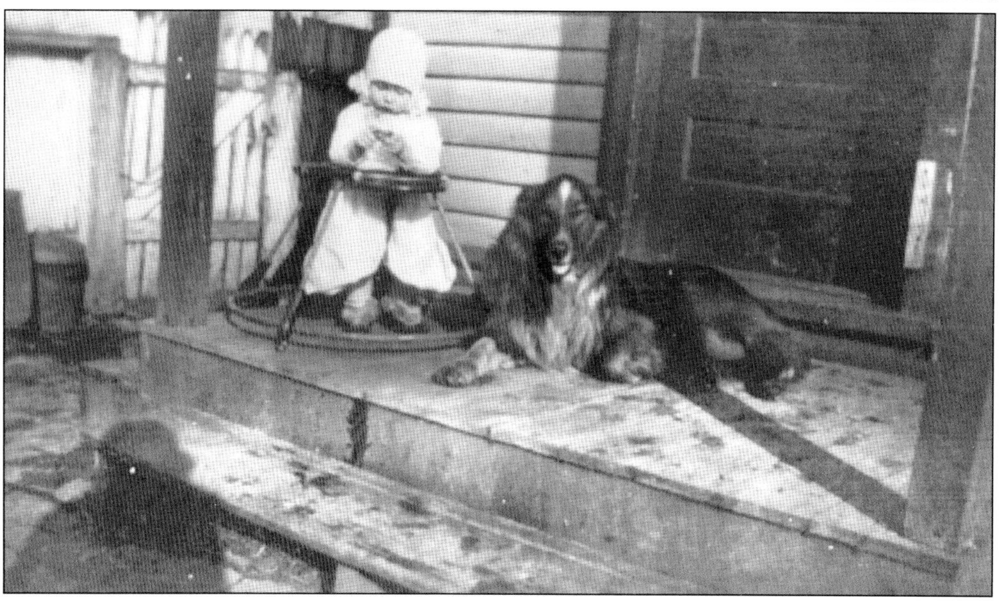

Little Virginia Kupper sits in her baby tender, guarded by her faithful dog in this *c.* 1920s photograph. These old-fashioned contraptions were well designed. The baby could play with toys on the small lap table, yet be in little danger of falling because of the wide circular base. She was safe on her porch with pooch, especially with mother only a few feet away with the camera. (Courtesy of Virginia Kupper Kaufman.)

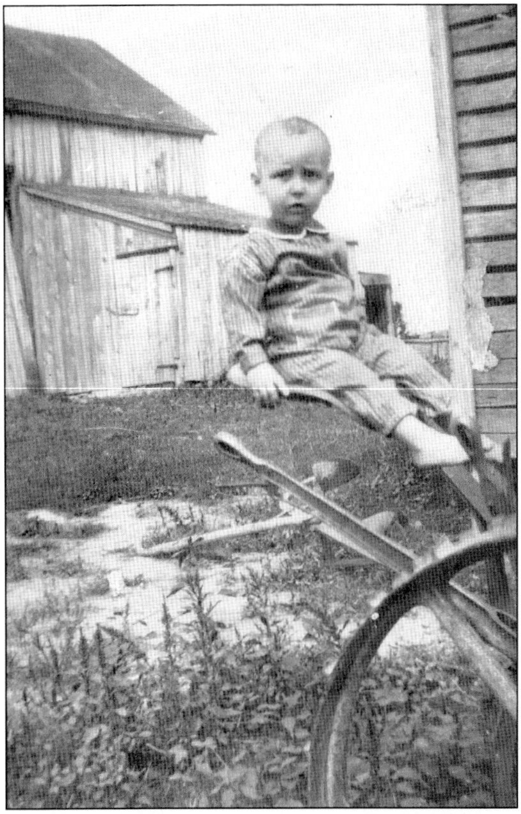

Paul Dorman perches on the seat of a plow in the early 1920s. Many parts of Latonia still had a rural feel, even in the 1920s. Farms were familiar to children then. Often grandparents or other relatives lived on farms, and families would visit or picnic there. Paul was born in an apartment over Swindler's Funeral Home on Southern Avenue. (Courtesy of Tricia Dorman.)

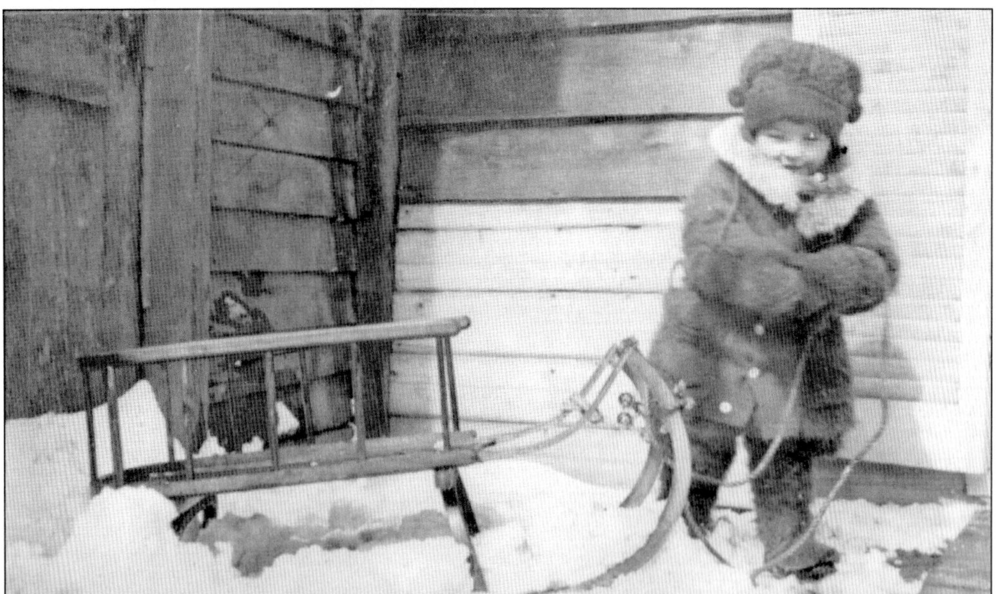

Mary Kochersberger tries to manage her sled in the snow, all bundled up against the Northern Kentucky winter in this *c.* 1920 photograph. She was an only child, and her father, Ray, who worked on the L&N, was a photographer by avocation. Her childhood was generously and artistically recorded. (Courtesy of Mary Cecil.)

The Petty boys, Gary (left) and Doug, celebrate patriotism and their family business in this c. 1956 photograph. Their parents, Charles and Helen Petty, owned the Latonia Bakery, and had taken it over from Helen's parents, Carl and Helen Schliff, so the bakery had been in the family since 1929. In spite of these convincing costumes, neither boy went into the family business. (Courtesy of Lorna Petty Harrell.)

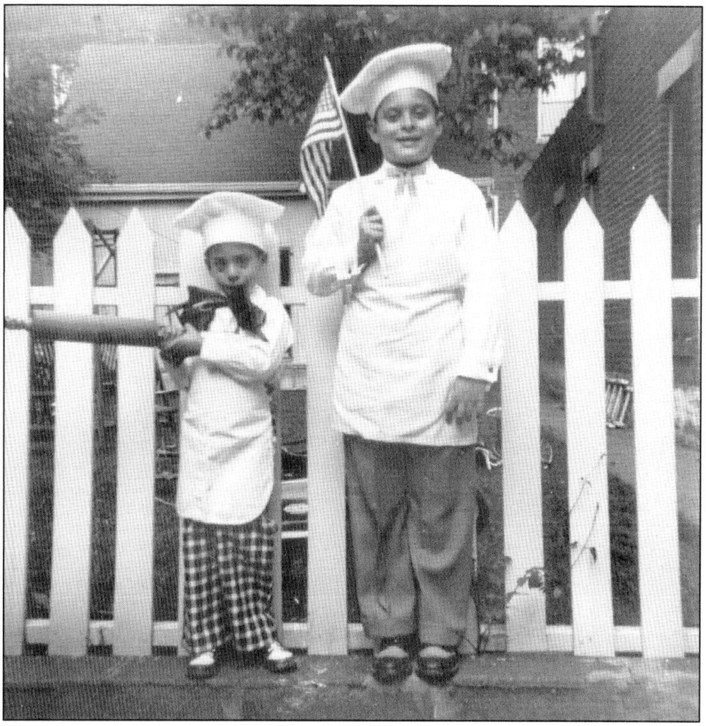

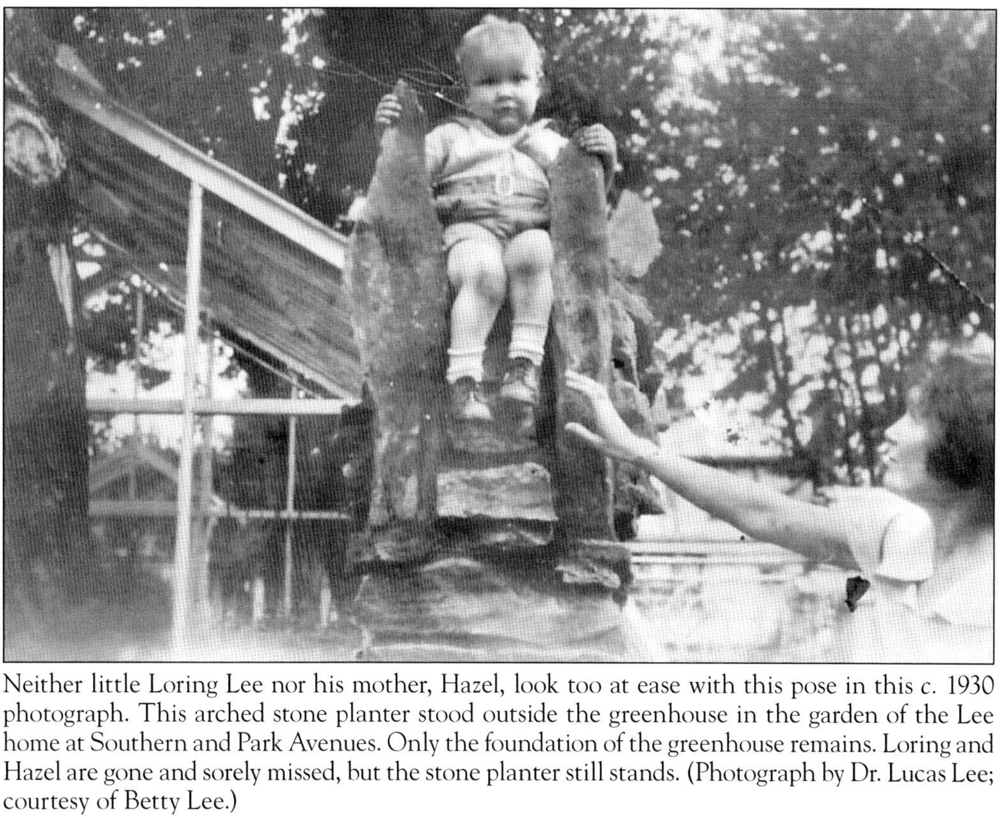

Neither little Loring Lee nor his mother, Hazel, look too at ease with this pose in this c. 1930 photograph. This arched stone planter stood outside the greenhouse in the garden of the Lee home at Southern and Park Avenues. Only the foundation of the greenhouse remains. Loring and Hazel are gone and sorely missed, but the stone planter still stands. (Photograph by Dr. Lucas Lee; courtesy of Betty Lee.)

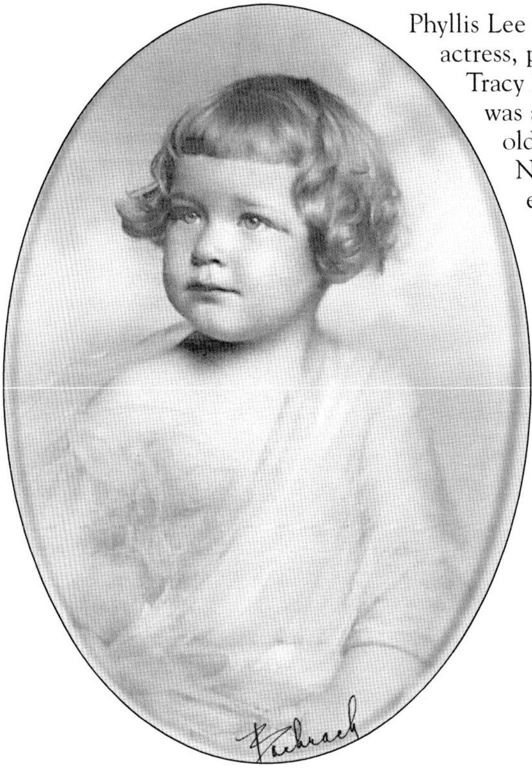

Phyllis Lee was glamorous even as a child. She was an actress, performing in the 1940s including a role as Tracy Lord in the *Philadelphia Story*, for which she was a natural. She and some friends fixed up an old farmhouse for parties and called it "Chez Nous." It had no electricity, so it was always evocatively lit by candlelight. In the 1950s, she left Latonia for New York City. (Courtesy of the author's collection.)

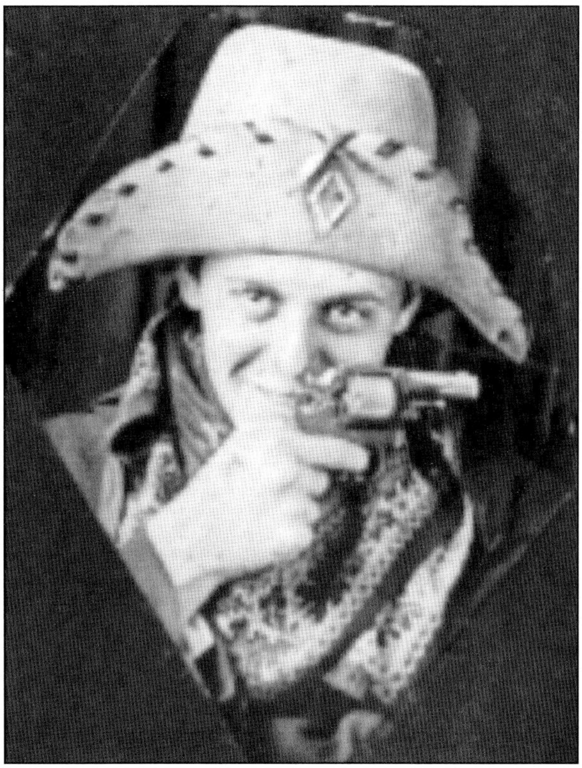

The little cowboy in this 1920s photograph is Jack Stratman, son of Bill and Margaret Kruse Stratman. Inspired by Tom Mix and Hoot Gibson, Jack is dressed realistically right down to the bandana. (Courtesy of Judy Mark.)

Seven

At Work

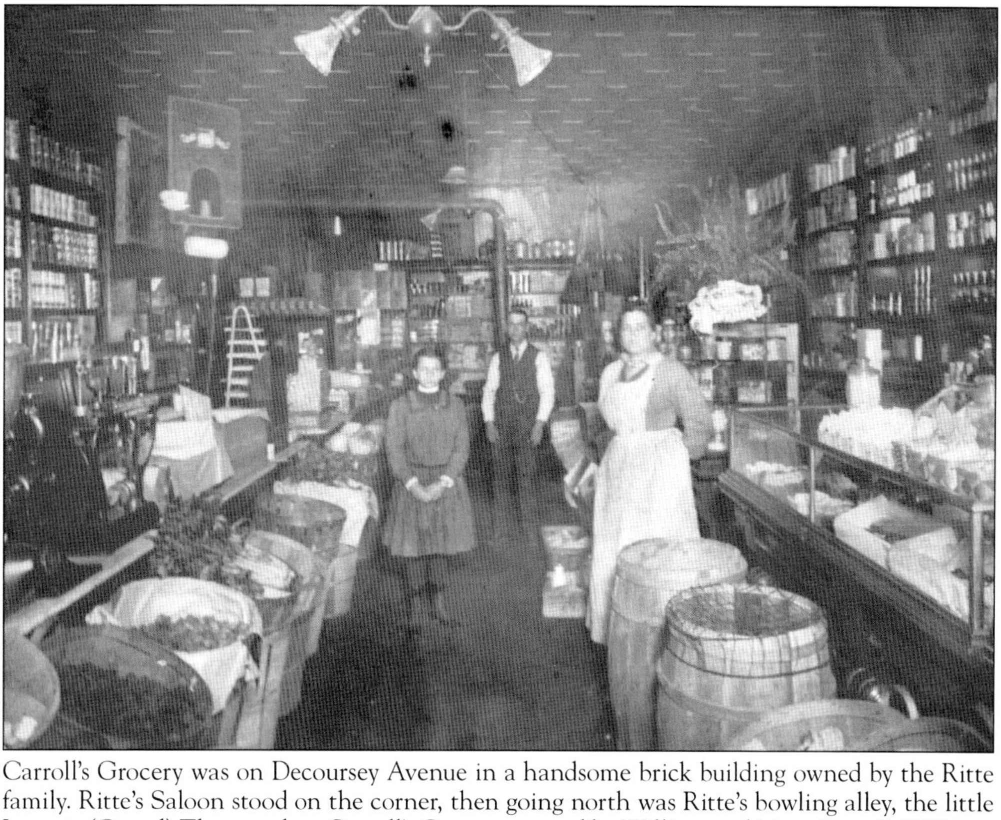

Carroll's Grocery was on Decoursey Avenue in a handsome brick building owned by the Ritte family. Ritte's Saloon stood on the corner, then going north was Ritte's bowling alley, the little Latonia (Grand) Theater, then Carroll's Grocery, owned by William and Mary Carroll. William, a former jockey, kept his hand in training his racehorses, but his old racing injuries bothered him as he grew older. In his late 40s, he and his wife became grocers, first here, then at Thirty-sixth Street and Decoursey Avenue. It was a family operation. From left to right are Levina (their daughter), William, and Mary. This was long before the days of self-service grocery stores. Here the shopper asked for items one at a time or gave the grocers a list, and they filled it. Everything was well organized where they could find things easily. Note the bushels and barrels, especially the barrel with the glass lid, which undoubtedly contained big dill pickles. There were many grocery stores in Latonia, because they were each within walking distance of their customers—and, they delivered. (Courtesy of Mary Cecil.)

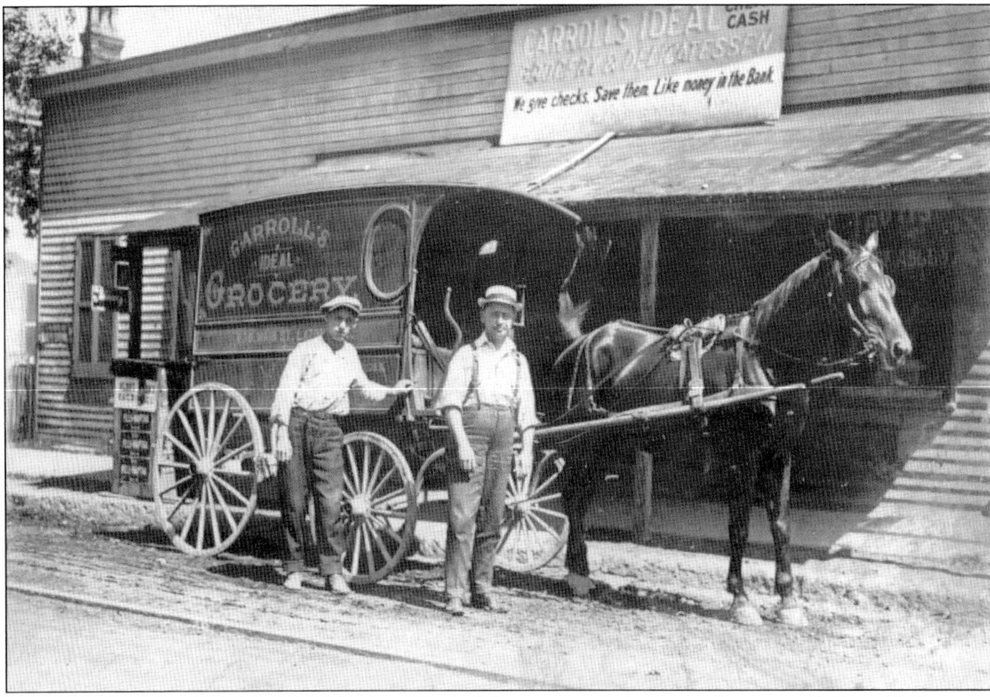

A helper (left) and Billy Carroll prepare to deliver groceries from the second Carroll Grocery location at Thirty-sixth Street and Decoursey Avenue. Sales and service people delivered or solicited business door to door with a horse and wagon, even into the 1930s. Besides the grocer, there was the iceman, scissors sharpener, butcher, milkman, baker, junk man, and even a man who sold clothes props for hanging laundry. (Courtesy of Mary Cecil.)

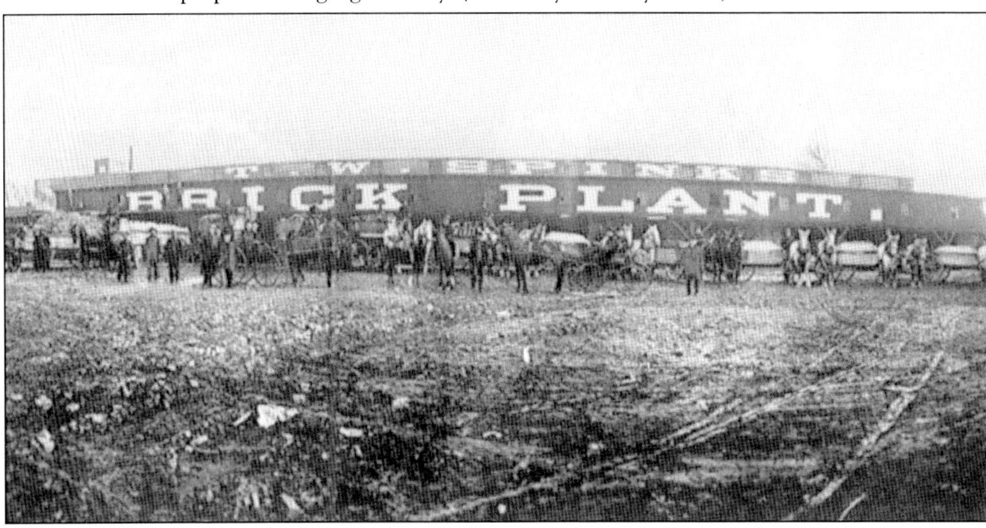

The T. W. Spinks Brick Plant was near Wolking's Lake (Forty-seventh Street area). In 1906, it became Busse Brick Yard. Spinks also had a Latonia coal business, which began around 1888. Milldale had industry before the racetrack or residential development. Kentucky Central and Louisville, Cincinnati, and Lexington Railroads (both L&N later) intersected at Milldale, making it desirable for manufacturing and warehousing, offering access to railcars and to the Licking River. (Courtesy of www.nkyviews.com.)

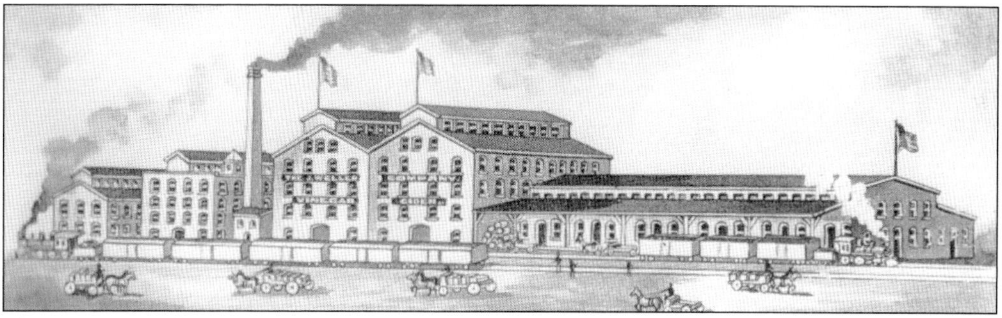

This extensive plant was the pickle factory, J. Weller Company's Milldale factory, established in 1870 near the Latonia Depot. They manufactured Acme Brand sweet-and-sour pickles, catsup, mustards, olives, malt and cider vinegar, jellies, and mincemeat, among other products. Weller's also manufactured My Wife's Choice–brand and Pure Gold–brand tomatoes and Silver Thread–brand sauerkraut. They had additional canneries and salting factories in Kentucky and Ohio. (Courtesy of www.nkyviews.com.)

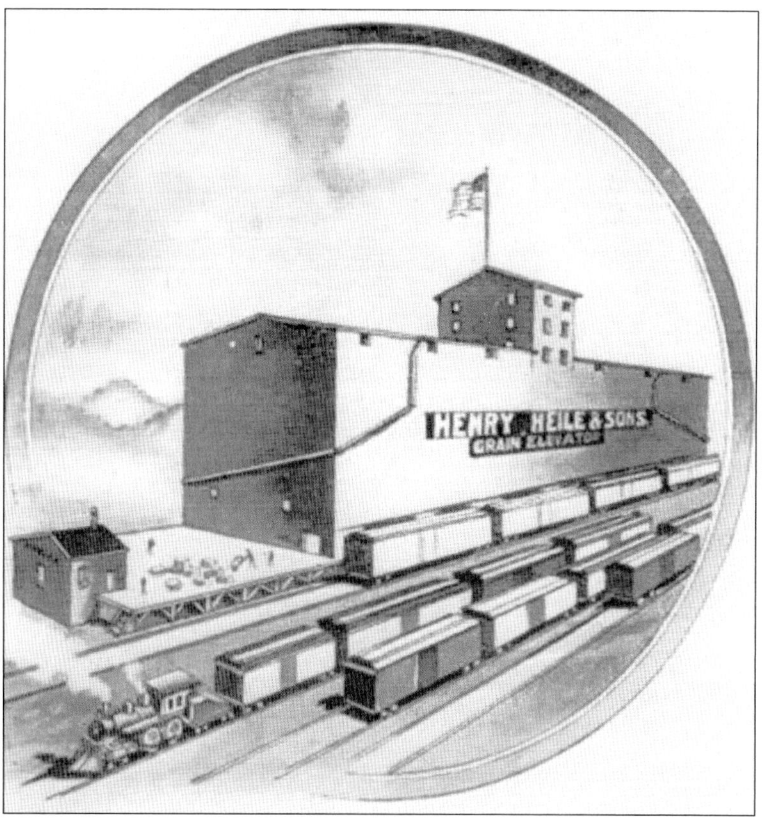

Henry Heile and Sons, established in 1858, came to Milldale around 1888 and maintained a grain elevator near the Latonia railroad yard. Henry and his sons, Frank J. and Anthony L. Heile, shipped hay and grain by railroad, and had a warehouse and offices in Cincinnati. Hay and Grain Merchants, J. H. Hermesch and Company, also had a warehouse in Milldale, near railroad access, by 1900 at latest. (Courtesy of www. nkyviews.com.)

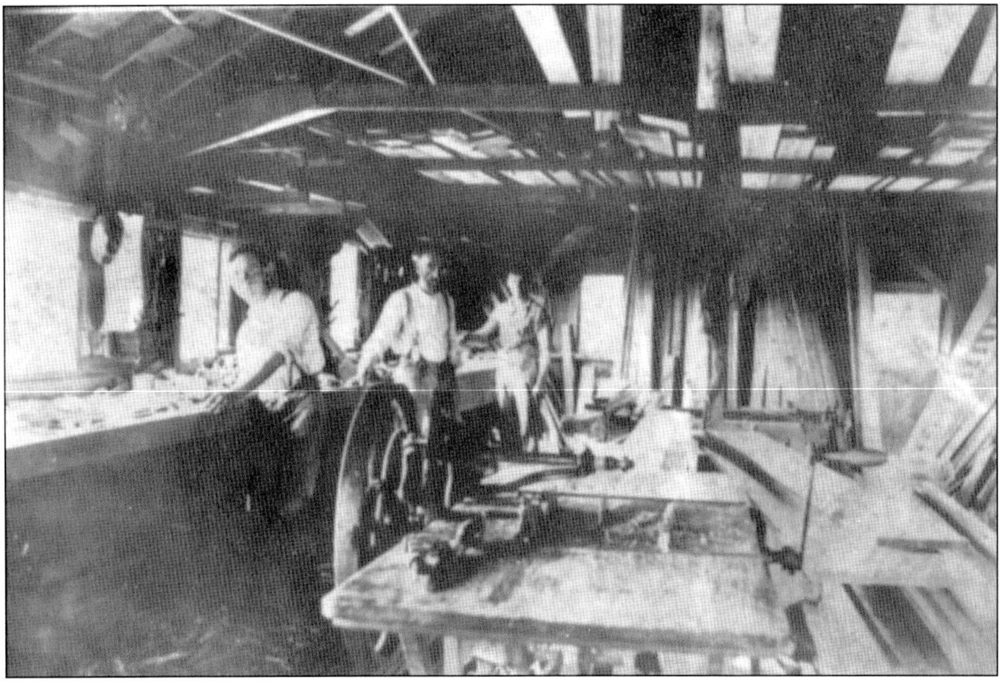

Matthew Felten's carpentry workshop, between Southern Avenue and Golding (now Thirty-eighth Street), was adjacent to his home, which faces Southern Avenue. From left to right are his son Albert; Matthew; and his son-in-law, Frank Olinger. They were responsible for much early construction, both residential and commercial, during Latonia's biggest growth surge. Matthew served on the Latonia town council. His home and workshop are still in the family. (Courtesy of Tom Martin.)

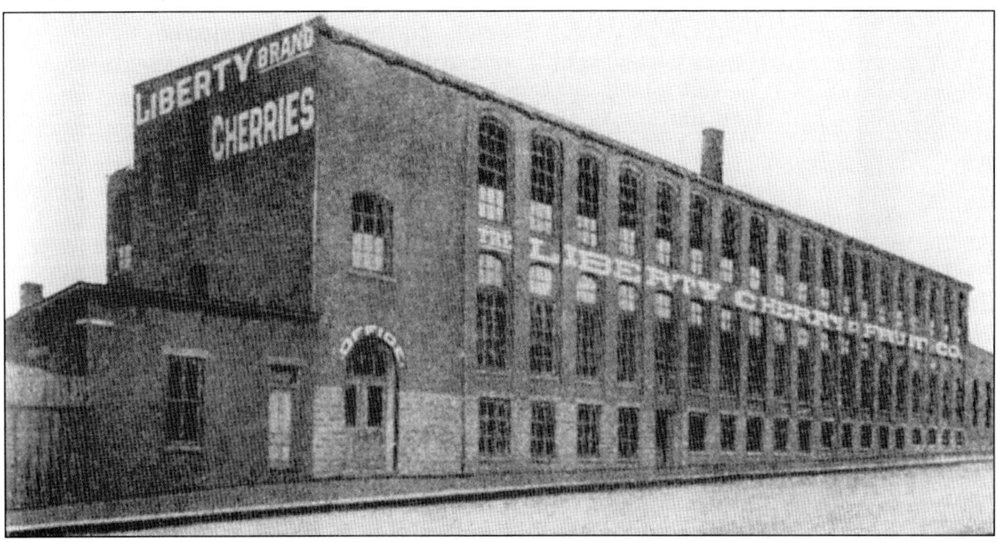

Liberty Cherry and Fruit Company processed glazed fruits, including the maraschino cherry of chocolate sundae fame. The Bettman family founded this plant in 1914 on Southern Avenue, near the rail yard. In 1941, they built a "sanitary daylight one-story" facility. Bettmans sold in 1991, and, in 1997, it was resold to Senaca Foods, who closed Liberty Cherry in 2000. Calvary Baptist bought the property and razed the buildings. (Courtesy of www.nkyviews.com.)

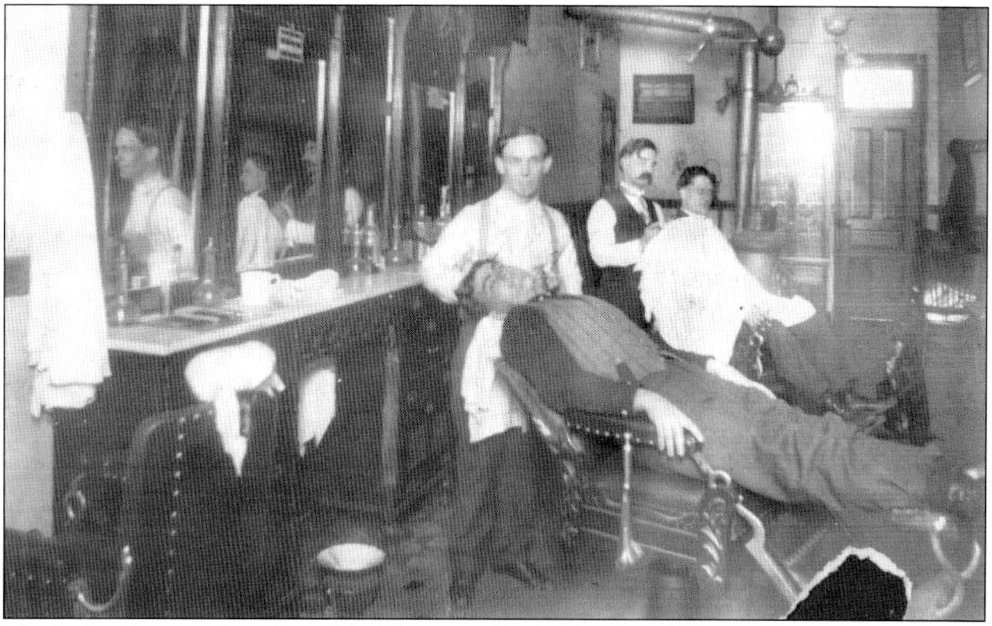

This barbershop may be in Rosedale. The second barber (moustache) is George Hartman, placing this photograph around 1890. In the barbershop, a man could get a shave, haircut, and hot towel in the reassuring company of other men. He could smoke, target the spittoon, and rest easy that his lies and exaggerations were no worse than the next man's. The barber might even pull a troubling tooth—with whiskey anesthetic. (Courtesy of the author's collection.)

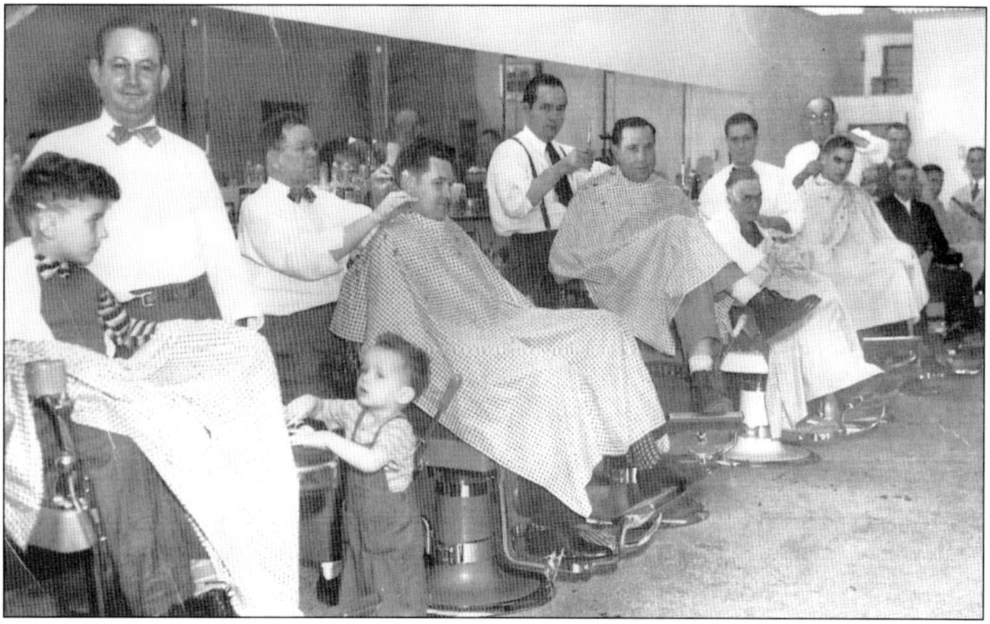

Jack Snider, standing at left, opened his barbershop at Thirty-fifth Street and Decoursey Avenue in 1930 and ran it for 31 years until his death at 57. After a 1948 remodeling, Jack's Latonia Barbershop was modern and well-equipped. He was proud of his seven barber chairs plus a steam room and two showers—and air-conditioning! He founded Jack's Rifle and Revolver Club and belonged to the Latonia Gun Club. (Courtesy of Dr. Bruce Snider.)

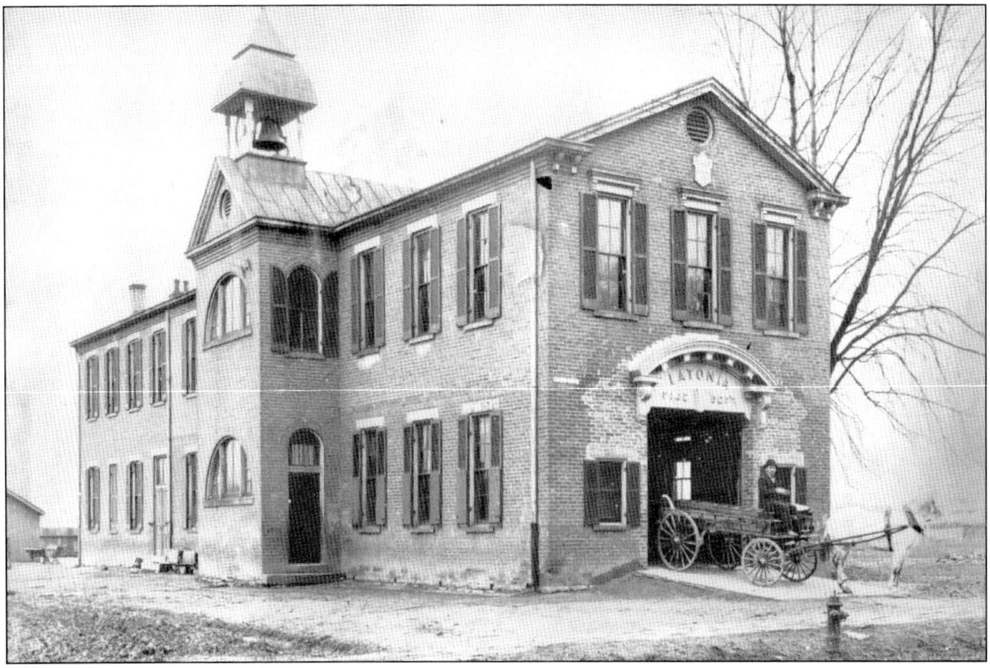

Latonia's first firehouse (above) stood on the southwest corner of Southern Avenue and Tibbatts Street. Enlarged from a two-room schoolhouse, it had courtrooms on the second floor and a jail in the rear of the first floor. The photograph below shows an addition to the front of the original firehouse. The drainpipe in front of the bell tower indicates where the addition began. The photograph above shows only three windows per floor in its front section. In 1900, when the two-room schoolhouse was still in service, the Latonia town hall stood across the road on the north side of Southern Avenue. It housed the city police court and the volunteer fire department. (Courtesy of Tom Mitchell.)

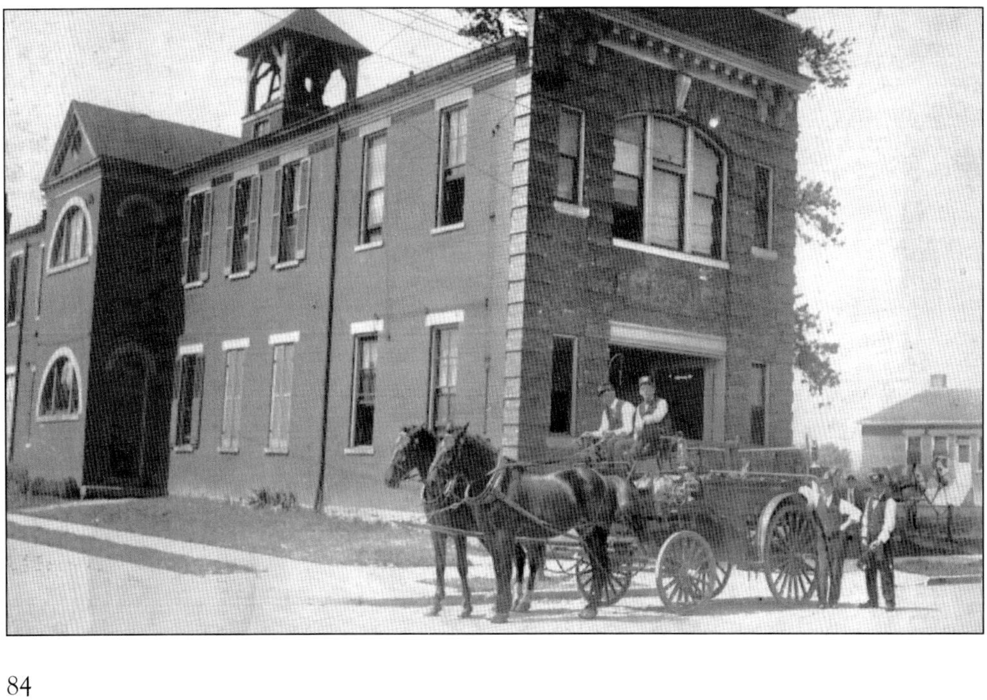

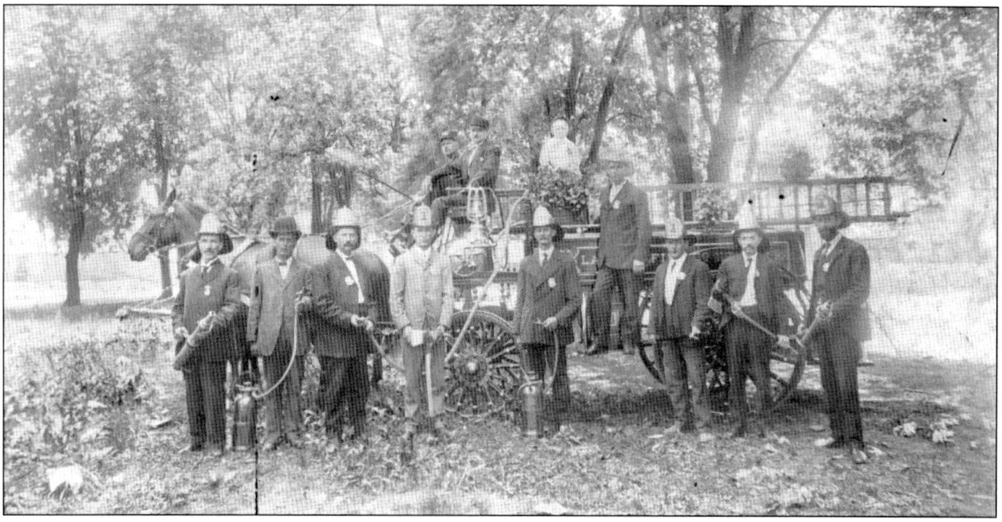

The Latonia Fire Department poses near the firehouse with a fire hose, ladder wagon, and horses in 1908. The firemen are unidentified. Shortly before World War II, property became available on the southeast corner, and Covington built a new firehouse there. Calvary Baptist bought the old firehouse and razed it to build its first church. In 2002, when the second firehouse was replaced, Calvary Baptist bought that too. (Courtesy of Tom Mitchell.)

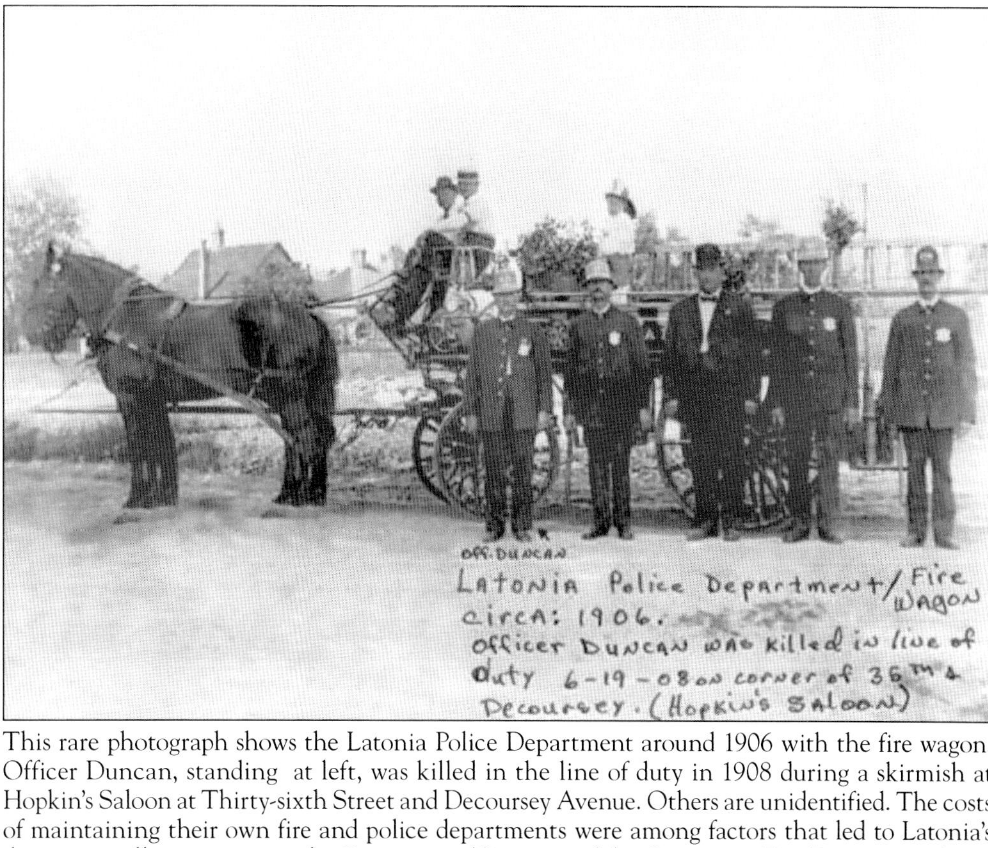

This rare photograph shows the Latonia Police Department around 1906 with the fire wagon. Officer Duncan, standing at left, was killed in the line of duty in 1908 during a skirmish at Hopkin's Saloon at Thirty-sixth Street and Decoursey Avenue. Others are unidentified. The costs of maintaining their own fire and police departments were among factors that led to Latonia's decision to allow annexation by Covington. (Courtesy of the Covington Fire Department.)

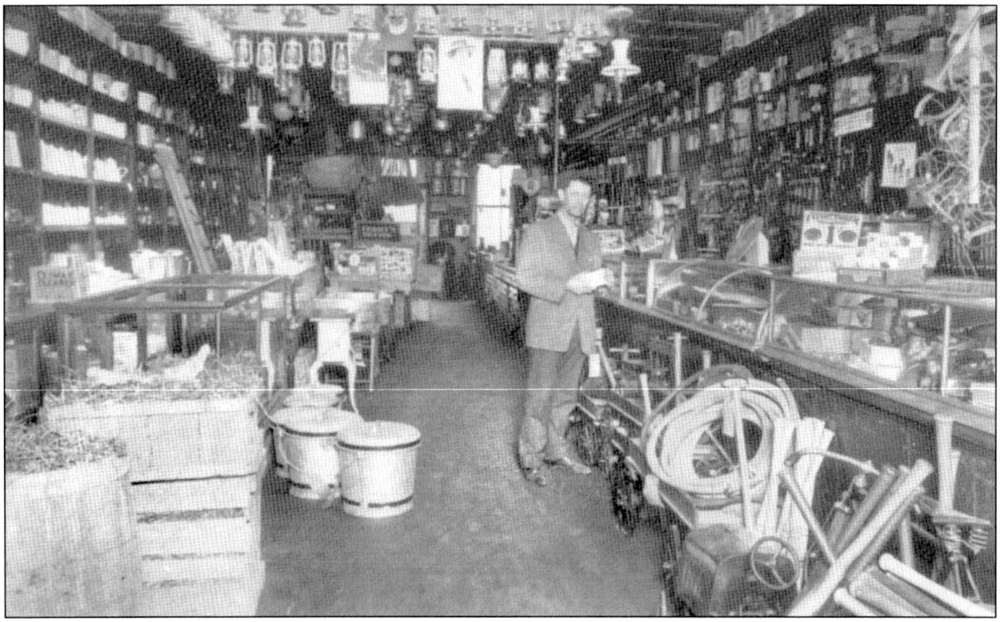

Tom Martin stands in his hardware store on Decoursey Avenue in this *c.* 1905 photograph. In the 1920s, Tom Holian joined him, and the store became Martin and Holian's. (Rookwood Pottery artist Edith Felten married Holian.) After Martin retired, Holian took over. During World War II, Martin helped run his son Bill's new store, Johnny's Toy Store. When Holian retired, Ed Hook took over, but he retired around 1995, ending the store's 90-year history. (Courtesy of Tom Martin.)

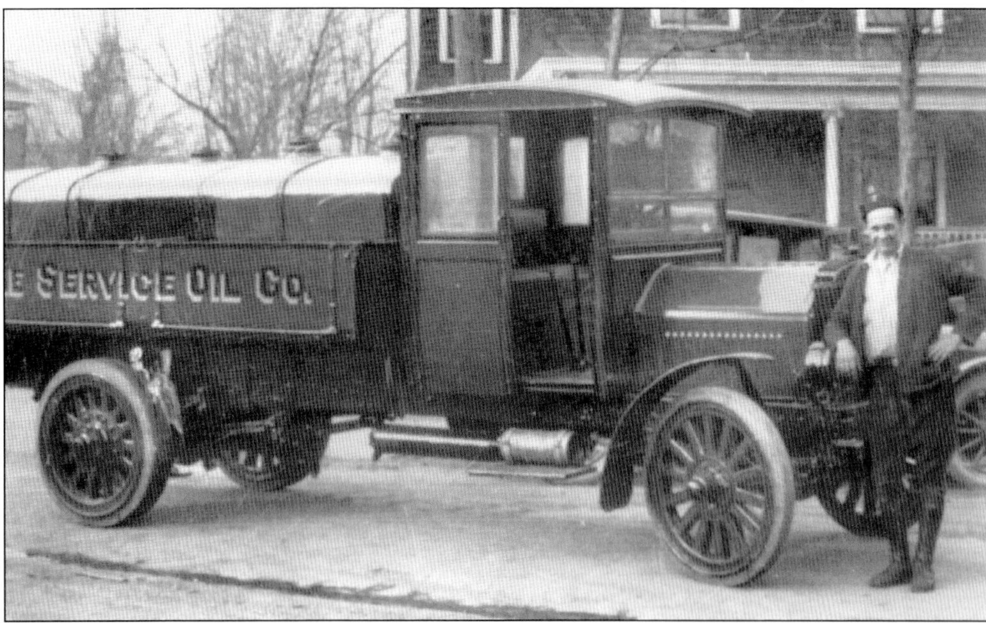

This is the first truck purchased by the Service Oil Company, which was owned by Stanley Vogelsang. Service Oil Company was an offshoot of the Latonia Service Station at Church Street and Decoursey Avenue, owned by Stanley and his brother-in-law, Ed Phelps. The driver is unidentified. Stanley also had milk brought daily from his farm near Taylor Mill Road. He and his family sold it from their Latonia kitchen. (Courtesy of Carol Dick and John Kennedy.)

The Muellers harvested ice from their lake on Madison Pike. Men cut the ice, and horses pulled it off the lake for storage in an icehouse. Ice was obtained this way before refrigeration. A horse-drawn ice wagon made rounds door to door. Customers put a numbered card in their windows indicating how many pounds of ice they wanted. The iceman would chop that amount off the slabs in his wagon, rest it on his shoulder on a leather pad, and carry it to the family's icebox. Mueller's Latonia Ice and Fuel, on Eugenia Avenue, seen here with trucks in this 1940s photograph, also dealt in coal. The slatted construction was an icehouse that preserved ice with water. It was near the railroad for easy access. Mueller's Lake was filled and is now the site of the Transit Authority of Northern Kentucky (TANK) bus barn. (Courtesy of Kenton County Public Library.)

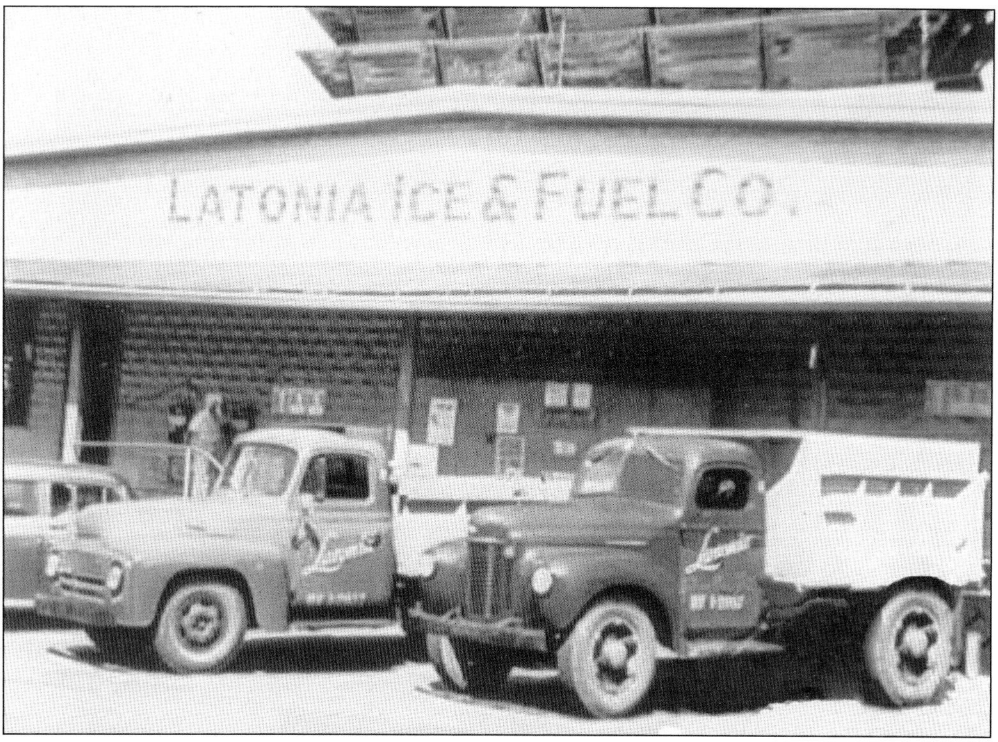

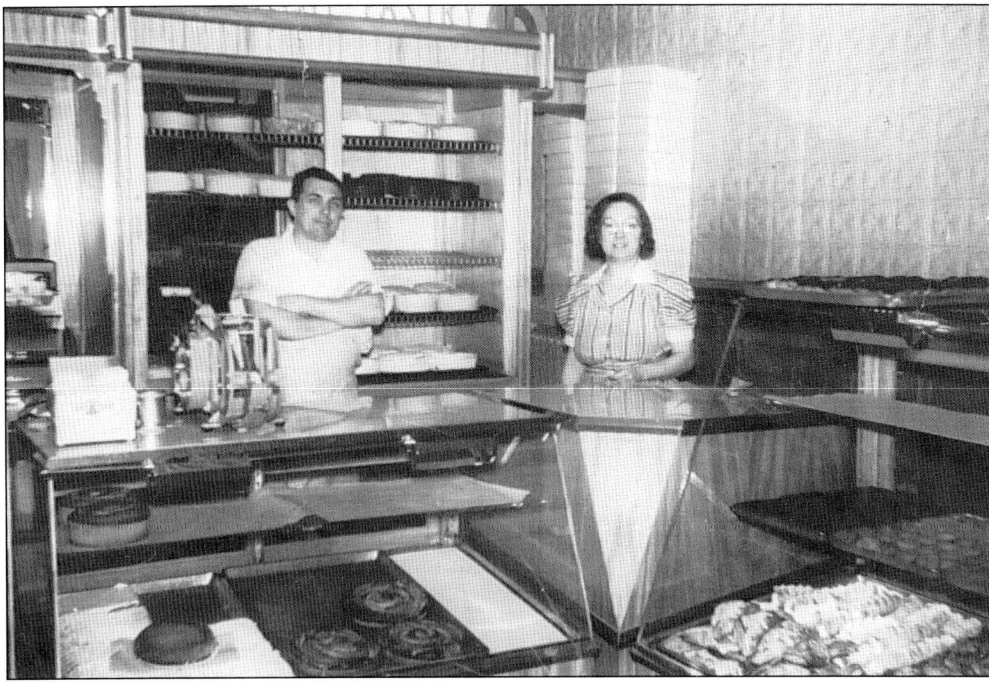

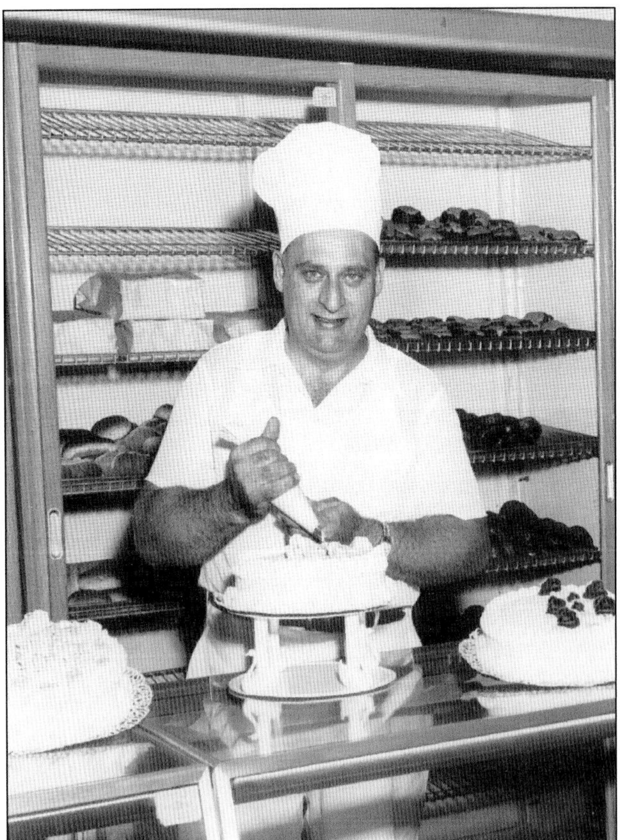

The Latonia Bakery has a long history. Carl Barfknecht started it in 1917. Then Carl Schliff and his wife, Helen, bought it in 1929. Carl had emigrated from Germany as a teenager and often spoke German with his customers. Their daughter, Helen, married Charles Petty, a bakery employee, and they took over the bakery in 1945. They redecorated, and Helen was creative with displays. Their most popular practice was selling baked goods fresh from the oven at night. Customers lined up at the side door off the kitchen, lured by the scent of baking dough. The Pettys offered specialties such as preparation of a dough-wrapped holiday turkey or ham, and no little child, shopping with mother, ever left without a complimentary cookie. Above are Carl Schliff and an employee. At left is Charles Petty, who is decorating a cake. (Courtesy of Lorna Petty Harrell.)

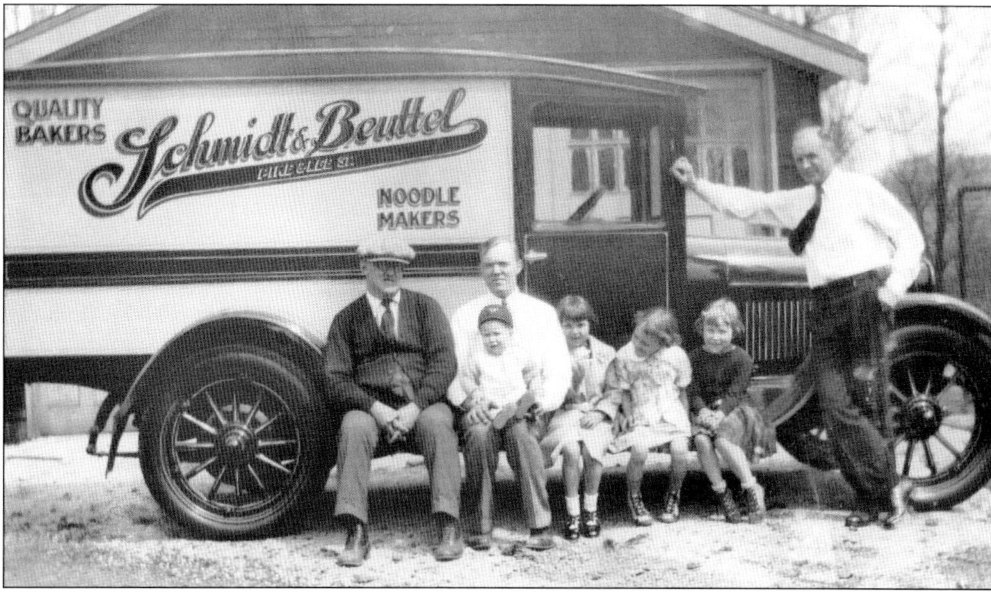

Latonia's Schmidt and Beuttel families had a bakery in Covington offering baked goods and freshly made noodles. The older generation of Schmidts and Beuttels founded it in 1886. Here in this c. 1928 photograph, the next two generations pose with a delivery truck. From left to right are Walter Beuttel, brother Carl Beuttel holding his son Bill, niece Audrey Danks (Lacey), Mary Schmidt (Fossett), Carl's daughter Virginia, and George Schmidt (Mary's father). (Courtesy of Bill Beuttel.)

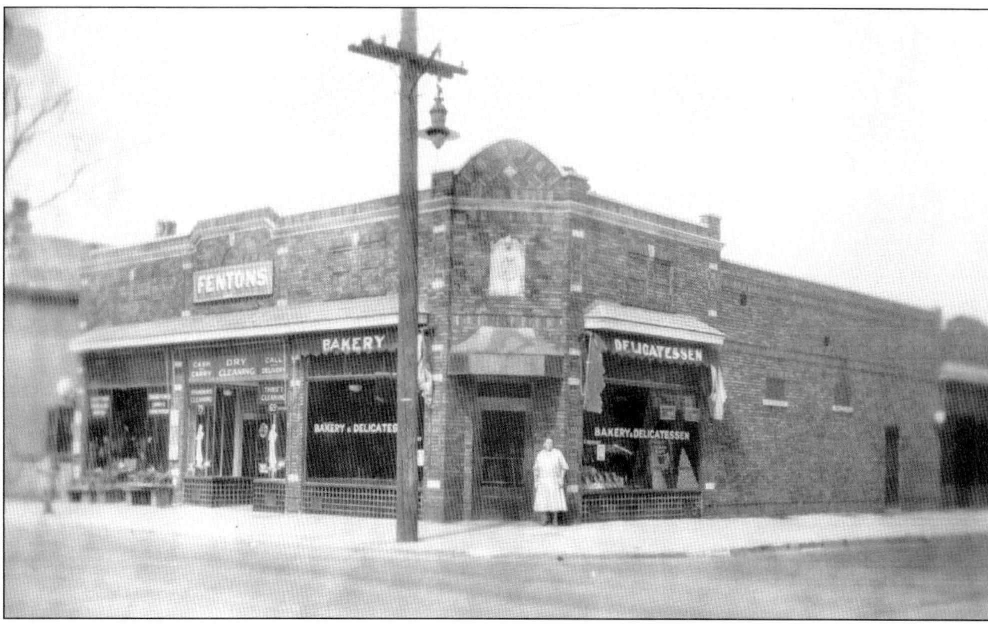

Mary Carroll stands before the building she had constructed at Thirty-sixth Street and Decoursey Avenue after the 1926 death of her husband, former jockey Billy Carroll. A. B. Dierke's Grocery was in front, and Charlie Sam had his Chinese Hand Laundry in the rear facing Thirty-sixth Street. He paid his rent in one-dollar bills and laid each one out in a row on Mrs. Carroll's sofa to count it. (Courtesy of Mary Cecil.)

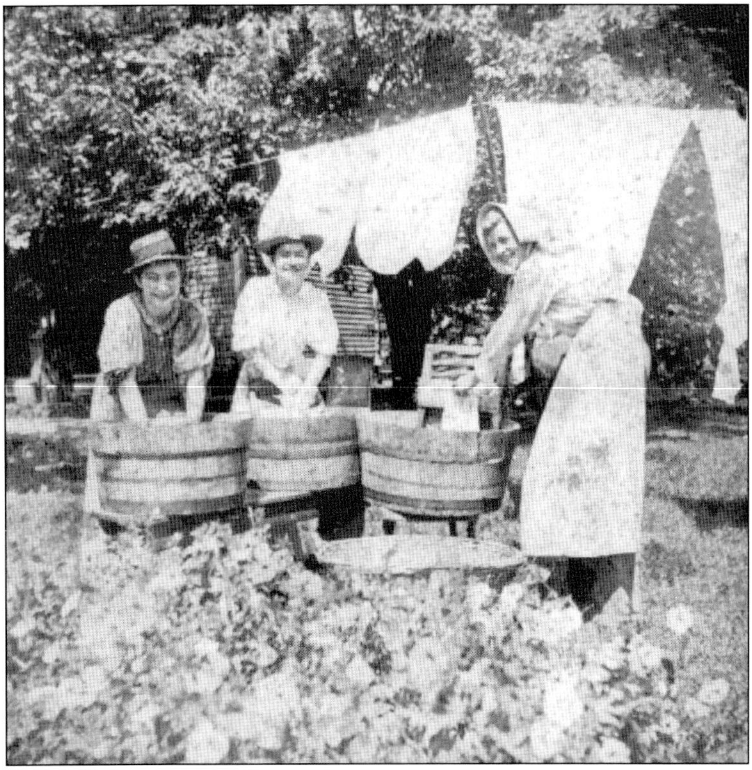

The Felten girls tackle the laundry. Water was heated on the stove to fill washtubs. Clothes were agitated with sticks. Stains were scrubbed on a washboard. When all was washed and rinsed, whites were soaked in bluing and shirts were starched. After being cranked through the handwringer, damp clothes were hung on lines outside or on drying racks in the basement. After they were dry, they were ironed. (Courtesy of Tom Martin.)

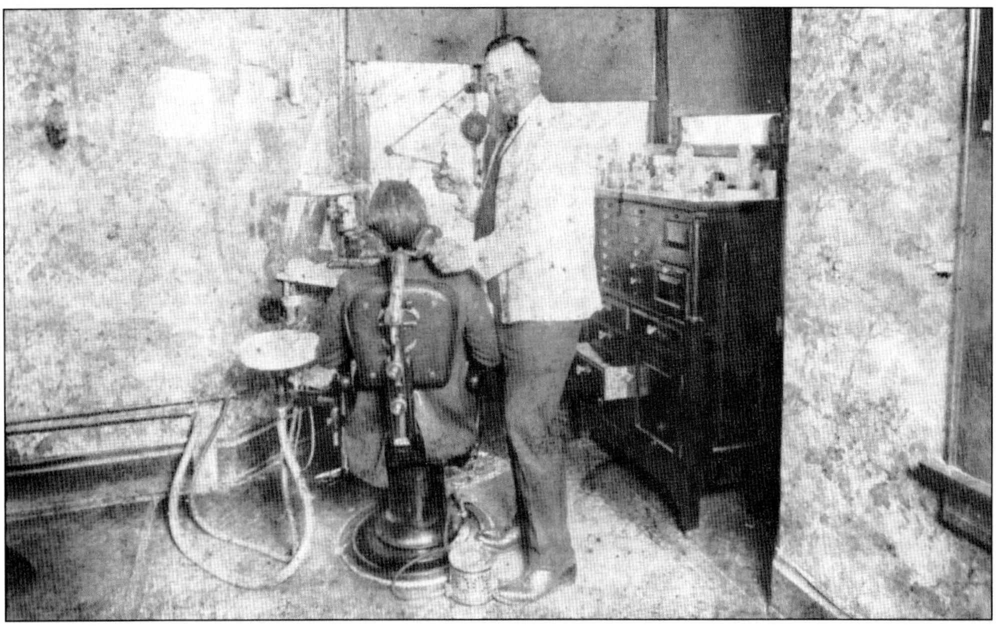

Dr. Lucas Lee attends a patient in his dental office in the First National Bank in this c. 1930 photograph. His office was closed on Sunday, so people just came to his house instead. He did not object. He kept dental tools in his closet, so he could work from home if necessary. During the Depression, people had to barter for dental service. One time, Lee was given canaries as payment. (Courtesy of the author's collection.)

Eight

At Play

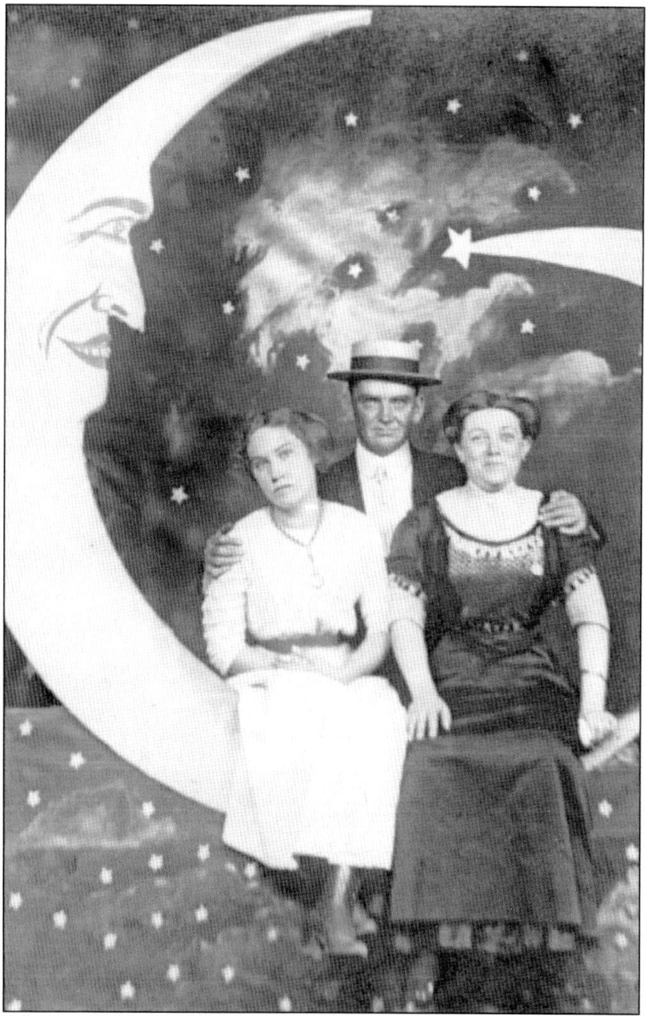

Amusement parks, expositions, and even racetracks had these fanciful photographic backdrops that were a popular way to create an amusing souvenir of a special day. Here Fern Smith (Gillham), at left, and her aunt Annie Luzader May sit on the moon while Annie's husband, John (Bub) May, keeps a protective hand on both. Fern is wearing her favorite gold locket, given to her by Aunt Annie. It had a crescent moon described in chip rubies with a diamond star. Annie also had some of her elegant clothes and hats reworked for Fern. John May owned and trained racehorses and was a well-known figure at the Latonia Race Track. Annie loved to go to the races, too, and watch their horses run. When he and Annie traveled from track to track on the racing circuit, they sometimes took Fern along. This *c.* 1910 photograph was taken in New Orleans, but over her entire lifetime Fern never liked to be away from Latonia for long. (Courtesy of the author's collection.)

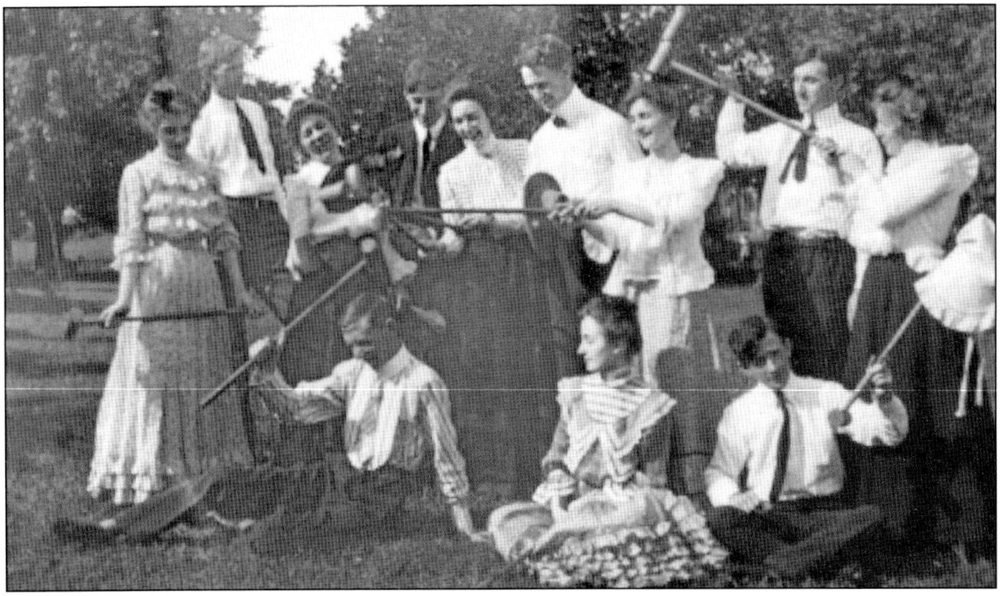

The Felten kids and their friends pose after a game of croquet in this *c.* 1900 photograph. Croquet was a popular game that young ladies and young gentlemen could play together in the fresh air. The five young Feltens were Edith (a Rookwood Pottery artist), Frida, Magdelena (a dressmaker), Lizzie, and Albert (a carpenter). Their father, Matthew, a carpenter and developer, had his workshop behind their Southern Avenue home. (Courtesy of Tom Martin.)

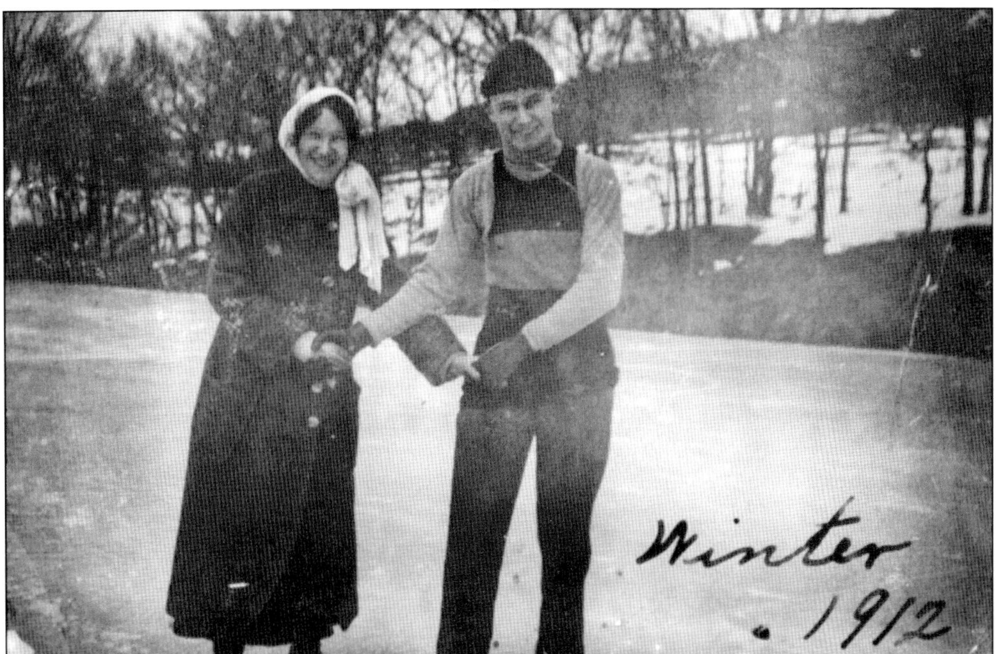

Flora and Charles Warnke are pictured in the winter of 1912 enjoying skating together on a frozen lake. Probably this was Wolking's Lake in the Rosedale section of Latonia, since the Warnkes lived nearby at Forty-second and Church Streets. Couples skated on Coppin's Lake too, but it was all the way across town, near the 3L Highway. (Courtesy of Jim Feldman.)

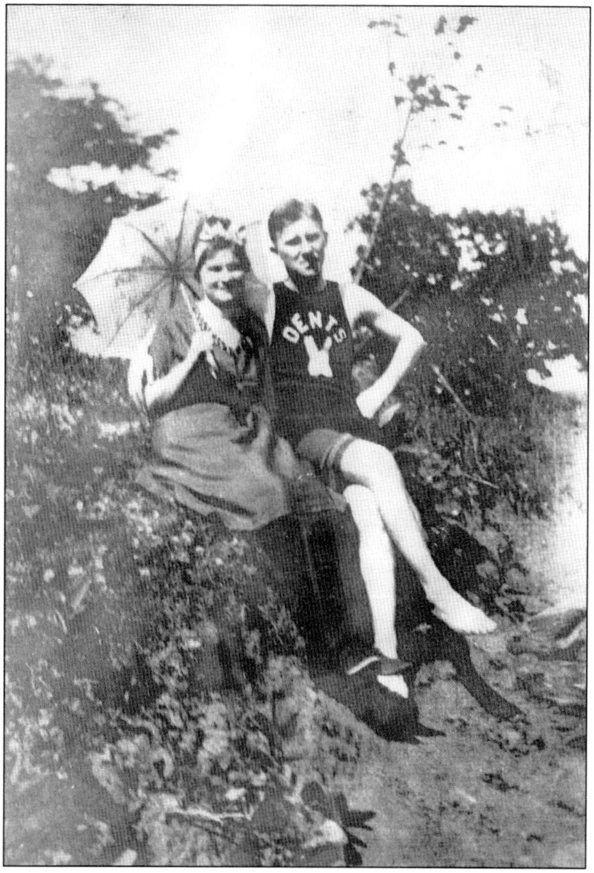

Margaret Kruse Stratman and her husband, Bill, take in a little sun at the edge of a swimming hole in 1916. Notice that the skirt of her bathing costume reached below her knees, and full-length, black stockings and slippers completed the outfit. The parasol was to protect her delicate skin from too much sun. A suntan was not desirable for a young lady in those days. Bill's costume is also modest, with a sleeveless shirt and shorts almost to his knees. Below is Margaret (fourth from right) and unidentified family and friends in their bathing suits. This was probably taken at the pool in Rosedale Park. (Courtesy of Judy Mark.)

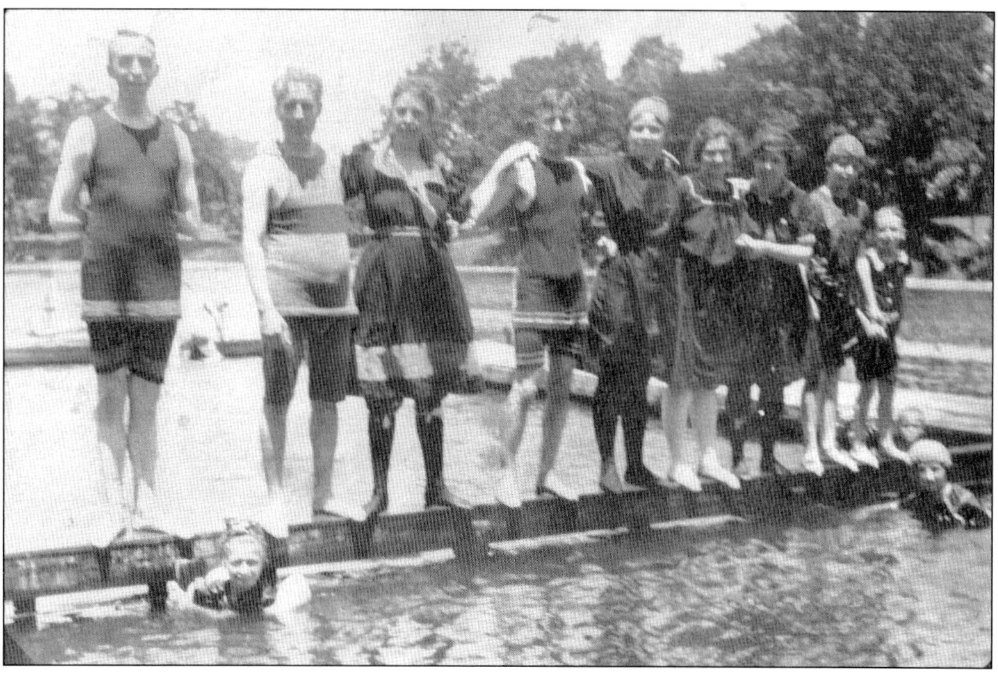

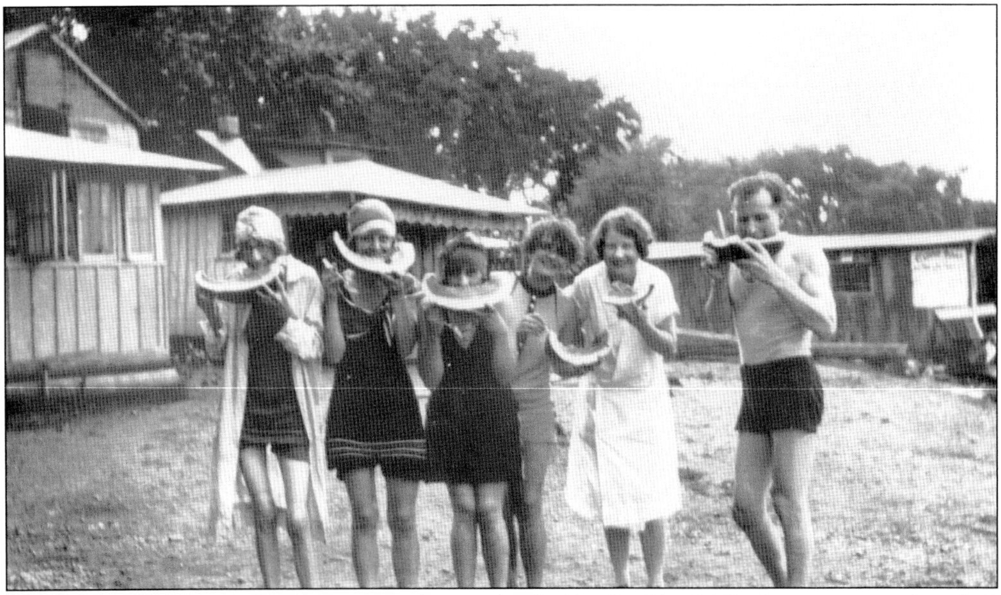

Here friends enjoy a watermelon party in the rain by the Beatley Hotel. The location is unidentified, but most of the people are members of Holy Cross Parish. They are, from left to right, Marie Tegge, Loretta Heithaus Lietzenmayer, three unidentified ladies, and Cyril Foust. By 1928, bathing costumes had gotten more daring. Women's suits were above the knee, and the top was tunic-like. (Courtesy of Karl Lietzenmayer.)

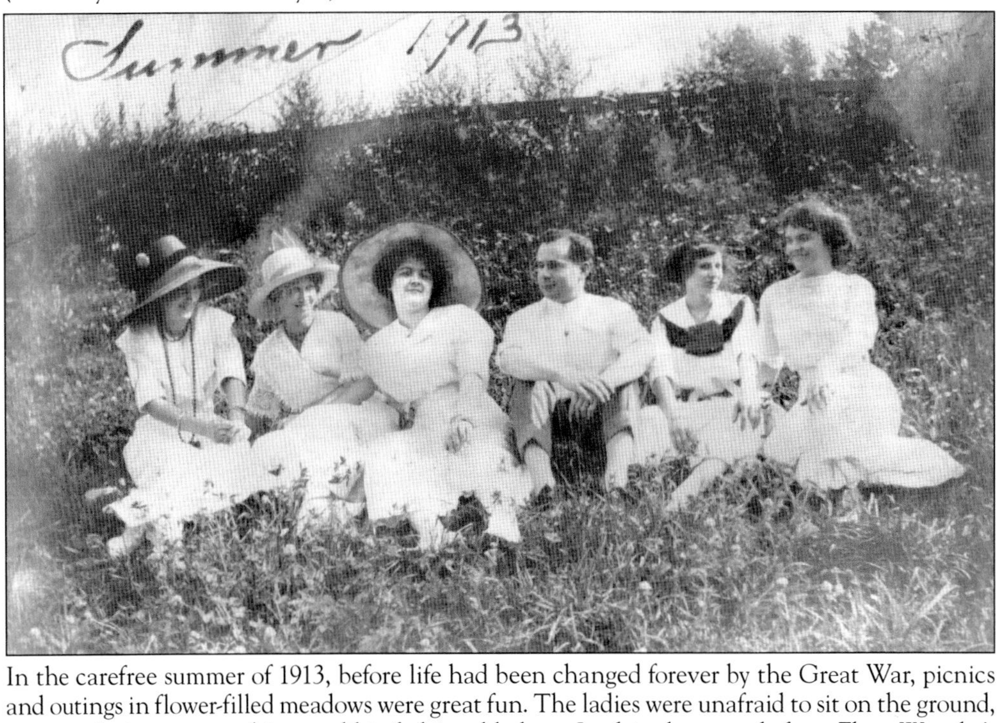

In the carefree summer of 1913, before life had been changed forever by the Great War, picnics and outings in flower-filled meadows were great fun. The ladies were unafraid to sit on the ground, even in their summer whites and big fashionable hats. In this photograph from Flora Warnke's album, the man is probably her husband, Charles, and she may be second from left. Others are unidentified. (Courtesy of Jim Feldman.)

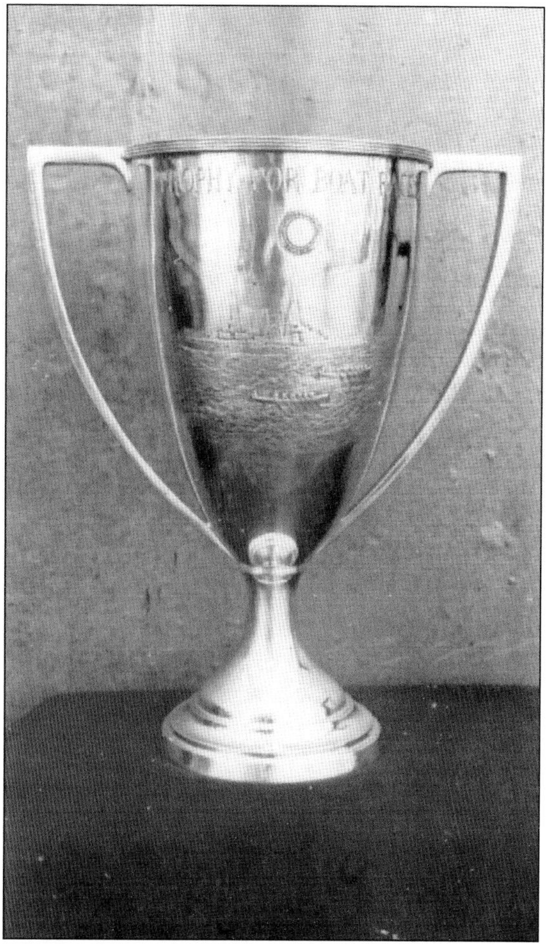

Pictured at right is a boating trophy won by Charles Warnke in a race on Wolking's Lake. Below is a postcard of Wolking's Lake, which offered fishing and boating and also some amusement park rides in later days. Rosedale Park adjoined the lake, and it had a Ferris wheel, merry-go-round, and a swimming pool. Charlie Burnam built a miniature train large enough for children to ride, and it was used in Rosedale Park in the 1930s and 1940s. He moved to Latonia in 1927, and he and his wife, Nanny, lived on the banks of the Licking River, near where Rosedale Manor now stands. Charlie, an African American, was loved by the children who played with him and his train, no matter their race. They remember him, too, even 75 years later. (Courtesy of Jim Feldman and www.nkyviews.com.)

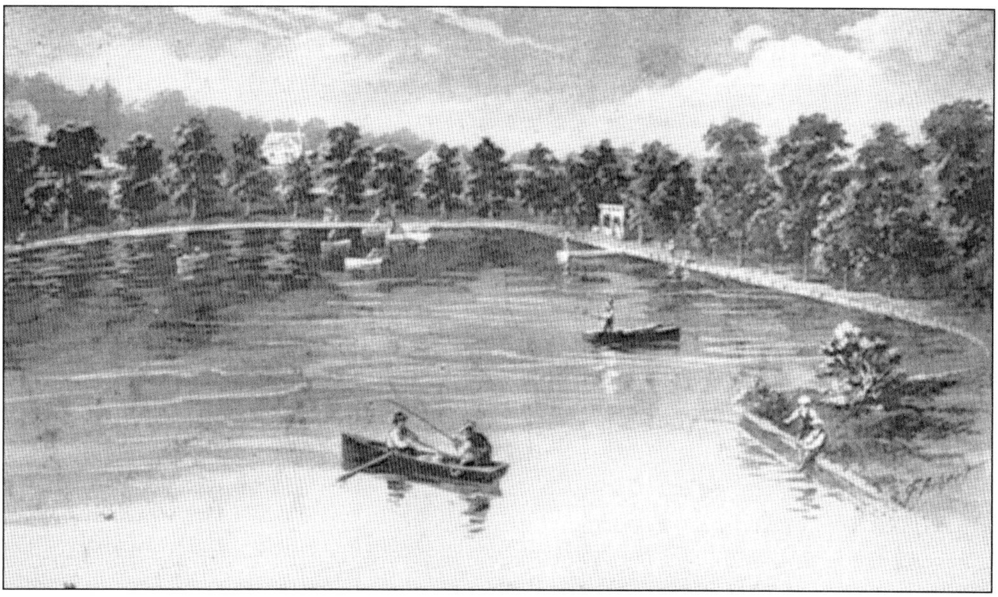

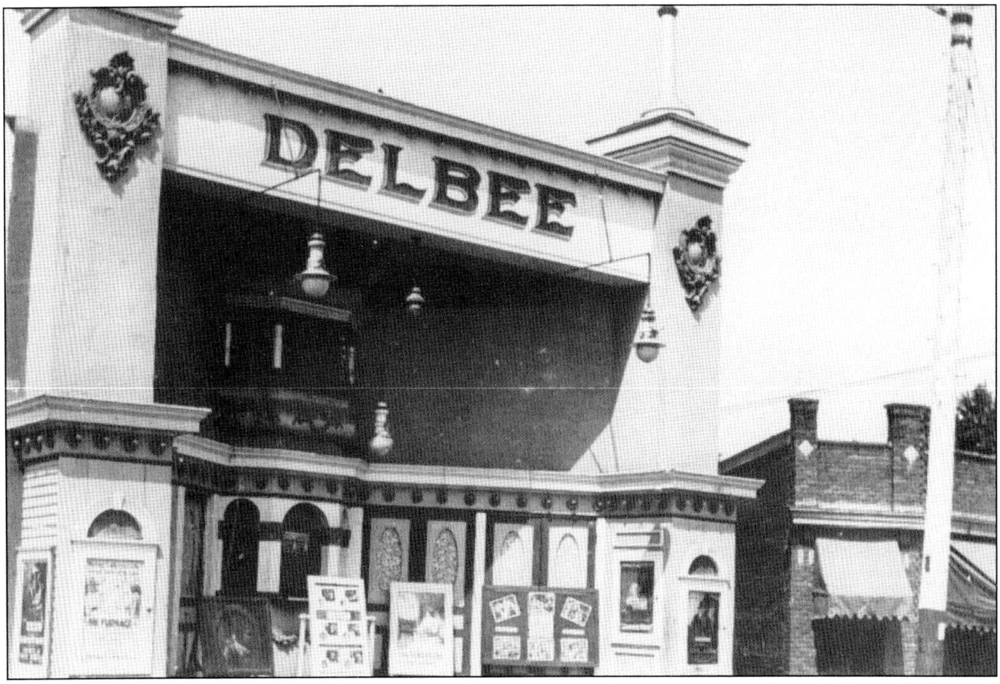

The Delbee Theater at Fortieth Street and Decoursey Avenue opened in 1910 and showed hand-wound silent movies accompanied by a live pianist. A. J. Dehlinger and Harry Beerman owned it. On winter evenings, patrons were kept warm by a coal-fired pot-bellied stove. (Courtesy of the Kenton County Public Library.)

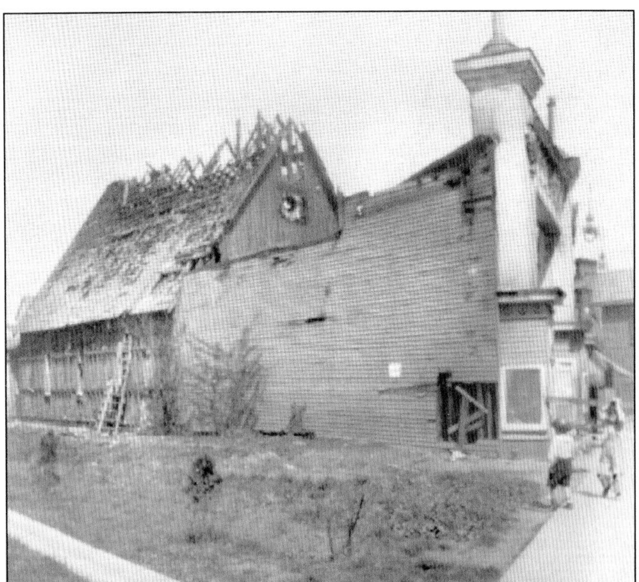

The Delbee Theater caught fire regularly, and the sixth time it burned beyond repair (at left). Easily visible at the rear of the fire-damaged building is the old Episcopal and Methodist Church building that Dehlinger had moved from Southern Avenue and Church Street in 1910. Dehlinger sold the property, a new brick movie house was built, and the name changed to the Derby. After another change of ownership, it was known as the Walker. During the Depression, the theater had grocery giveaways and amateur shows. (Courtesy of Tom Martin.)

Plays and theatricals were quite popular before radio and television, and one of the most popular was the minstrel show. This was a combination of music and jokes performed with a certain amount of slapstick by white actors in blackface. Frank Rothert, left, and Harry Smith performed in Latonia minstrel shows in the 1890s, once even including Harry's baby sister Fern in the cast, also in blackface. (Courtesy of the author's collection.)

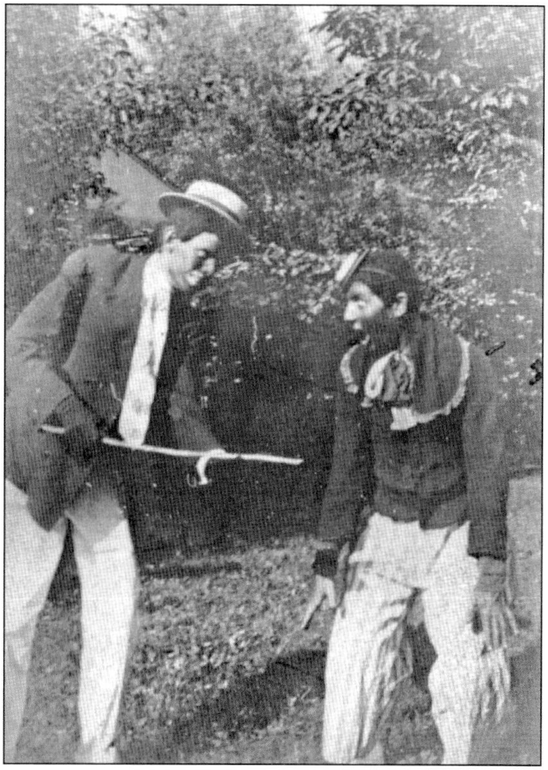

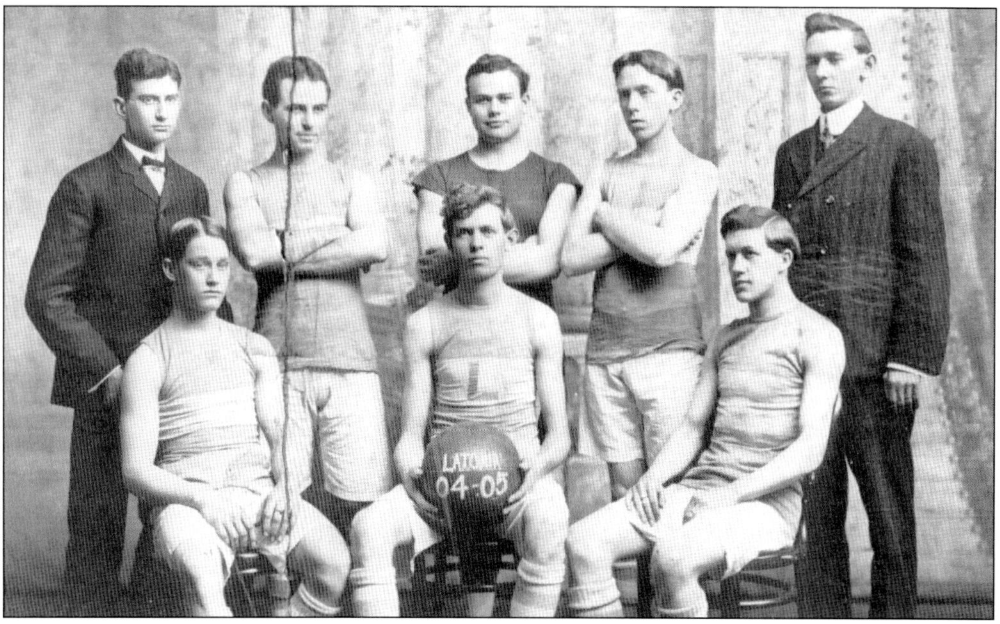

The Latonia Athletic Club poses for a team picture in the 1904–1905 season. Pictured from left to right are (seated) Charles Luzader, George Rothert, and Walter Ritte; (standing) unidentified, A. J. Dehlinger, Grover Morgan, Charley Schlapp, and Frank Rothert. Frank is athletic as well as theatrical, and A. J. Dehlinger (Delbee Theater) will be moving little churches in a couple more years. (Courtesy of Tom Martin.)

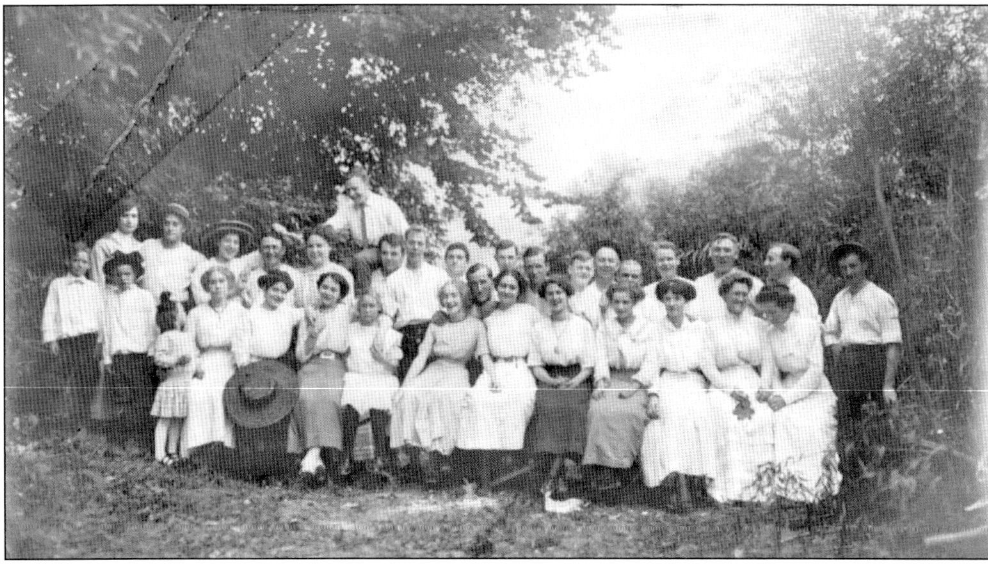

The group featured in this *c.* 1912 photograph was known as the Delbee Social Club. The nature of its connection to the Delbee Theater is unknown. From left to right are (first row) unidentified, Fern Smith (Gillham), two unidentified people, Hazel Smith (Lee), four unidentified ladies, Frederica Dias Smith, Lizzie Luzader Smith, and ? Dias, Frederica's mother; (second row) two unidentified children, then Nora Johnson Luzader and her husband, Al Luzader. The rest are unidentified except Harry Smith, third from right, and Georgie Smith, fourth from right. (Courtesy of the author's collection.)

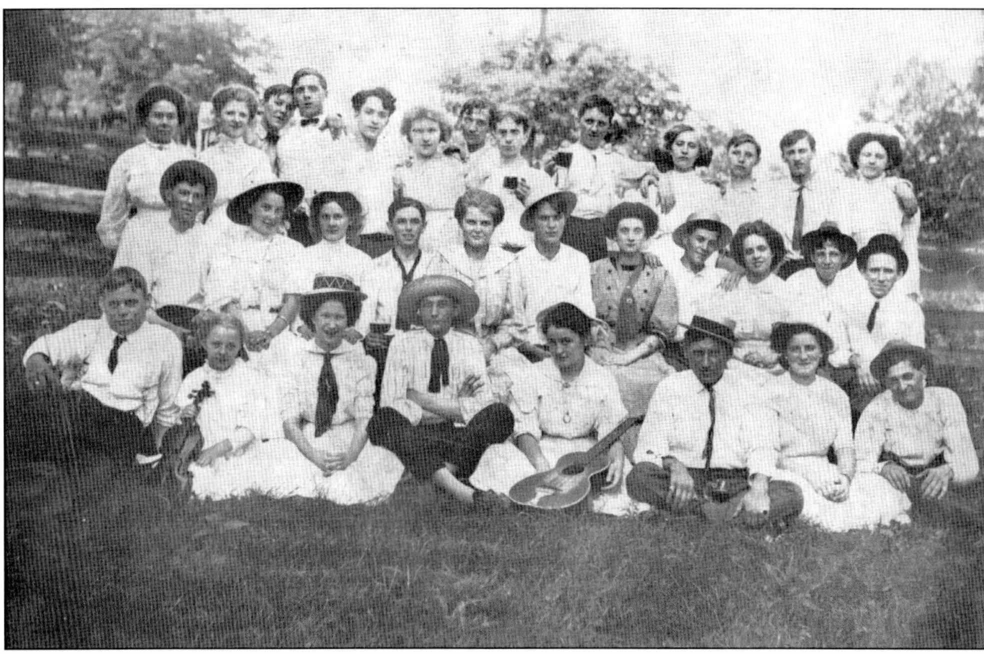

Here another large group of picnickers are posing, though no one is identified. Although it is from the album of Flora and Charles Warnke, neither is identified. With a fiddle (first row, second from left) and a guitar present, they were equipped to make their own music. Before the days of radio and television, people made their own entertainment. (Courtesy of Jim Feldman.)

Young Georgia Roe (Gibson) was photographed at Coney Island on a dappled artificial pony. Coney Island was Cincinnati's favorite picnic ground and amusement park. Named for its forerunner in New York, this one was reached by a riverboat ride up the Ohio River on the Island Queen. The trip was as much fun as the destination, according to those who were lucky enough to have done it. (Courtesy of the author's collection.)

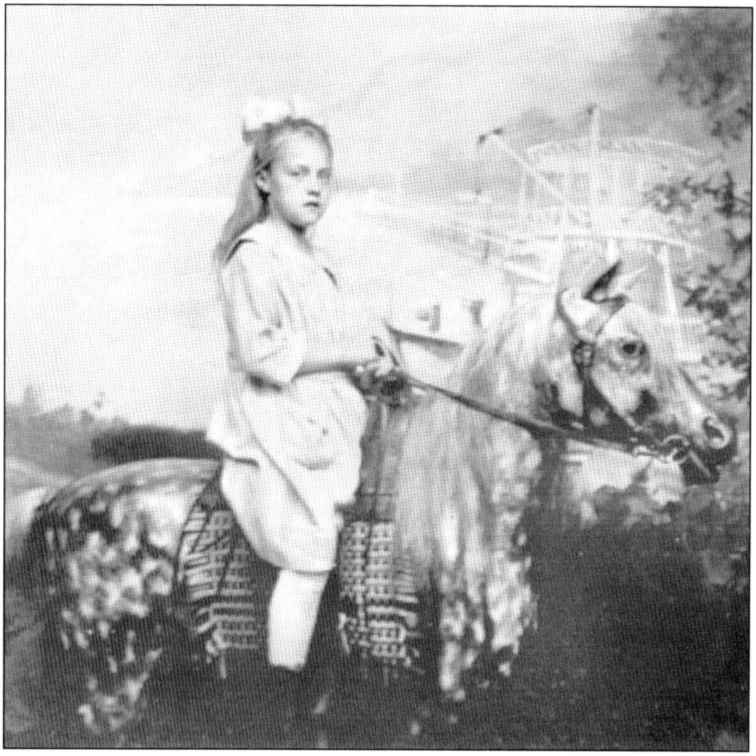

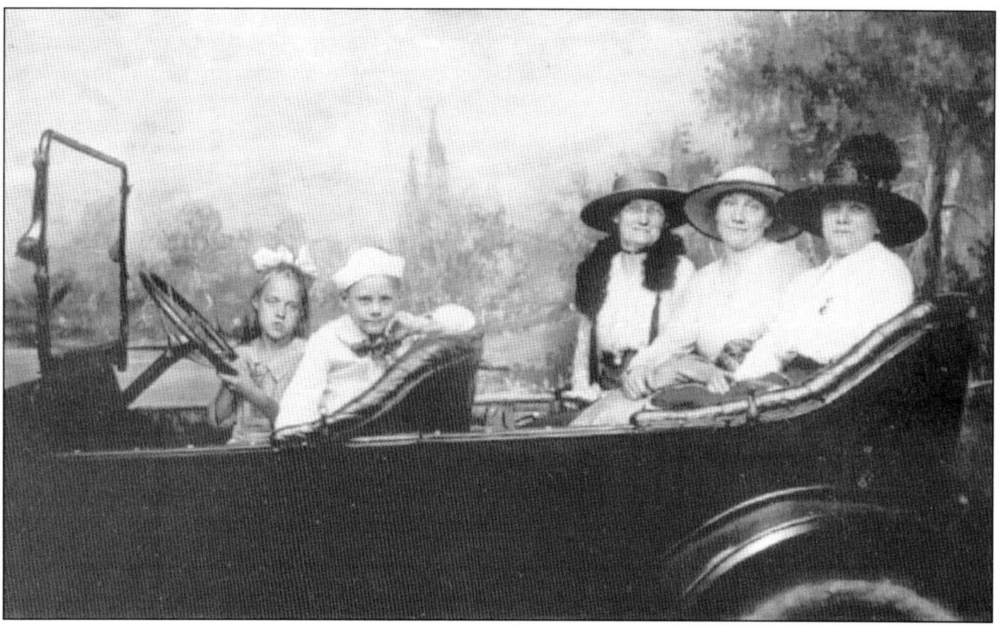

This photography set is either at Latonia Racetrack or Coney Island. The automobile has literally entered the picture now, and life in America will never be the same. From left to right are Georgia and Richter Roe, Lizzie Luzader Smith, Myrtle Smith Roe (Lizzie's daughter), and Annie Luzader May (Lizzie's sister). (Courtesy of the author's collection.)

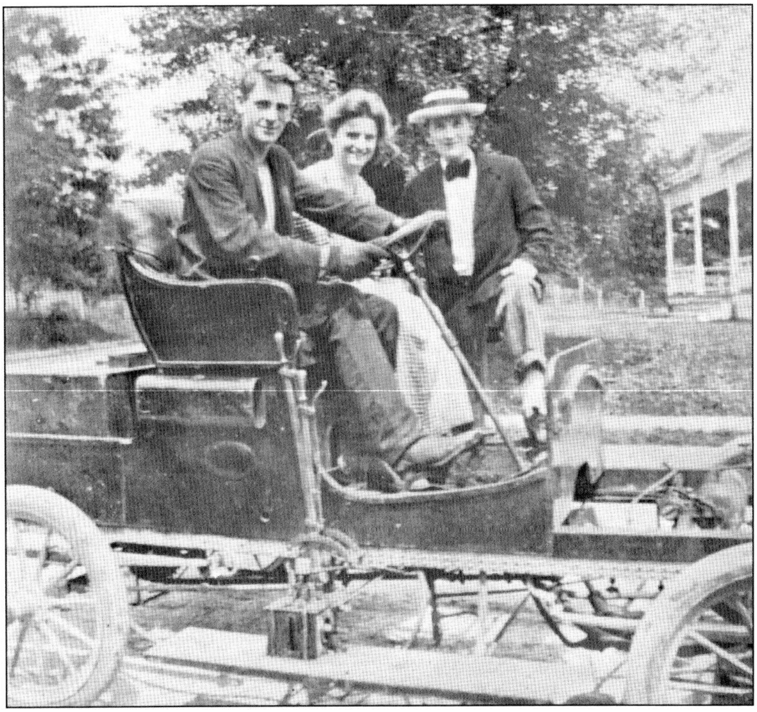

Once it arrived on the scene, the automobile took over. Here young people go for a drive in what must have been one of the earliest motorcars on the streets of Latonia. From left to right are Dudley Grey, Etta Earle, and Howard Johnson. Etta was the daughter of J. T. Earle, the mayor of Latonia. (Courtesy of Kenton County Library.)

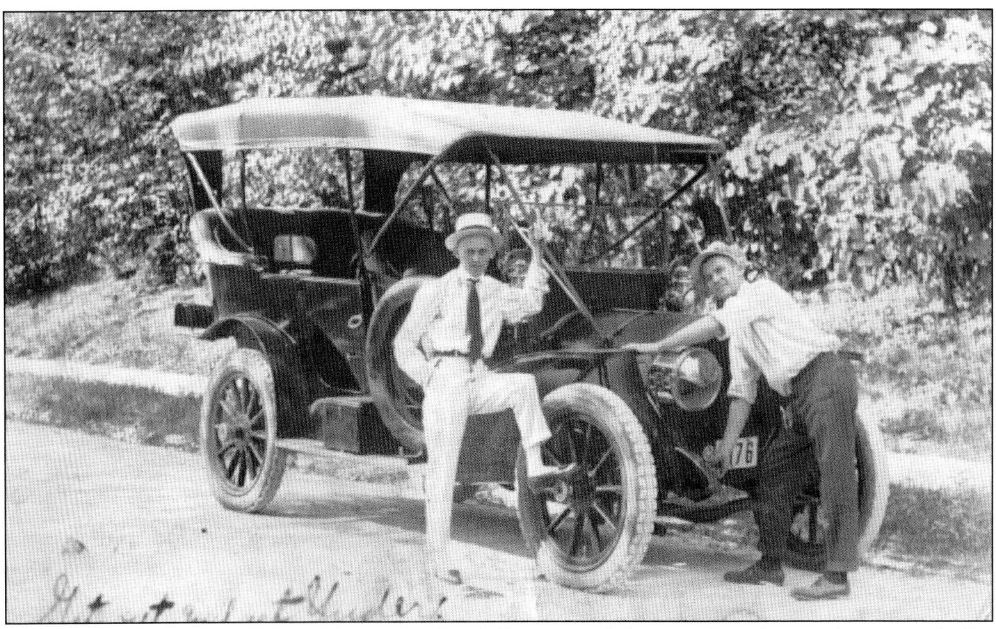

Clifford Kruse, left, and a friend pose with Cliff's automobile. His friend is ready to crank the engine to start it up. Automobiles took a fair amount of tinkering and minor repair to keep them running. A popular song of the day was "Get Out and Get Under the Car." Hopefully that did not happen to Clifford while he was wearing his white driving togs. (Courtesy of Judy Mark.)

Cliff's sister, Margaret Kruse Stratman, rests on the ground after disembarking from a motorcar. With the advent of the automobile, "going for a ride" for its own sake became a popular pastime. It was also a pleasant way to cool off. A ride in a car offered a breeze not available to someone sitting on a hot, humid porch with a paper fan. (Courtesy of Judy Mark.)

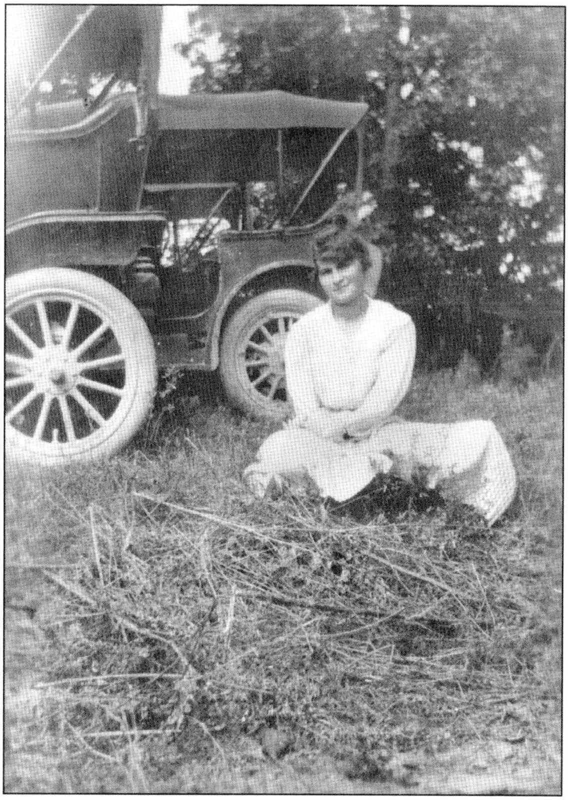

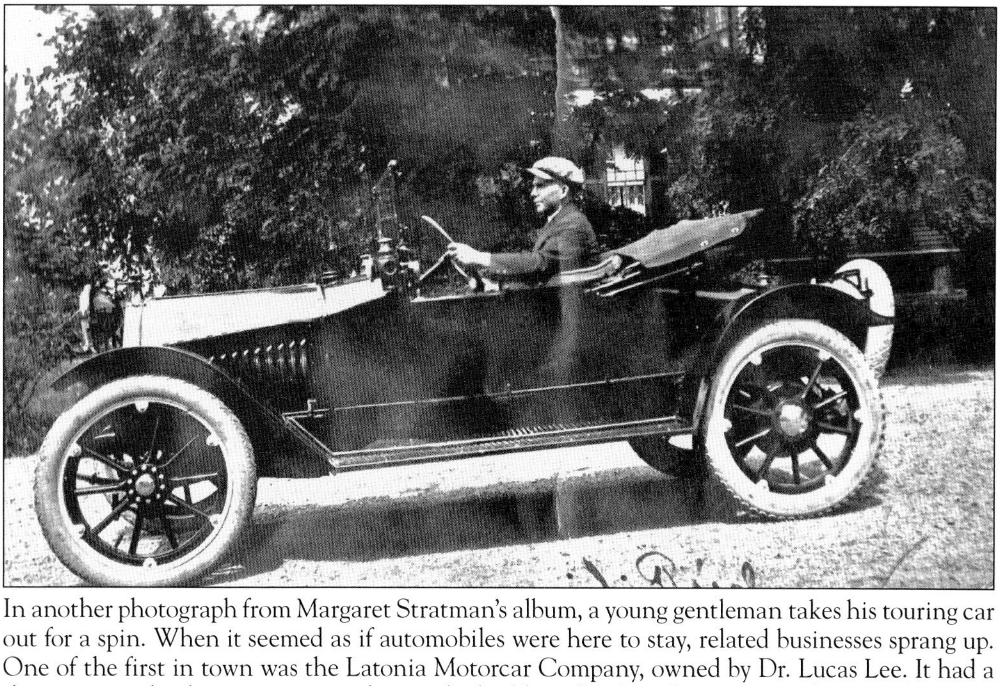

In another photograph from Margaret Stratman's album, a young gentleman takes his touring car out for a spin. When it seemed as if automobiles were here to stay, related businesses sprang up. One of the first in town was the Latonia Motorcar Company, owned by Dr. Lucas Lee. It had a showroom with a large picture window in the building that later became Hand's Crescent Dairy. (Courtesy of Judy Mark.)

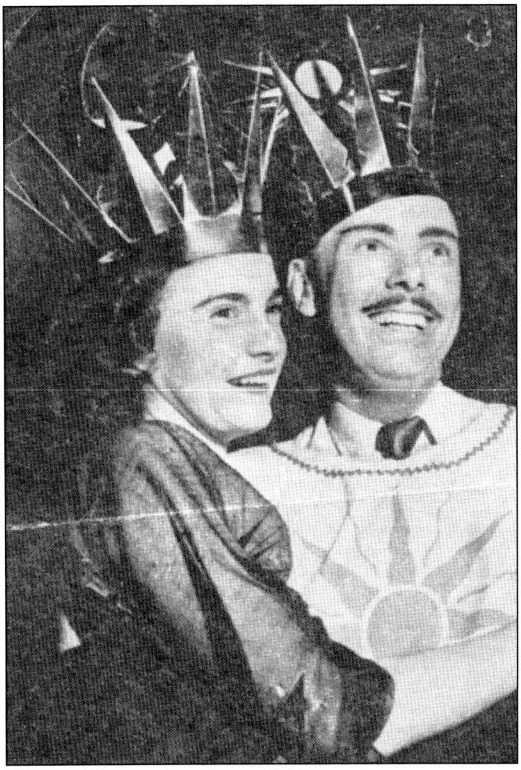

Art students Marcia Mullen (Gillham) and Charles Gillham were photographed for the newspaper at the 1948 Cincinnati Art Academy Beaux-Arts Ball. Academy students made their own costumes for the annual event. Marcia was dressed as the Goddess of Night in a filmy black gown and moon crown. Charles was the Sun God in a sun-emblazoned tunic and sun crown. (Courtesy of the author's collection.)

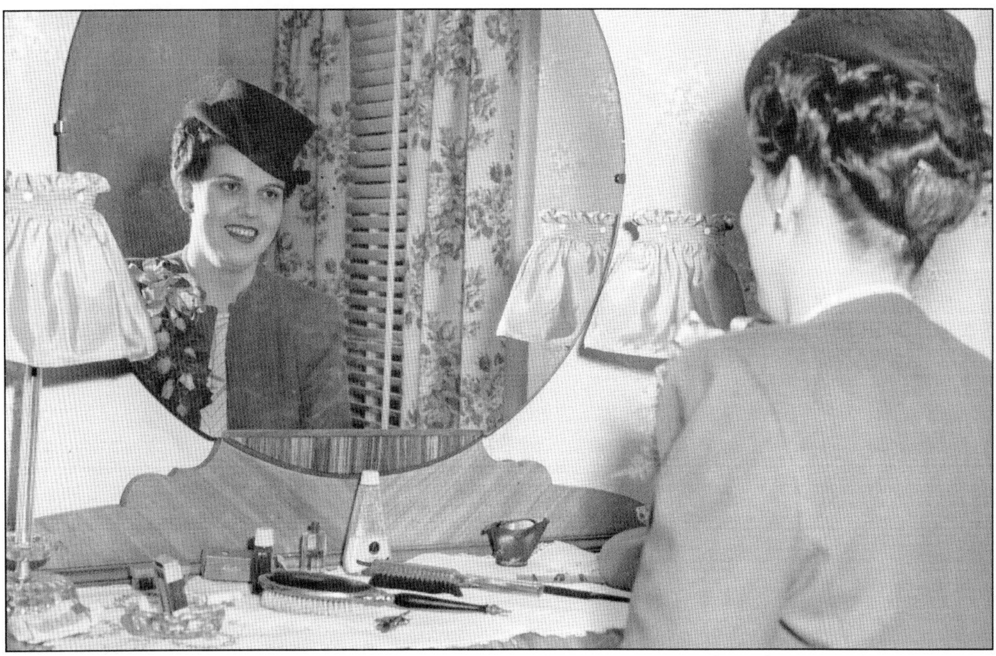

This unidentified Latonia girl is ready for a night on the town. Notice her classic art deco dressing table with patterned veneer, round mirror, and matching lamps. In 1940, she and her date could go to the movies, a beer garden, a Newport nightclub, or dancing to big bands at Coney Island's Moonlight Gardens. (Courtesy of the author's collection.)

Nine

At War

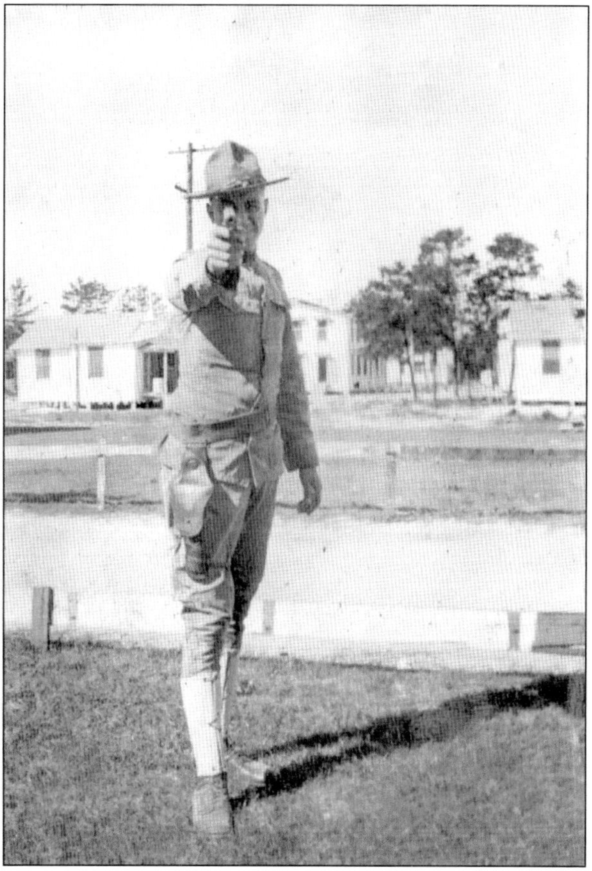

Bill Stratman of Latonia enlisted as soon as the United States entered World War I. After induction at Fort Thomas, he was sent to Fort Barrancas, Florida, for training. In the Great War, 4.7 million American soldiers—known as "doughboys"—fought the Kaiser's German legions across France and Belgium and into Germany. In the end, some 60,000 died in battle and more than 200,000 were wounded. An additional 60,000 died of disease, many from the influenza pandemic that killed more than 20 million worldwide in 1918 and 1919. Many surviving combatants suffered psychological damage, known as shell shock, from the horrors of trench warfare. (Courtesy of Judy Mark.)

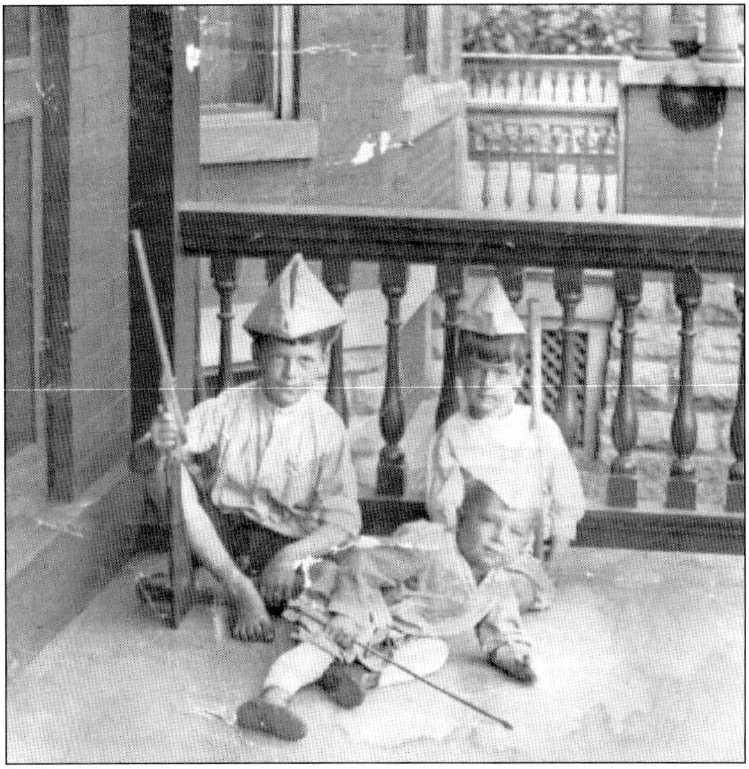

Little boys always play at war, but mothers always hope that it remains only a game. Dressed in paper soldier's hats, Ray Kochersberger, (left) his brother Harry (right), and their unidentified baby brother wield toy guns and wooden swords. They pause from battle for a picture, safe on their front porch. (Courtesy of Mary Cecil.)

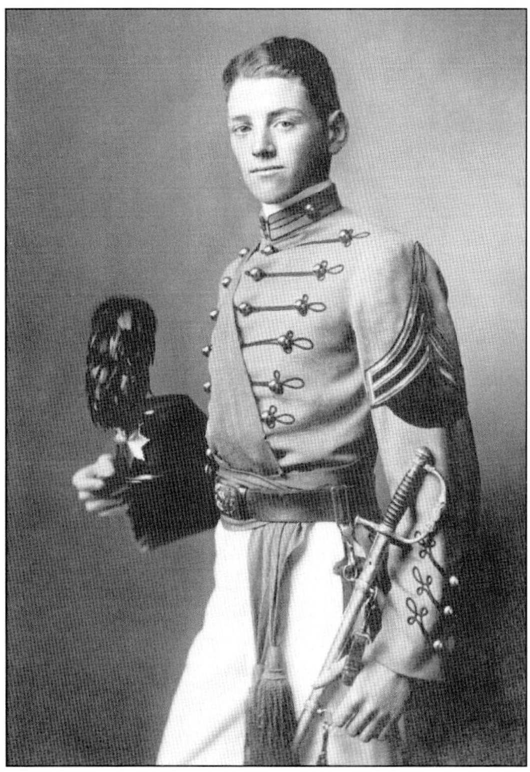

Older boys were sent to military schools to prepare them for their rank in society, to teach them discipline, or to provide them a home at boarding school. John William May cuts a fine figure in his cadet's uniform at Millersburg Military Academy in Kentucky in this c. 1907 photograph. He was the son of racehorse owner and trainer John May and his wife, Annie. (Courtesy of the author's collection.)

Here is a somewhat uncertain-looking George Smith posing at boot camp before being sent to France—and the trenches. Before his nephew Charles left for World War II, George gave him a pocket Bible and said, "If you want to get along, on your first day there, say 'I can lick any so-and-so here.' They'll beat the hell out of you, but afterwards you'll all be friends." (Courtesy of the author's collection.)

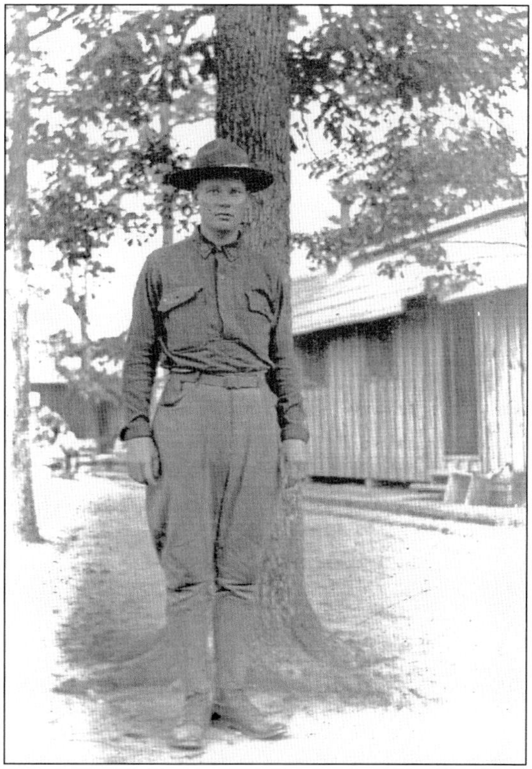

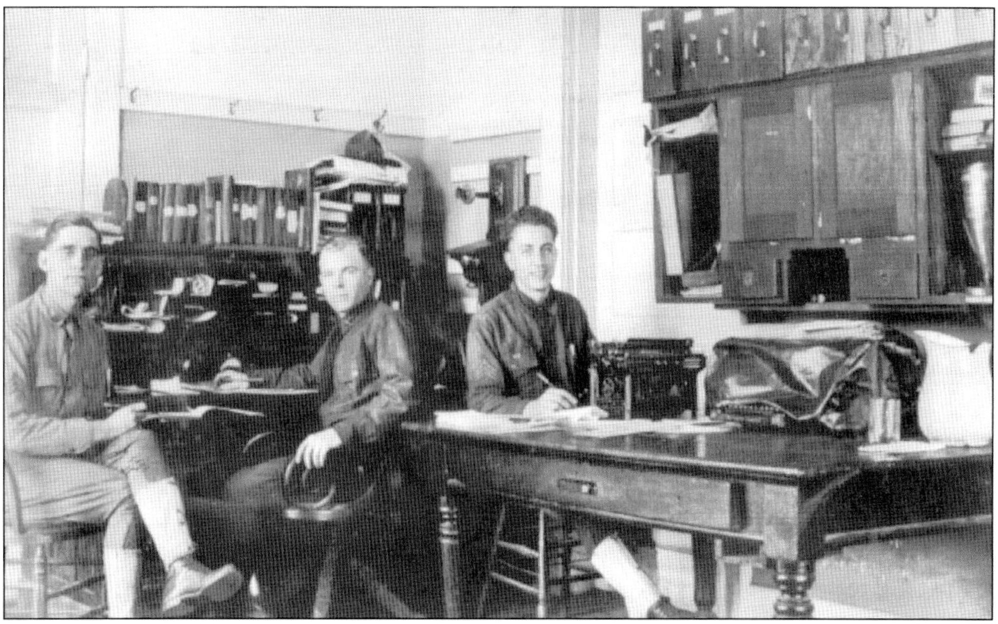

Bill Stratman (right) and two unidentified soldiers of the Third Company were photographed at their desks at Fort Barrancus, Florida. They look earnest, but when he sent the photograph home, Bill wrote, "Not working, just posing." Back in Latonia, along with the rest of the country, Bill's family and friends were coping with rationing and high levels of inflation, plus strong anti-German sentiment. (Courtesy of Judy Mark.)

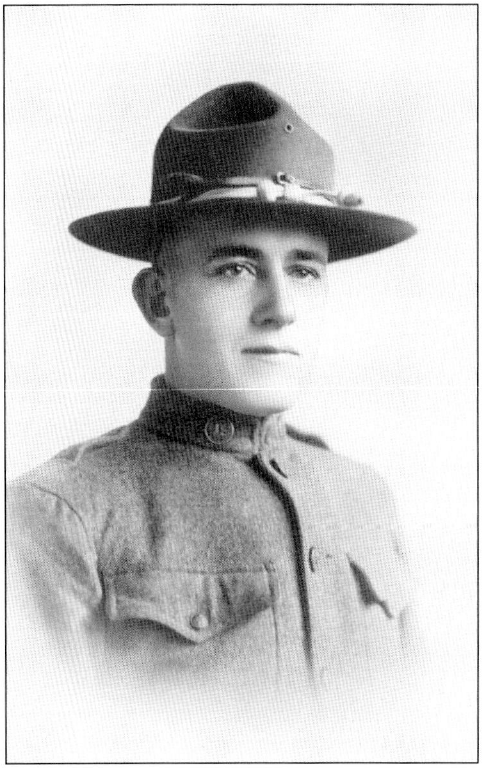

Tom Knot posed in his World War I army uniform, but he never returned. Flavia Curtiss Gillham, William F.'s wife, was related to Tom. W. F. was a pacifist, a rare bird in the era of the Great War. He was a young boy during the Civil War, and his family's reaction to that grisly and tragic war might have formed his antiwar beliefs. W. F. Gillham died in 1920. (Courtesy of the author's collection.)

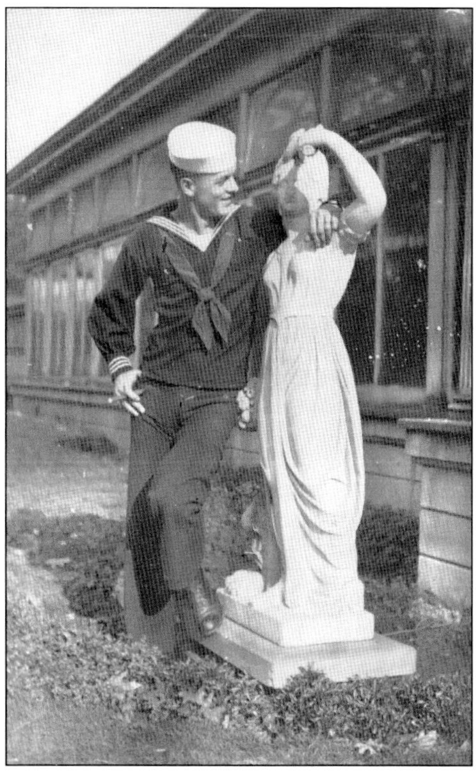

Meet Ray Kochersberger as "Pygmalion" with his Galatea, a lifeless statue. A photographer himself, he couldn't resist a good photo op. In World War I, Ray served in the U.S. Navy, stationed at the base in Chicago for the duration of the war. His wife, Levina, could visit him occasionally from Latonia, where she was working for her parents at Carroll's Grocery. (Courtesy of Mary Cecil.)

"Fuzzy," a relative of the Dorman family of Latonia, served in the U.S. Navy in World War I. Small-town boys were seeing a world unlike anything they had ever known. Combat aside, they were experiencing exotic people, cities, and customs. Like the war-era song said, "How You Gonna Keep 'Em Down on the Farm, After They've Seen Paree?" (Courtesy of Tricia Dorman.)

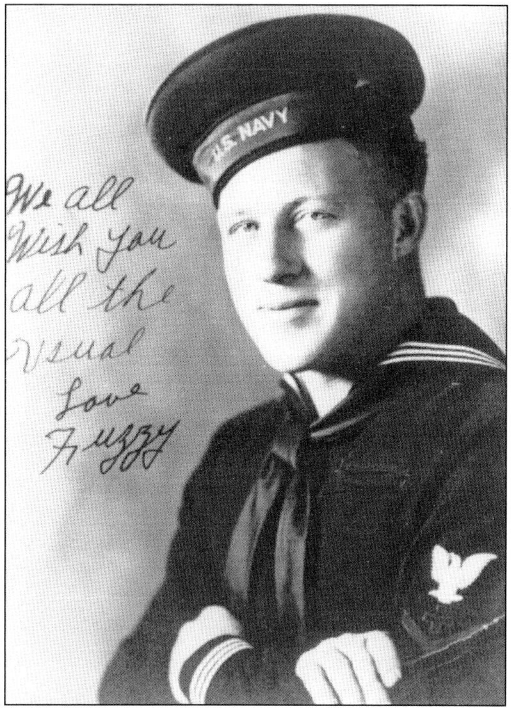

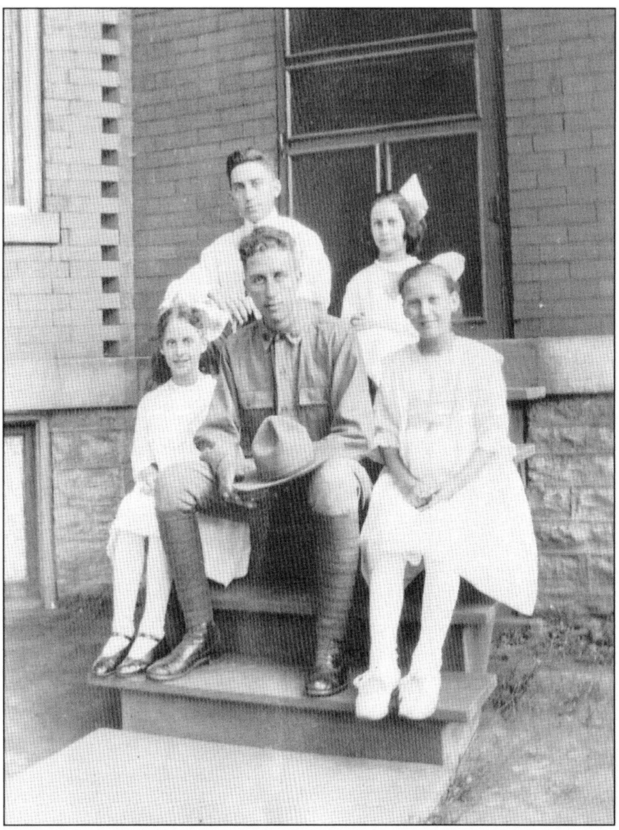

Going to war was an unimaginable change for these boys. They went to serve their country willingly, but the carnage and horrific conditions of World War I were exceedingly hard to assimilate. They wanted to be good soldiers, see the world, and fight the enemy, but most of the time they just wanted to go home. Bill Stratman sits on the stoop with his siblings. (Courtesy of Judy Mark.)

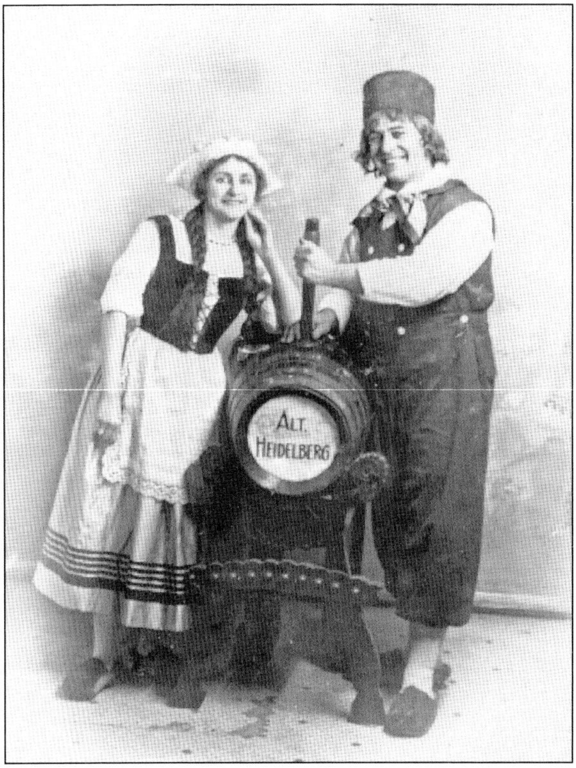

Multitudes of German immigrants settled in Northern Kentucky in the late 1800s and early 1900s. German was spoken on the street, church services were held in German, and German newspapers were widely available. German-Americans were deeply involved in their communities. Prominent Latonia entrepreneur Albert Dehlinger and his wife pose in German costume, celebrating their heritage. All that would change during World War I in Latonia. (Courtesy of Tom Martin.)

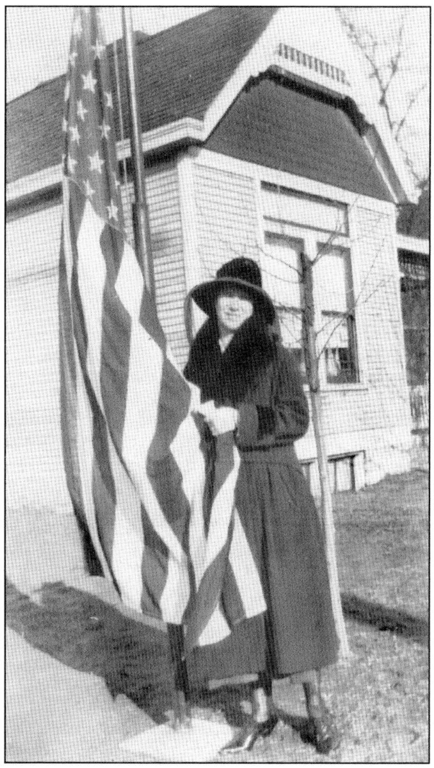

Kate Cooper displays a huge flag outside of the Warnke home at Forty-second and Church Streets in this 1918 photograph. When the United States entered the war that year, citizens swelled with patriotism and flew their flags. Most supported the war effort without hostility toward their German-American neighbors; however, anti-German tensions grew, and groups with vigilante intentions began to spread a virulent, intimidating threat under the banner of "patriotism." (Courtesy of Jim Feldman.)

The Citizens' Patriotic League (CPL) used propaganda, intimidation, and violence, and Latonia became ground zero for their worst attack. Attorney Stephens Blakely led the CPL; his second-in-command was Harvey Myers, president of the Latonia Racetrack. German-Americans Charles Schoborg, J. H. Kruse (right), and Henry Feltman (below) gathered daily at Schoborg's shoe shop, where they smoked pipes and talked. In 1918, they talked about the war. The CPL planted a listening device in Schoborg's shop to "prove" they were pro-German. Using unverifiable transcripts of alleged conversations held in private, CPL had the men arrested for espionage and sedition. (Courtesy of the author's collection.)

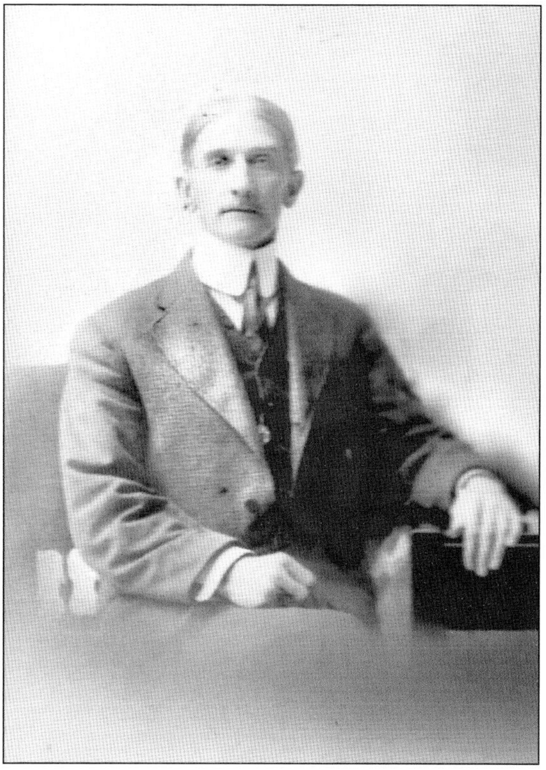

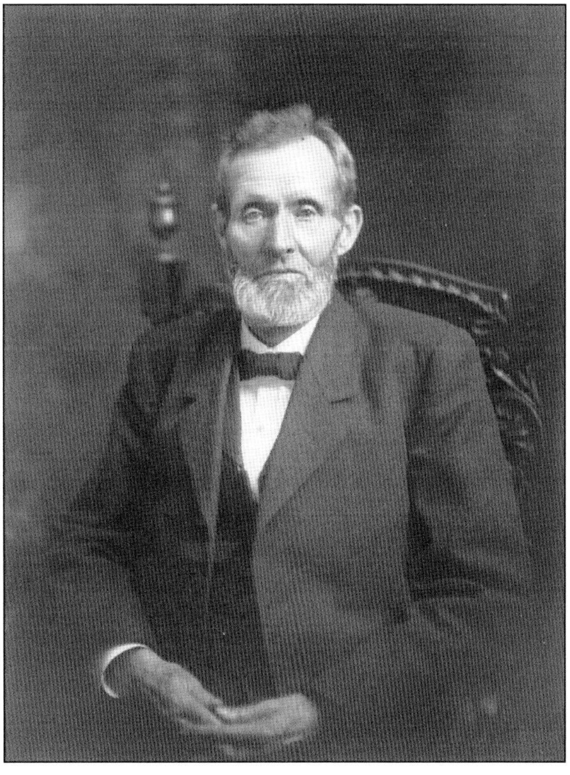

The case drew national attention. All three were respected and wealthy—and no longer young. With a stunning disregard for justice, three honorable, innocent men were convicted and sent to prison in disgrace, though their actions never undermined the war effort. CPL was never held accountable. (Courtesy of Trinity United Methodist Church.)

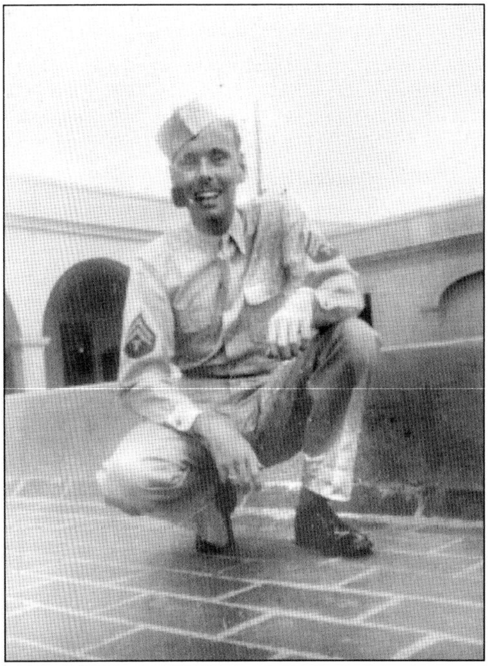

Of course, "The War to End All Wars," as it was commonly called, did not; and, less than 25 years later, the United States was embroiled in World War II. As always, Latonia men served their country. Here is army staff sergeant Charlie Gillham at Headquarters Company in San Juan, Puerto Rico. After a job loading ammunition, for which he was not well suited, he ended up in the U.S. Department of Engineers, Caribbean Theater, doing cartography and making use of his artistic and graphics skills. He also learned Spanish and the rumba, and developed a lifelong love of the tropics. Unable to get furlough to go home to Latonia for Christmas, he drew this card (below) for his parents, Charley and Fern, back on Iowa Avenue. The local newspaper picked it up, since it expressed the sentiments of so many soldiers and their families. (Courtesy of the author's collection.)

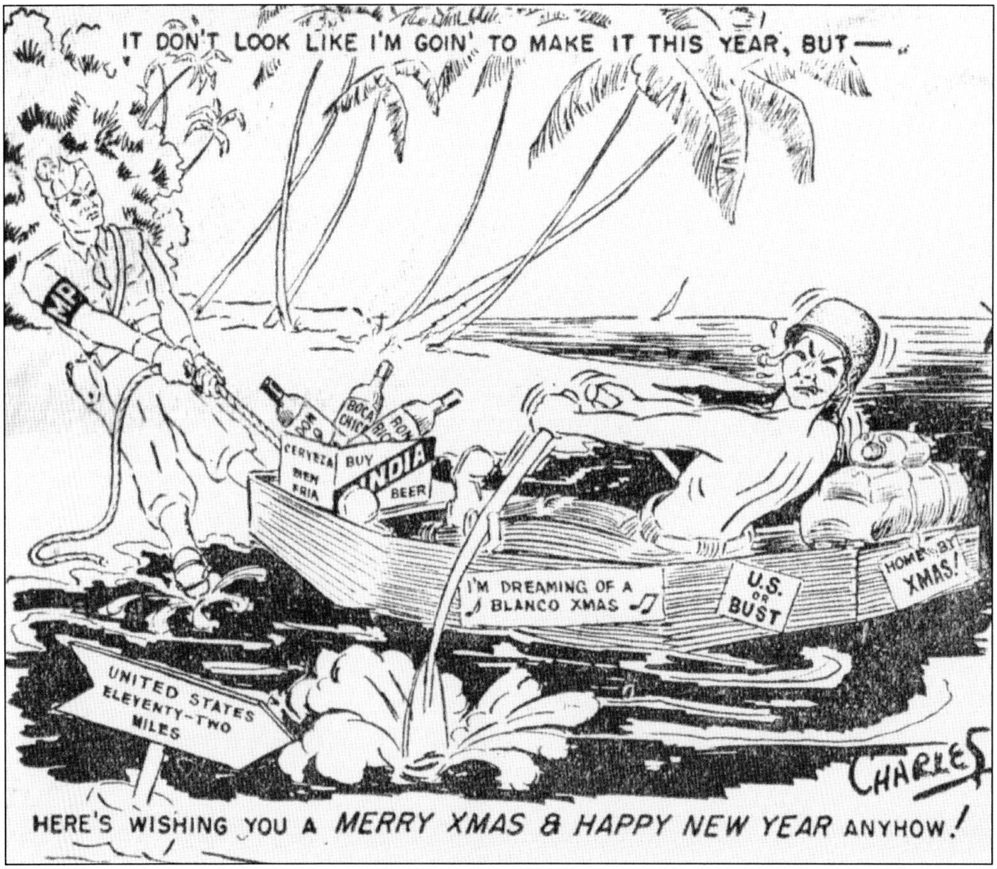

Jack Cecil, right, was an investigator in U.S. Navy Intelligence. He was stationed in Cincinnati for the duration, so he was able to live at home in Latonia with his wife, Mary, but he was often required to be out of town. Richter Roe, (below) Charlie Gillham's first cousin, served in army infantry in Europe. He fought in the Battle of the Bulge and was deeply affected by what he experienced. (Courtesy of Mary Cecil.)

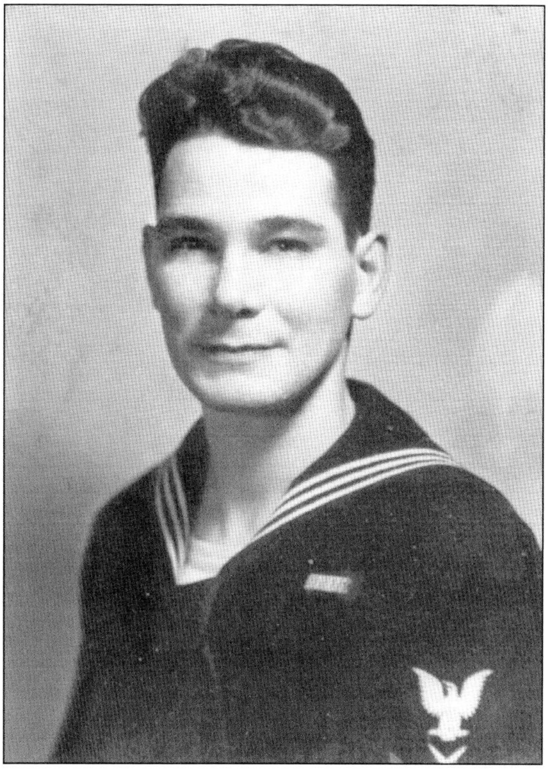

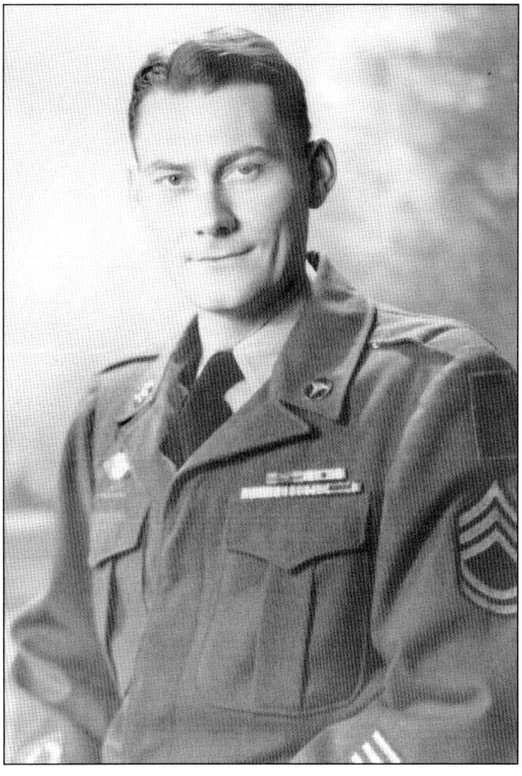

Often all the men in a family, graduating class, or church group were in the service. An entire Sunday school class at St. Mark's Church served, including the pastor, Rev. Frank Scholl, an army chaplain. Some of the Latonia men who went to war did not return, like Bill Bolling, Allen Clare, Joe Arlinghaus, and Warren Richardson, who was killed at Pearl Harbor. (Courtesy of the author's collection.)

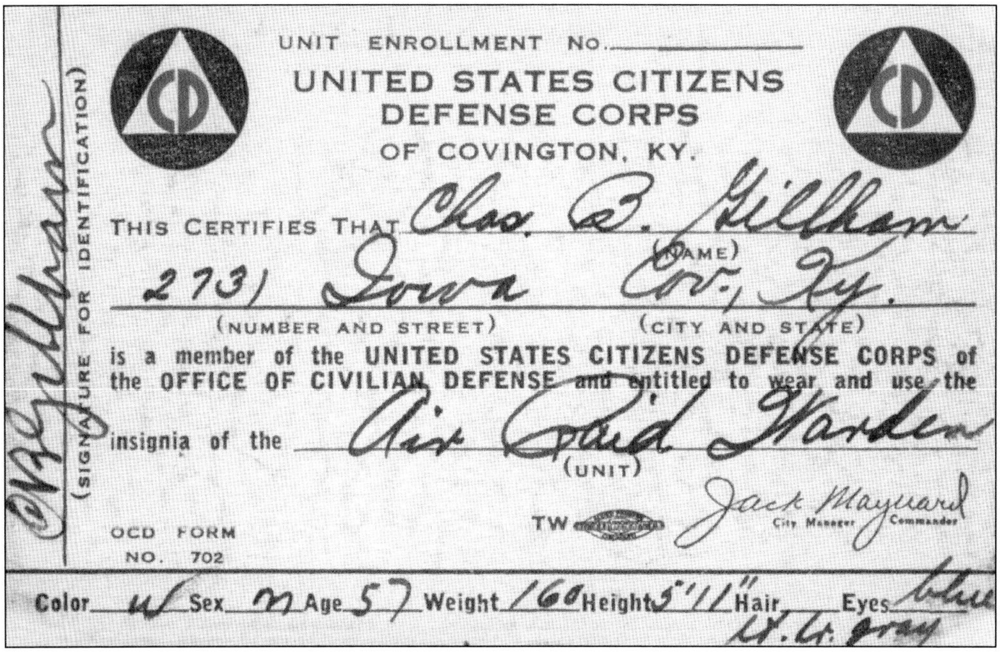

UNIT ENROLLMENT No.________

UNITED STATES CITIZENS DEFENSE CORPS OF COVINGTON, KY.

THIS CERTIFIES THAT Chas. B. Gillham
(NAME)

2731 Iowa Cov., Ky.
(NUMBER AND STREET) (CITY AND STATE)

is a member of the UNITED STATES CITIZENS DEFENSE CORPS of the OFFICE OF CIVILIAN DEFENSE and entitled to wear and use the insignia of the Air Raid Warden
(UNIT)

Jack Maynard
City Manager Commander

OCD FORM NO. 702

(SIGNATURE FOR IDENTIFICATION)

Color W Sex M Age 57 Weight 160 Height 5'11" Hair lt. br. gray Eyes blue

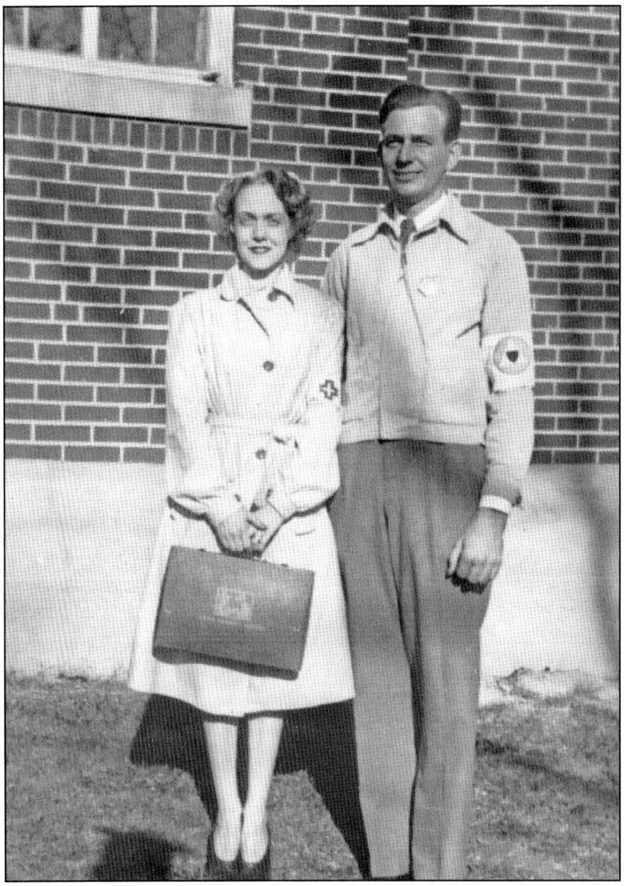

There were ways to serve the war effort on the home front, too. Civilians served as air raid wardens or nurses for the American Red Cross, they collected scrap metal and rubber, young ladies helped entertain soldiers at USO dances, and mothers sewed blankets and socks and wrapped bandages. Women stepped into jobs vacated by soldiers to keep industry moving. Families grew victory gardens and observed rationing. While his son was serving in Puerto Rico, Charley Gillham was in Latonia serving as an air raid warden. His job was to look after his neighborhood and to monitor air raid drills and blackouts to ensure they were effective. Pictured above is his ID card. Pictured at left, Georgia Roe Gibson and her husband, Joe, served at home, she as an American Red Cross nurse and he as an air raid warden. (Courtesy of the author's collection.)

This is from an Airplane Spotter card deck. These were regular playing cards, except that each featured a silhouette of an American or German airplane to teach citizens to recognize aircraft. When an airplane was spotted in the sky, it could be identified as friendly or enemy craft. One night during the war, an American airplane buzzed Latonia, swooping back and forth. Everyone was puzzled by the pilot's erratic behavior. Thinking he was in trouble and needed to land, air raid warden Charley Gillham organized neighbors to line up their cars and turn their headlights in the direction of Lunken Airport to guide the flyer. But the airplane flew away, and it remained a mystery. Below is a ration coupon that belonged to Ray Kochersberger of Church Street. (Courtesy of the author's collection and courtesy of Mary Cecil.)

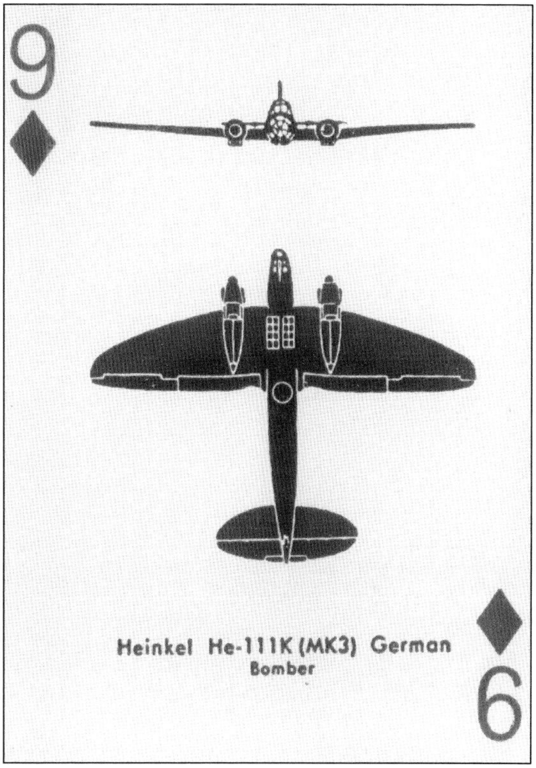

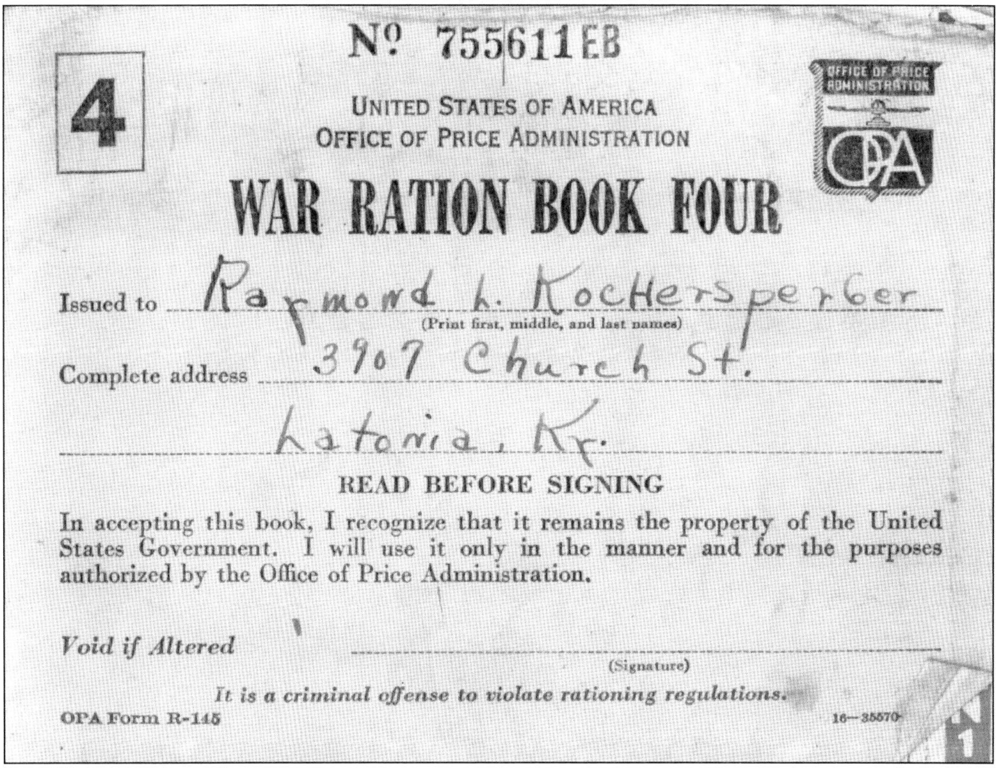

4

N° 755611 EB

UNITED STATES OF AMERICA
OFFICE OF PRICE ADMINISTRATION

OFFICE OF PRICE ADMINISTRATION
OPA

WAR RATION BOOK FOUR

Issued to Raymond L. Kochersperber
(Print first, middle, and last names)

Complete address 3907 Church St.

Latonia, Ky.

READ BEFORE SIGNING

In accepting this book, I recognize that it remains the property of the United States Government. I will use it only in the manner and for the purposes authorized by the Office of Price Administration.

Void if Altered ______________________
(Signature)

It is a criminal offense to violate rationing regulations.

OPA Form R-145 16—35570

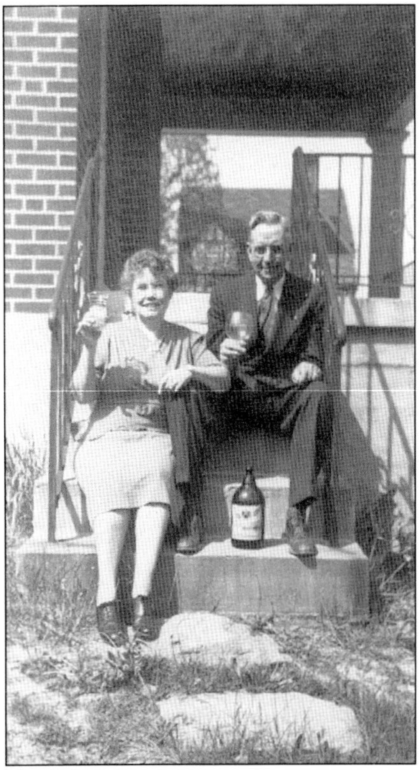

When the war was finally over, the whole country was poised in anticipation. From the steps of their front porch on Iowa Avenue, Fern and Charley Gillham toast their son's homecoming. They sent him a copy of the picture, so he could see them saluting his return. In 1945, most soldiers were on their way home, and many took advantage of the GI Bill to go to college. America changed with that homecoming in ways that few could have imagined. Below is Charles Petty, owner of the Latonia Bakery, presenting a special cake to a young soldier and his mother to celebrate his homecoming. (Courtesy of the author's collection and Lorna Petty Harrell.)

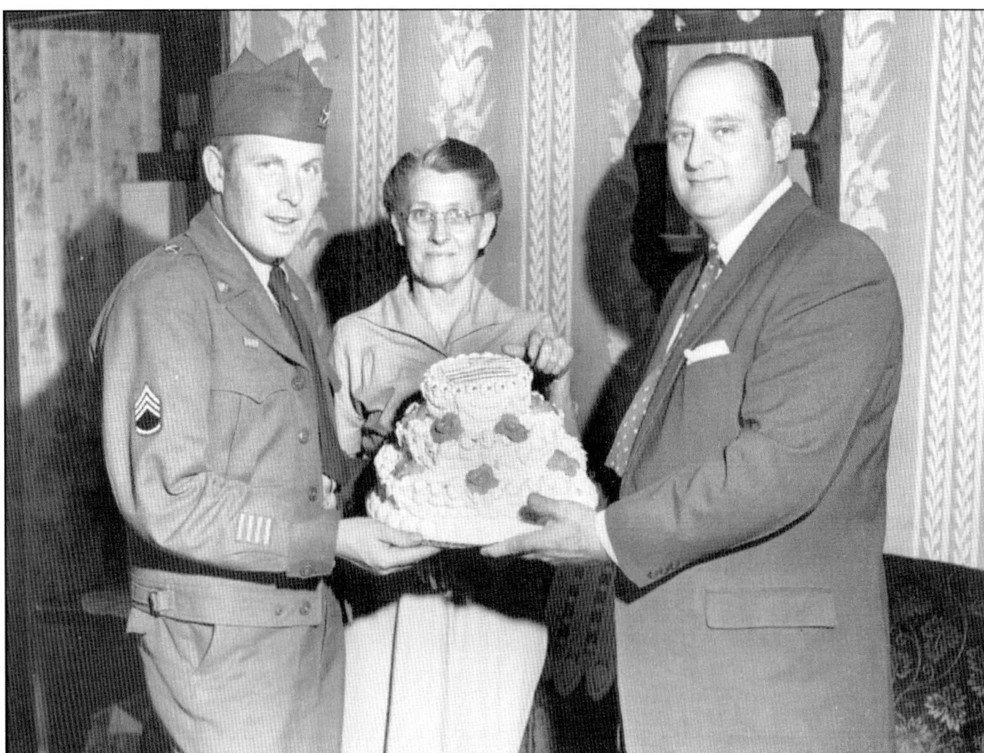

Ten

Back Home Again

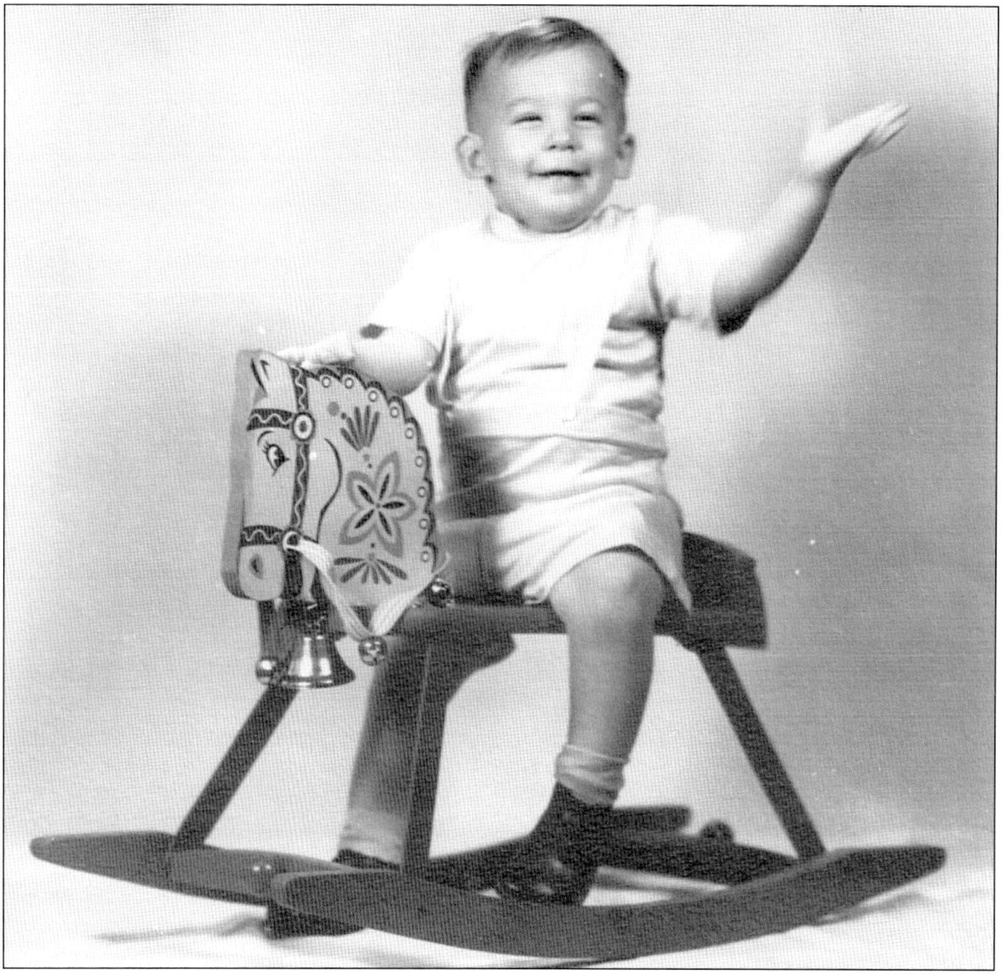

After World War II, soldiers returned to Latonia and, as they did all over the country, settled down to start families. It was a new era. After sustaining the privations of the Depression and suffering through the war, young married couples were eager to have quiet, peaceful, and prosperous home lives. Men who had gone to college on the GI bill were eager to rise in their careers. There were new products, new industries, and new technologies. Dressed in their suits and ties, they drove their new cars to work on Eisenhower's new freeways. Moms went to the new supermarkets and PTA meetings in full skirts, pearls, and high heels. New homes went up; kindergarten ranks swelled. Barbecues were built. Lawns were mowed. It was boom time. Little Jeff Cecil's smile and confident wave say it all. (Courtesy of Mary Cecil.)

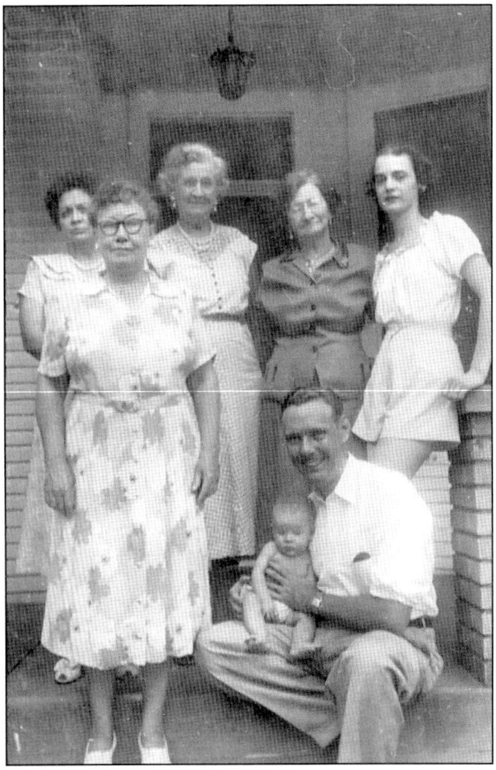

Here a young father holds his infant daughter on the front porch of his Southern Avenue home while surrounded by his young wife and some older ladies of the family. From left to right are Louise Smith, Fern Gillham, Matilda Mullen, Lucy Scherrer, and Marcia Mullen Gillham. Charles Gillham sits on the porch step with daughter Lisa. Another boomer baby greets Latonia. (Courtesy of the author's collection.)

The family pictured below is celebrating the birth of first grandchild Carla. From left to right are (seated) Ruth Beuttel (Bill's wife), Bob Beuttel, Audrey Danks, young Bill Beuttel, Virginia Beuttel Gridley (mother of baby), Ruth Beuttel (Virginia and Carl's daughter), and Mary Schmidt Fossett; (standing) George and Mayme Schmidt, Mary Beuttel (mother), Walter Beuttel, Elsie Beuttel Danks, Virginia Beuttel (holding granddaughter), Carl Beuttel (Virginia's husband), and Ella and George Beuttel. (Courtesy of Bill Beuttel.)

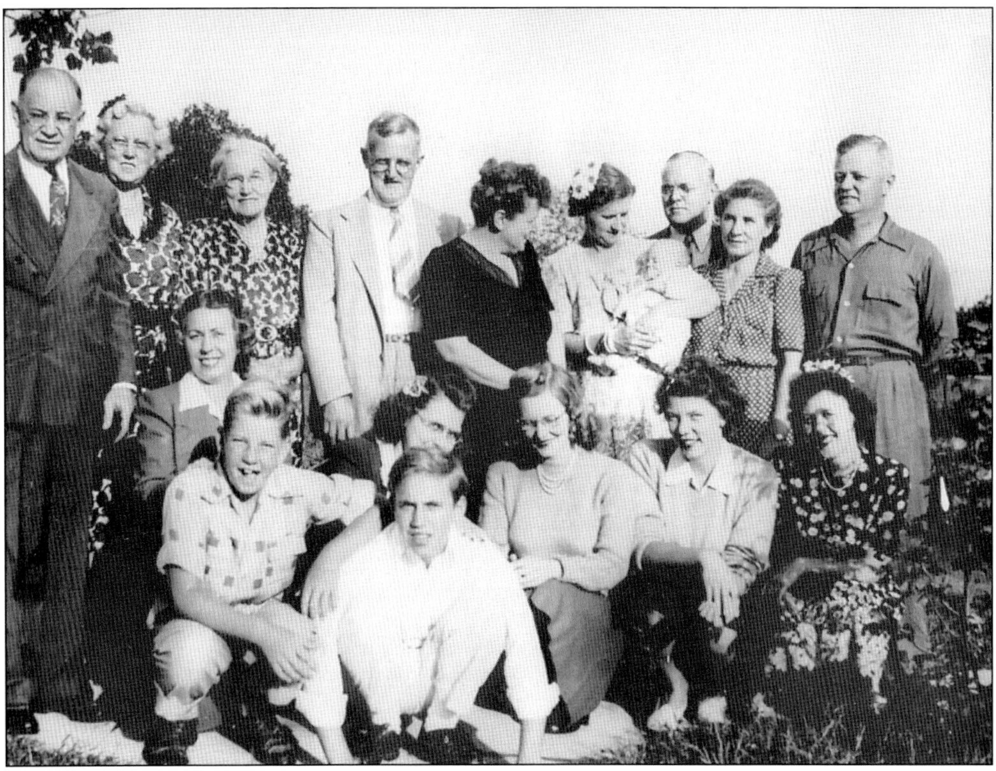

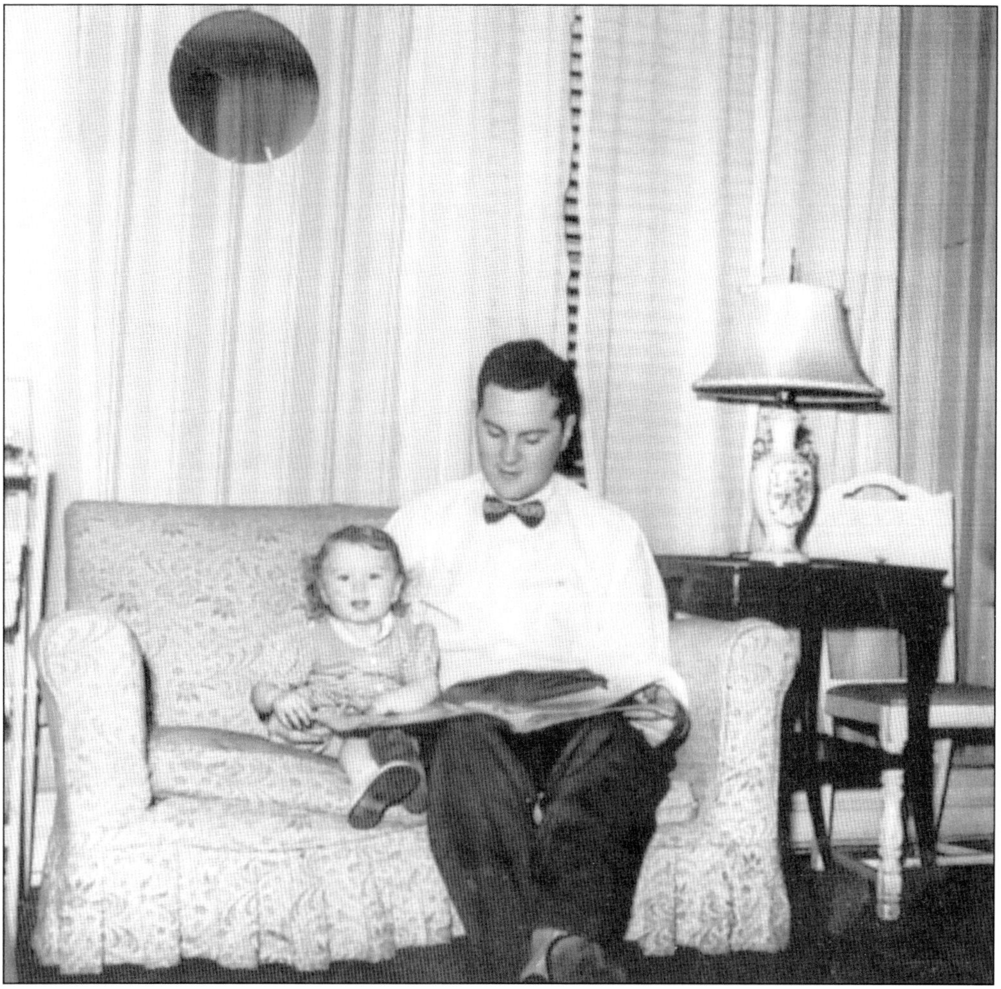

Benjamin Baker reads to his daughter Kathy Ann in their home on Rosina Avenue in this c. 1950 photograph. Ben had been born on Rosina Avenue, had gone to war, met his wife, Kathy, in San Francisco, and returned to Rosina Avenue. In World War II, he had worked in communications on a radio ship, so his experience had prepared him for a job at Cincinnati Bell when he returned home. One lesson from the 1950s worth keeping is that there are few things more valuable than a mommy or daddy reading a storybook to their little child. (Courtesy of Ben and Jim Baker.)

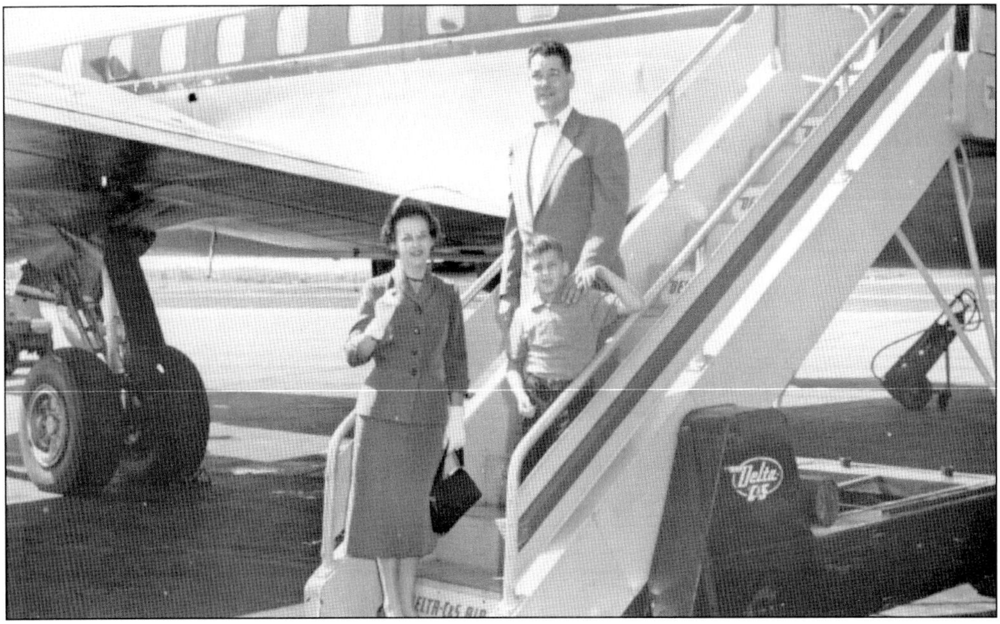

Jack Cecil worked for the Ford Motor Company, where he was awarded a free airplane trip to Florida with his wife, Mary, and their son Jeff. This was the first airplane ride for Mary and Jeff, and it was a big deal. Airplane travel was not yet commonplace, but transportation was surging into the future. Everything was on the move and speeding forward. It was the jet age, and anything was possible. (Courtesy of Mary Cecil.)

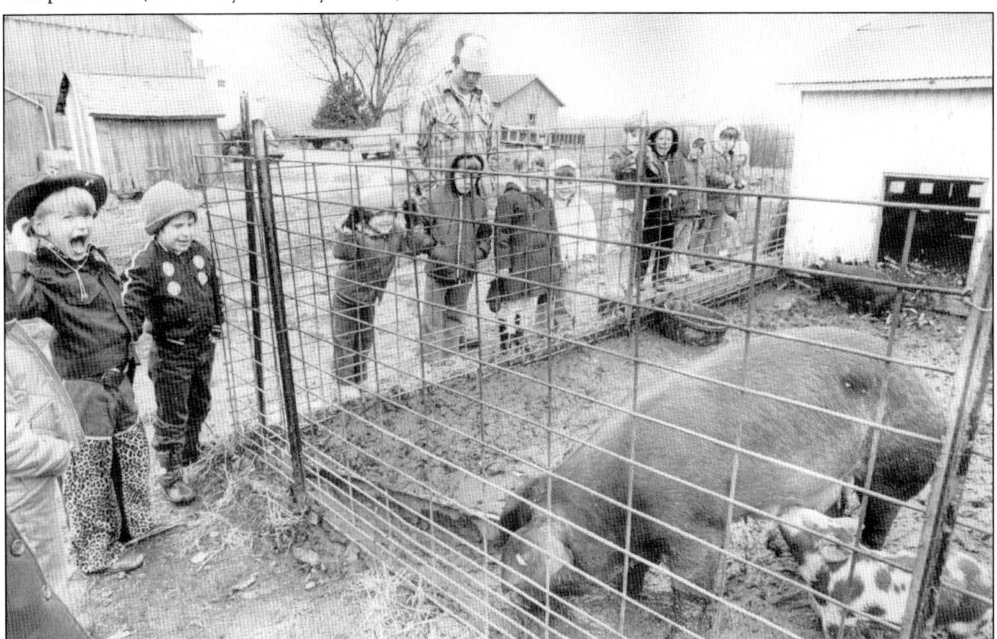

By the 1950s, few children were familiar with farm life. Most children knew cows, pigs, and sheep only from the pictures in their storybooks. Here the Ruoff Family Farm in Cincinnati hosted a tour for Latonia Baptist Church's kindergarten. The boy at left, making faces at the pigs, is Kevin Eilerman. The others are unidentified. (Courtesy of Kenton County Public Library.)

This couple was beginning a different kind of new life after the war. Lillian Pope and Ray Kochersberger are photographed here on their honeymoon in 1951. Ray's first wife, Levina, had passed away at an early age, and Lillian's first husband, Forest Pope, had died in 1941. The two widowed friends became closer, got married, and enjoyed the rest of their lives together. (Courtesy of Mary Cecil.)

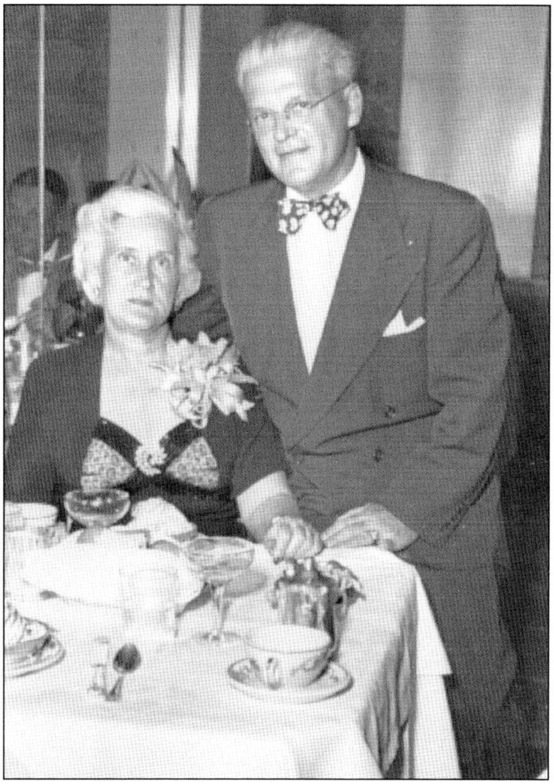

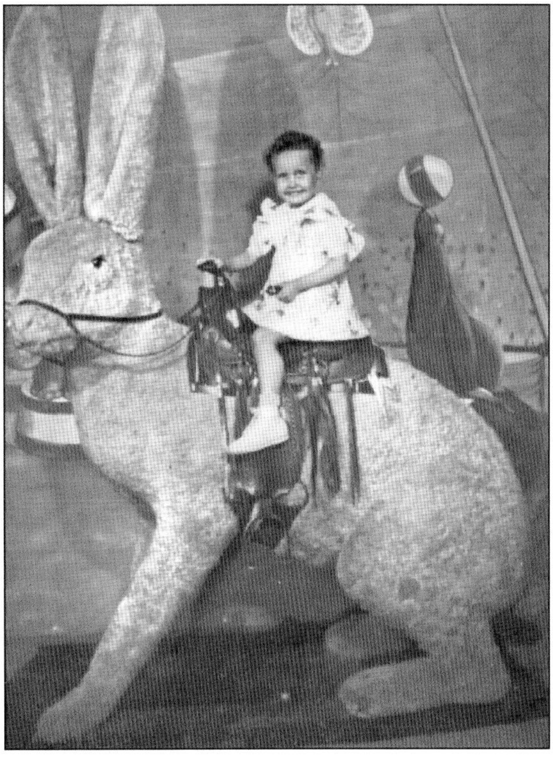

Here three-year-old Pamela Ann Dorman takes a ride on a gigantic rabbit. A huge animal does not seem strange to a little girl who has seen creatures talk in Walt Disney movies and who is already watching *Captain Kangaroo*, *Jellybean Acres*, and *The Uncle Al Show* on that little, round, gray screen at home. She looks confident and knows that whatever happens next will be fun. (Courtesy of Tricia Dorman.)

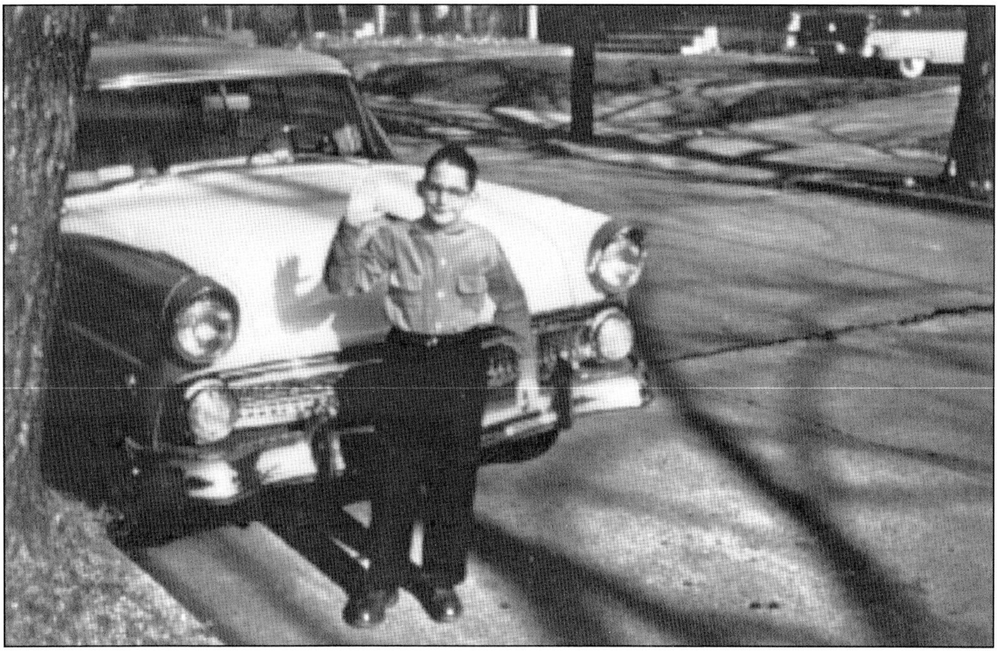

It was the 1950s and the era of the car. Jeff Cecil is waving again, this time in front of his parents' shiny Ford parked on Church Street. On the new freeways, cars could drive fast without stopping, but the freeways bypassed little towns and their old train tracks. Soon older city neighborhoods across the country would begin to slide into a long, slow decline. (Courtesy of Mary Cecil.)

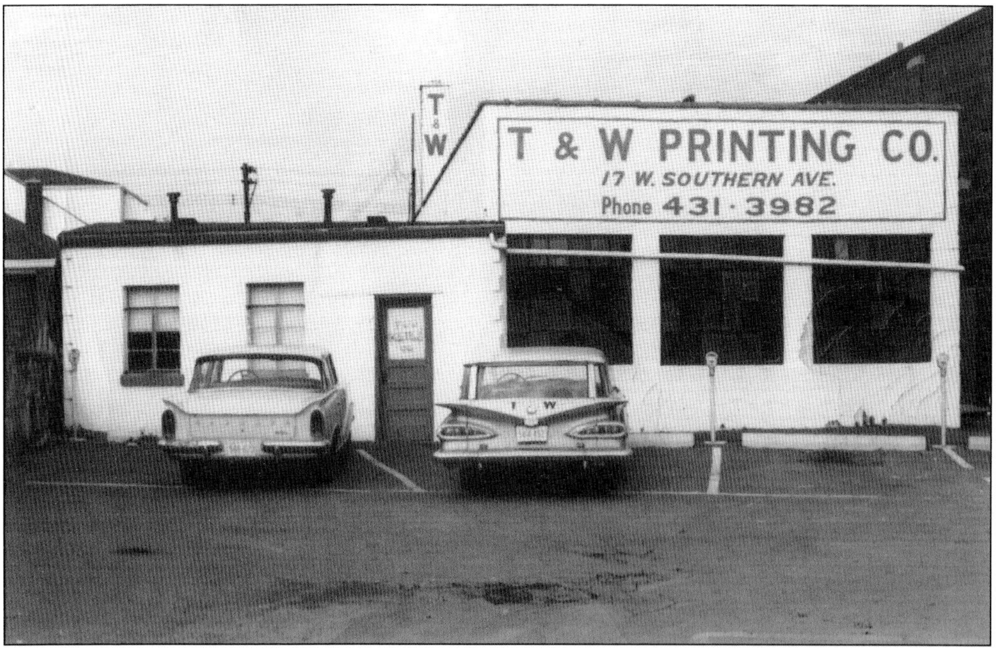

Harry Mitchell's T&W Printing Company was going strong on Southern Avenue, and in his parking lot are a couple of the latest cars, wing fins and all. Parking lots were becoming an obsession in the 1950s. Irreplaceable buildings that had stood for 100 years fell to provide all-important parking. T&W is still in business there and is now run by Harry's son Tom. (Courtesy of Tom Mitchell.)

This Iowa Avenue couple thought their new car was so special, they gave it its own party. Charlie and Marcia Gillham celebrate purchasing their first new automobile, an Oldsmobile Super 88 with a "Rocket Engine" and "Hydra-Matic Drive." Charlie made party hats with big silver 88s on them for each of their guests. At right, he plays piano while Marcia accompanies him with Puerto Rican maracas made for him during the war. (Courtesy of the author's collection.)

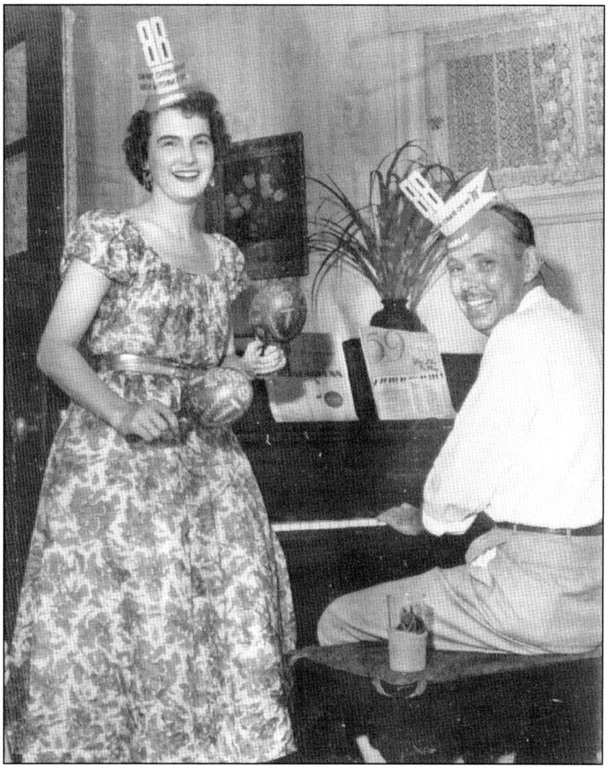

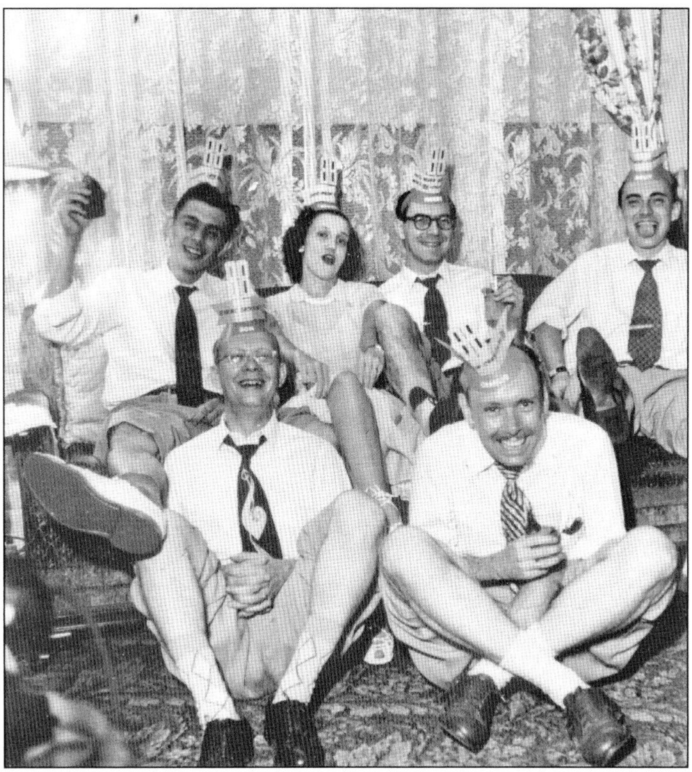

Of course, a party for a shiny green Oldsmobile Super 88 can get a little wild. The newlyweds made mint juleps and stored them in a big tub of ice. By the time the party started, they had to chisel the glasses out and wrap napkins around the chunks of ice clinging to the bottoms. Those mint juleps were cold. Pictured from left to right are (first row) Don Mathias and Charlie Gillham showing off their legs; (second row) John Richter, Willie and Harry Henderly, and Wally Armstrong. (Courtesy of the author's collection.)

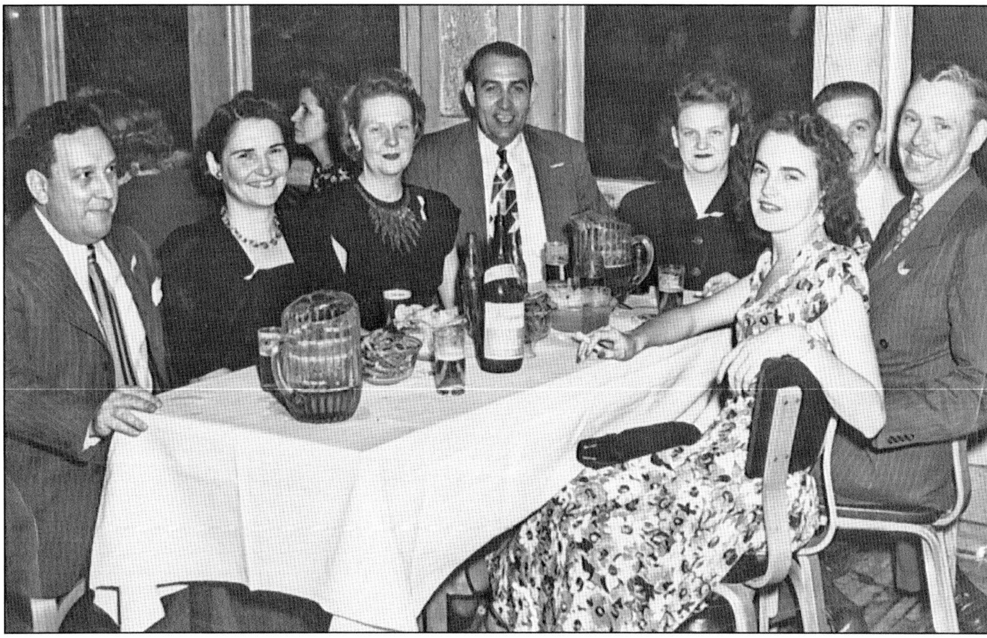

House parties were popular, with a pitcher of martinis or a couple of highballs, and so were nightclubs, like Beverly Hills and Newport's Glen Rendezvous. Here a group of cousins and their spouses enjoy a night at the Latonia's Twin Oaks Golf Club in 1948. From left to right are Benny and Janet Duke, Helen and Allen Samuels, Joan Born, Marcia Mullen (Gillham), Jack Born, and Charles Gillham. (Courtesy of the author's collection.)

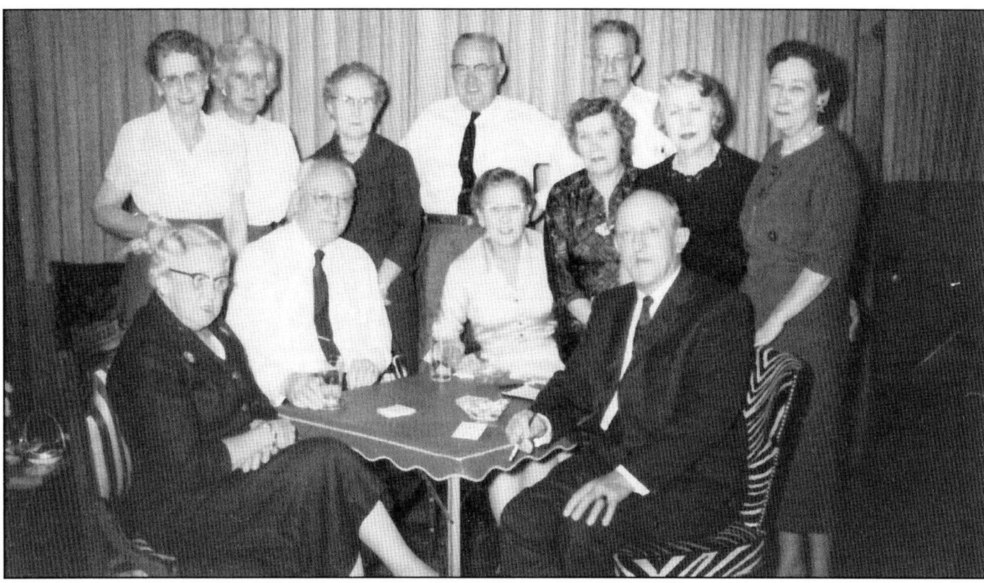

The older generation enjoys a card party at Hazel Lee's house in 1958. Seated from left to right are Mayme Schmidt, Oscar Boeckley, two unidentified ladies, and former Covington mayor Bill Beuttel. Standing from left to right are Mrs. Boeckley; Lillian Kochersberger; Virginia and Carl Beuttel; Walter Beuttel; Bill Beuttel's wife, Ruth; and Hazel Lee. Dr. Lee had died in 1946. These people had been friends for most of their lives. (Photograph by Ray Kochersberger; courtesy of the author's collection.)

During the 1950s and 1960s Latonia held a big Halloween block party every year. Ritte's Corner was closed to traffic, and revelry prevailed with food, games, and prizes. At right, Jack Cecil wins first prize for his convincing angel costume. His wife, Mary, made it, and he completed the outfit with white long underwear. Since 2006, the Latonia Business Association has brought back the tradition of the annual Halloween party, cosponsoring it along with Latonia Baptist and Latonia Christian Churches. An all-free event, it draws thousands of people every year; however, it is no longer in the middle of Ritte's Corner. (Courtesy of Mary Cecil.)

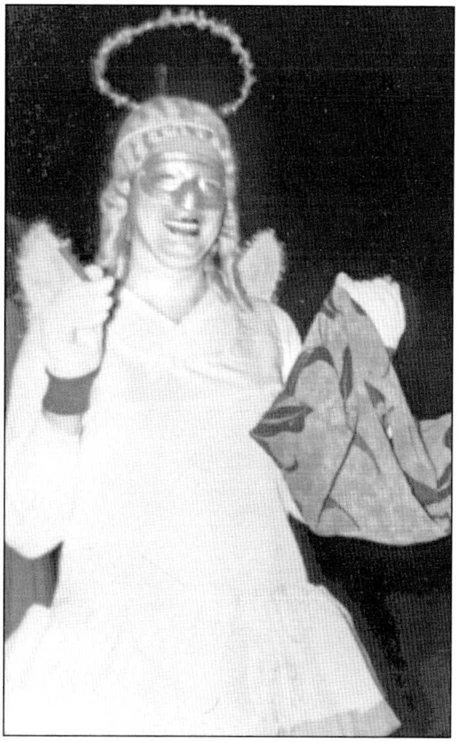

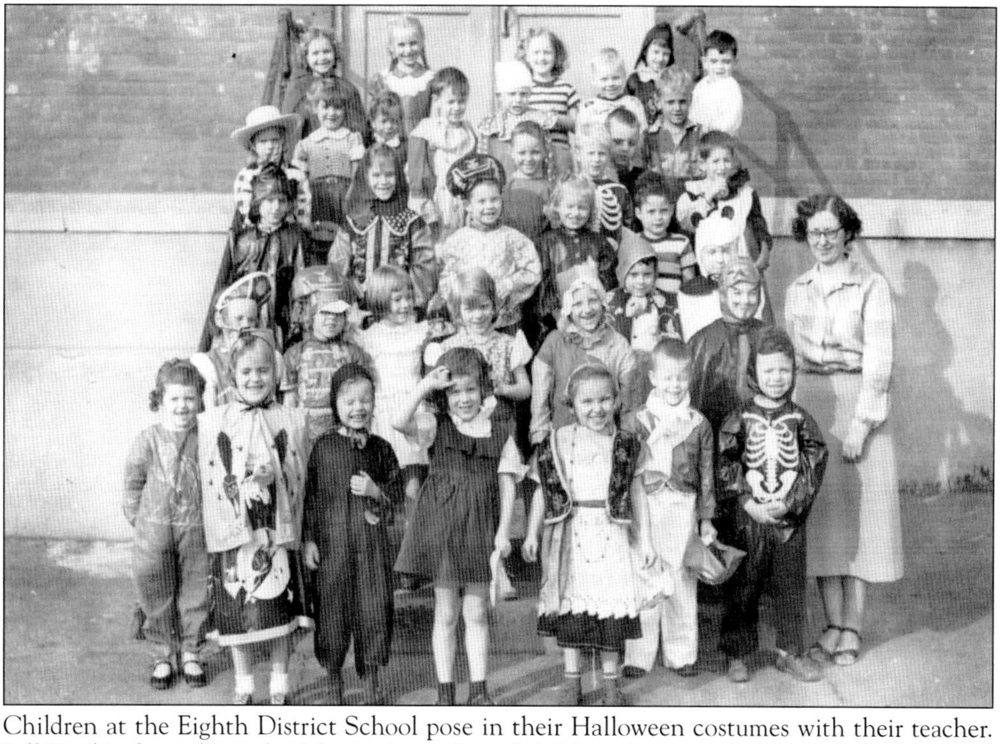

Children at the Eighth District School pose in their Halloween costumes with their teacher. Jeff Cecil is dressed as a devil (second row, far right). The others are unidentified. Students and teachers had been posing on these stairs since 1900. (Courtesy of Mary Cecil.)

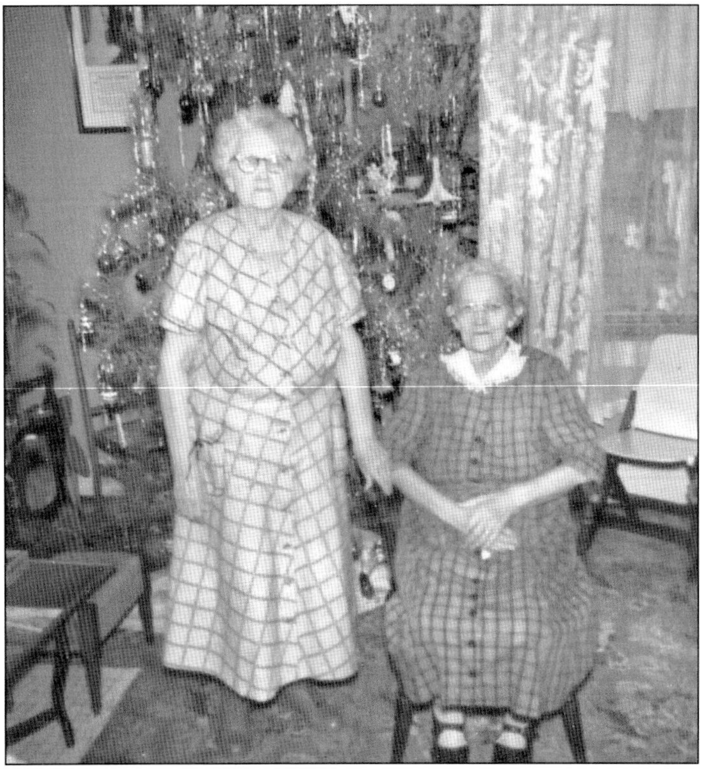

The 1950s brought a new era of Christmas, too. Christmas was lean during the war years, but it was back and better than ever. Since the war's end, finely crafted glass tree ornaments were available from Germany and Czechoslovakia again. The smiling Santa was drinking Coca-Cola. Grandparents were buying presents, and the family again went "over the river and through the woods to Grandmother's house" but in the car rather than the sleigh. Cora Osborn Dorman (left) and her sister Addie Chrisman (right) pose in front of the Christmas tree. (Courtesy of Tricia Dorman.)

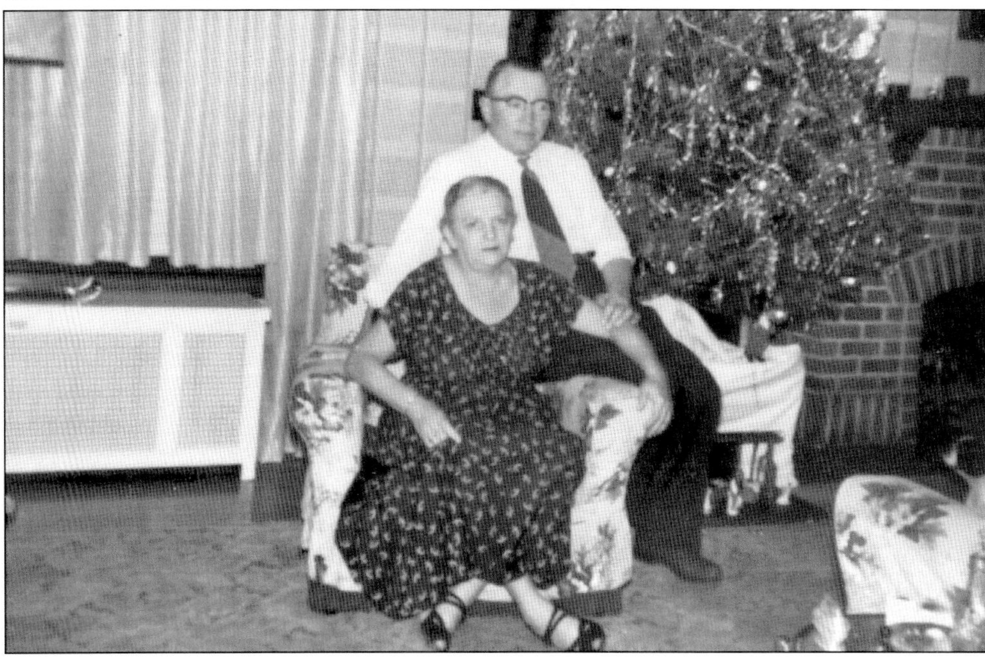

Stanley and Mildred Vogelsang are at their home on Winston Avenue in 1958, awaiting arrival of grandchildren. It was turkey and dressing, bowls and platters heaped high, then children playing with new toys, women washing dishes in the kitchen, and men taking naps in chairs. (Courtesy of Carol Dick and John Kennedy.)

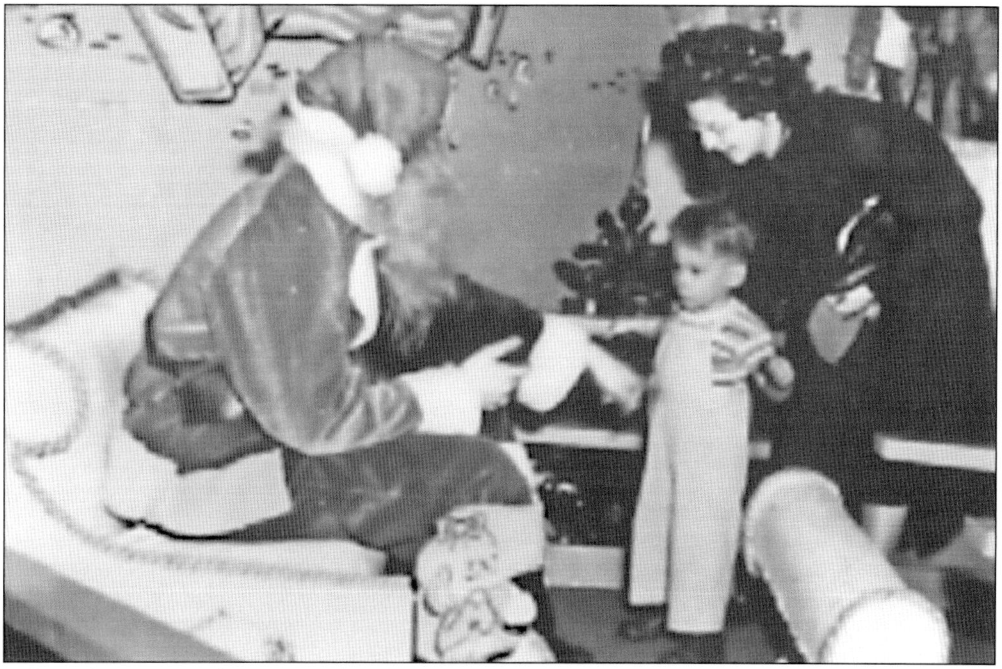

Jeff Cecil is presented to Santa Claus by his mother, Mary. He looks rather shy. What he does not know is that Santa Claus is actually his daddy, Jack. Maybe next they will go see the electric train display at the Gas and Electric Company on Fourth Street in Cincinnati. Jack played Santa Claus at a department store downtown and at hospitals where he delivered gifts and candy. (Courtesy of Mary Cecil.)

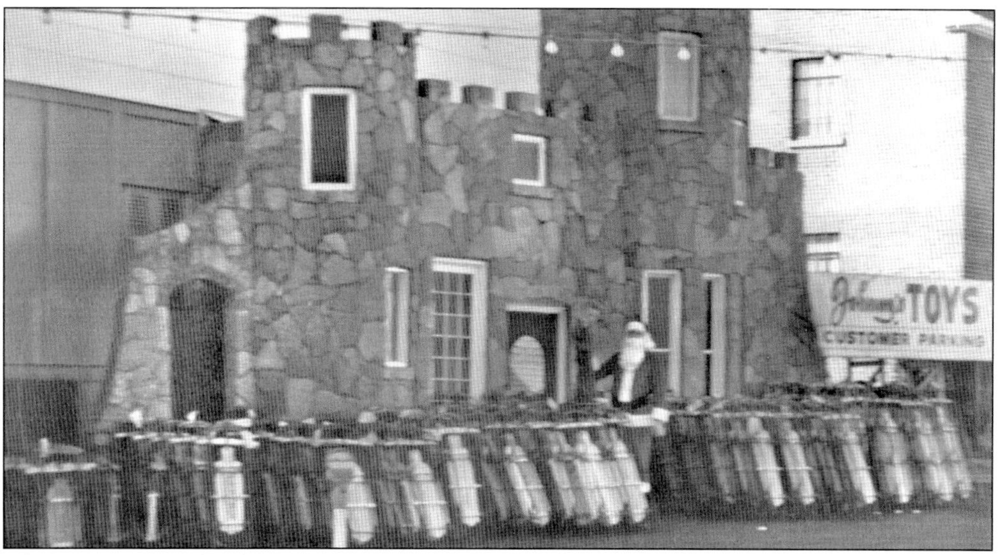

Johnny's Toy Store has been an institution in Latonia since 1939. Several generations of children have vivid memories of waiting for the Johnny's Toy Store catalog to be delivered, then wandering the aisles wide-eyed, and finally—the Christmas surprises. An enormous shipment of sleds is displayed outside the castle, which has become a symbol of Johnny's Toy Store. This photograph confirms what many have long suspected: Santa gets his toys at Johnny's Toy Store. (Courtesy of Tom Martin.)

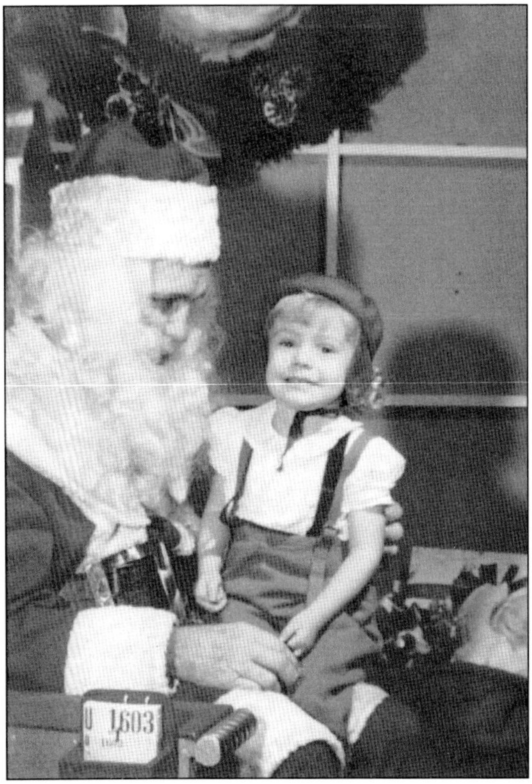

Children were welcomed into magical silver, white, and red "Santa Lands" in the department stores in downtown Cincinnati: Pogue's, Shillito's, Mabley's, and McAlpin's. Pogue's had what was called the "Fawn Shop," a tiny shop with doors only big enough for a child, containing a treasure trove of inexpensive gifts for grown-ups, where little ones could do their own shopping. Two-year-old Lisa Gillham sits on Santa's lap at Pogue's Department Store. (Author's collection.)

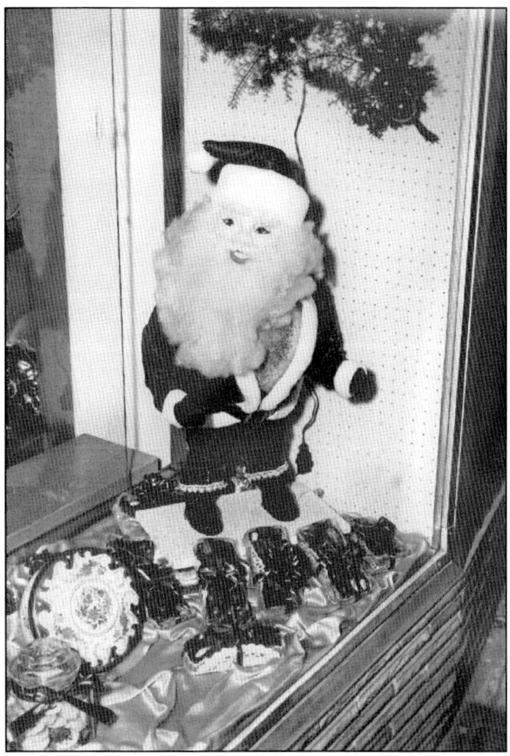

While not on the scale of downtown department stores, the Christmas displays in Latonia shops were festive and inviting, as this merry Santa in Latonia Bakery's window shows. Helen Petty decorated enthusiastically. She had round racks overladen with Christmas cookies, and no two packages were alike. Special cakes were decorated with Santa's face, or reindeer and elves, and cake stands were piled with little presents wrapped in colored foil. (Courtesy of Lorna Petty Harrell.)

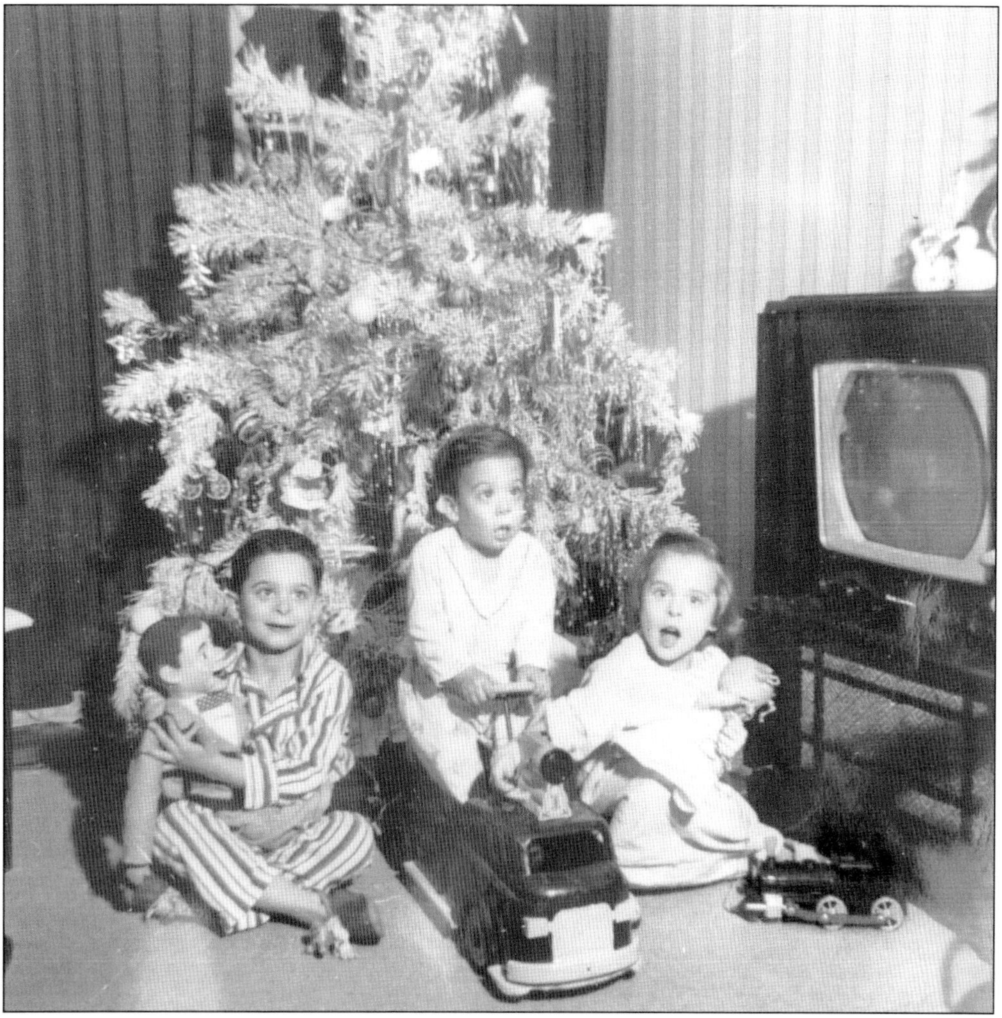

It's the New World of the 1950s, and the New World is filled with silver Christmas trees and big televisions. This is Christmas 1951 in the Petty apartment above their Latonia Bakery. Doug holds a Howdy Doody doll, while brother Gary rides on his fire truck. Lorna, holding her doll, is overcome by the wonder of it all. It may be a New World, but in Latonia, it's still about home and family. (Courtesy of Lorna Petty Harrell.)